2012

TWO PATHS:

END OF DAYS

OR

A NEW BEGINNING?

Public Statement to the World from Maya Elder
Don Alejandro Cirilo Perez Oxlaj

April 8th, 2011

Antigua Guatemala, Guatemala

To my brothers and sisters around the world:

In the name of the Heart of the Heavens and the Heart of the Earth, greetings from Guatemala and the National Council of Elders Mayas, Xinca and Garifuna.

I, Wakatel Utiw, "Wandering Wolf," Cirilo Perez Oxlaj, humbly offer this message to you. I speak now of what we see happening in the world today. According to the Maya Calendars we are living in the time of the 13 B'ak'tun and 13 Ajau. This is a time that comes accompanied with great pain. We are seeing a series of events approaching us as never seen before, these events come charged with tremendous sufferings and pain. They will happen in different places. They will touch us equally, men and women, old and young, indigenous or non-indigenous.

All this is due to the contamination. The atmosphere has lost its control. We the Maya see it with much sadness that we will see hunger and drought. Plagues will invade the fields and affect the agriculture; new illnesses will appear and will be difficult to cure. The sun rays are getting stronger and stronger as time goes by.

Our recommendation to avoid more suffering is this: No more nuclear testing, no more wars, no more mining and other explorations, no more use of chemicals. This is the only way the human race, the animals and the ancient trees could survive and see the new Sun. If we do not change, few will be the ones to survive and see the arrival of the 6th Sun.

Let's reconcile with our Creator and our Mother Earth, each one in our own way. For us the Maya will be with our Sacred Fire.

Respectfully, Wandering Wolf[1]
Head of the National Council of Elders in Guatemala[2]

2012

TWO PATHS:
END OF DAYS
OR
A NEW BEGINNING?

A Guide to Understanding 2012

And Changing the World's Current

Path to Impending Doom

BRUCE BURTENSHAW

Idaho Falls, Idaho

2012: Two Paths: End of Days or A New Beginning?
A Guide to Understanding 2012 and
Changing the World's Current Path to Impending Doom

Published by:
Winds of Change Publishing
Idaho Falls, Idaho 83404 USA
www.WindsofChangePublishing.com

This book can be purchased in paperback or e-book through:
http://www.Amazon.com
http://www.2012TwoPaths.com
http://www.BarnesandNoble.com
-Bookstores

First printing June 2011

ISBN: 978-0-615-41641-0

All book illustration paintings and drawings by Bruce Burtenshaw

Cover by Kal Chapman and Skylar Burtenshaw

Front cover paintings of President Obama and nuclear explosion scene by artist Bruce Burtenshaw (Maui jungle photo also by Burtenshaw)

See Burtenshaw's paintings on the Internet at *Burtenshaw Gallery of Fine Art* (Photo-realistic Hawaiian, Rocky Mountain, and nebula paintings) http://www.BurtenshawArt.com

Every effort has been made to research all copyright holders. If any mistakes or oversights have occurred, we will be happy to revise or credit information in any future edition.

To contact the author, please use Bruce's personal e-mail address:
Bruce@2012TwoPaths.com

Dedicated to the Memory of

Darrel L. Burtenshaw

CONTENTS

FOREWORD

Since the moment that each one of us was conceived, we have all been *slowly* introduced to the world around us and made aware of our existence. In order to fully understand this concept, one must picture the opposite. Imagine that you do not yet exist, and in one split second you awaken for the first time and find yourself in a body with a fully developed brain, but with *none* of your present abilities or memories.

As your eyes open, your brain is immediately overwhelmed by sensations that are received simultaneously from every sensor and nerve receptor in your body. You see images and can differentiate color, contrast, and brightness, but all of the information you perceive is completely meaningless. The awareness of your existence hits you so hard that your mind and body are traumatized, and you go into shock and possibly cardiac arrest.

Being slowly introduced into existence as our brains develop and adapt to our environment saves us from living this horrible nightmare, but it dulls our sense of reality. Everyone must comprehend the true value of our existence, the miracles of life, and the world around us that we all take for granted!

We should all cherish this world and its many creations! Earth* is an absolutely amazing place, as no other planet in the entire Universe can match what it has to offer. Earth and all its creations are unbelievably rare and unique! The mere existence and evolution of nature, let alone the existence of the planet itself, are wonders beyond human comprehension. Everybody should be extremely thank-

Note on Earth terminology: I observe protocol in which the word "Earth" is used in reference to the proper name of our planet. It is improper to say "the Saturn, the Pluto, and the Mars," thus it is also improper to say "the Earth." Therefore, I refer to the planet Earth as "Earth" and not as "the Earth."

ful for nature; can you imagine how life on Earth would be if it were taken from us? It's horrifying to envision, because if nature ceases to exist, so do we!

Most of us have a deep appreciation for nature, but we also love civilization and all the conveniences and pleasures of modern life. Unfortunately, we take modern conveniences for granted, such as electricity, running water, transportation, appliances, and our electronics. It is only when our conveniences stop working that we wonder why we didn't give them the respect they deserve. We also take the availability of food and supplies for granted. We assume that if we have the money, we can run to the store and purchase anything we may need or desire.

Our civilization has become so dependent on these modern conveniences that it would be hard to imagine life without them. Well, start imagining! The next time you turn on a faucet, wonder where you would get water if none flowed from the fixture. In the next days, as you turn on light and power switches, imagine getting no results. As you watch your television, imagine it shutting off, knowing that you might never watch another broadcast. When you grab a drink or a snack from the refrigerator or a cabinet, envision not having any way to restock that item. As you go about your daily routine in the next few weeks, picture everything you could soon lose. Envision being thrown hundreds of years back in time, living without running water, electricity, appliances, and the readily availability of food, medicine, or supplies. Only then can a person truly realize how much we've come to rely on our modern conveniences and the pleasures that they bring!

Visualize life without any of the modern amenities we have today (and possibly losing your home or your life), because that's exactly what will occur in 2012, *unless* our country rallies the world's people together to save our planet, its inhabitants, and the life we have come to know and love!

Acknowledgments

Many thanks go to my daughter Natalie, who recently graduated from Duke University, for her insightful suggestions and writing, proofreading, and editing skills. Many thanks go to my son Skylar, the electronics and computer genius, for his knowledge and extensive help with computer operations, formatting, illustration text, and graphics. My appreciation goes to graphic artist Kal Chapman, for designing a magnificent book cover. Many more thanks go to Skylar for his help with all the book cover's final touches. Thank you, Michael Bergen, for your assistance with preliminary editing and suggesting the book's title, *Two Paths*. Recognition also goes to my sister Beverly, for her help with proofreading and editing. Many thanks go to Brenda I. Harker for her proofreading talents. I also convey extreme gratitude to my beautiful soul-mate Kim and intelligent son Zack, who have put up with my speeches on the topics of 2012 and the country's problems for many years.

A special thanks to goes to everyone listed in this book's bibliography and notes, especially the courteous and helpful staff members of The History Channel, NBC News, The Discovery Channel, NORML, The California Physicians Alliance, and Greenpeace. Thank you for supplying and/or your consent to pass on the information that I have been privileged to acquire and share with others.

PREFACE

Is Armageddon fast-approaching? Many people believe so, after witnessing increases in the frequency and magnitude of earthquakes, hurricanes, global warming patterns, wars, terrorism, and outbreaks of uncontrollable diseases. For many years people have watched and waited for signs that the end of days is drawing near. Prophecies from numerous sources echo the threat of worldwide destruction that is to occur in our time.

Predictions of an imminent catastrophe resulting from worldwide computer system crashes surfaced a few years before the year 2000 (soon to be called the "Y2K scare," Y2K means "year two thousand"). The crashes were supposed to occur when computers around the world turned their yearly two-digit dates from 99's to 00's at midnight December 31, 1999. Obviously, Y2K was mostly just a big "scare." Since nothing major occurred on January 1, 2000, the scare has discredited many prophecies of 2012. People may now believe that 2012 is merely another Y2K.

The upcoming date of December 21, 2012, is far from just another Y2K. Prophecies of 2012 have been painstakingly passed down for *thousands of years* from the Maya, the Aztec, the Egyptians, and many other sources in order to warn us of a reoccurring cycle of global destruction, which the Maya have calculated to occur every 5,125 years (some say 5,160 years, others say 5,200 years, which I discuss in Chapter 6: Prophecies of the Maya and the Egyptians). The Maya, the Aztec, the Egyptians, the Hopi, and others believe that four previous worlds have been destroyed; will ours be the fifth?

What can having knowledge of the catastrophic events of 2012 prior to them occurring and gaining wisdom and ideas to rebuild our country in order to prevent this destruction from taking place do for you, your family, and everyone across the nation? Quite a bit!

First, this book will give you a preview of the events that could transpire between December of 2012 and April 2013. It will reveal to you the ramifications of mankind trashing the planet, and shows that unless we change our "evil" ways, *now*, we may soon be eradicated as an infestation! Picturing the possible events of 2012 described in this book will enable you to formulate your own plan of action.

Next, rather than following through with proposed stimulus plans, this book shows how we could put a $100,000 check from the government into the pocket of every adult American ($200,000 per couple), and when we look back five years from now, the "People's bailout" would have been achieved *FOR FREE!* The average American home owner could pay off their mortgage and our country's renters would be able to purchase homes. If everybody's homes were paid off, most people would have a lot more money to spend! The economy, which is built on spending, *would absolutely explode!* My family would have an extra $22,000 a year! What would you do with all the money that you would save?

This plan would instantly fix the economy! No one would *ever* be homeless again. Enacting other recommended plans from this book would result in everyone having free health and dental care. College or trade school educations would be free to anyone desiring to further their careers. Terrorists would marvel at our new ideals and join our cause; there wouldn't be any more wars. We could then concentrate on repairing the damage we've done to the planet. Issues on global warming, our oceans, toxic chemicals, nuclear weapons, and the overpopulation of Earth could more feasibly be dealt with after the economy is repaired. We could also focus on eliminating poverty, crime, and our country's drug problem, and Americans could retake their jobs that we've sold to China and other foreign countries.

After reading this book you will agree that *a new beginning* is what this book can do for you, your family, and everyone across the country! Please help me pass its information to the country's people, so that we might enlist enough voices to change our current path to impending doom and turn the American dream of home ownership into a reality for everyone!

Main Introduction

I began writing this book four years ago, as a quest to lead Americans toward a different path, far away from the present one of failing economic systems and the depletion of Earth's resources. These counter-active ways of living have become completely unsustainable and must be modified immediately!

The dollar amounts of our country's national debt and total unfunded obligations continue to avalanche with no end in sight. We can't even begin to pay off our national debt, let alone the country's total unfunded obligations, which total over ten times the national debt! Many of our country's systems are in need of a major overhaul or must be changed completely. Our moral standards are slipping away; the United States is supposedly the leader of the world, yet we have homeless and hungry people who live in the same cities as the multi-millionaires that we place upon pedestals.

In the last fifty years, we've trashed our planet's oceans, lakes, rivers, soil, and atmosphere. Scientists say we're now approaching a tipping point—a point of no return—where the damage that we have inflicted upon the planet will be irreversible.

Many of us carry a feeling of impending doom and disaster. We feel we're running out of time to change the country's current path, which everyone must realize was built on greed, selfishness, and envy, and is leading us to self-destruction. We must all revert to a path where our ways of life coincide harmoniously with nature, taking care of our people and the planet as our level of technology increases.

This book differs from others concerning 2012. It explores the problems facing the world today, their causes and cures, as well as research on prophecies of the upcoming date of December 21, 2012, which are both intertwined. It demonstrates that the "apocalyptic" outcome of the year 2012 will be determined by how mankind proceeds in the next few years. The future is not set in stone, but rather depends on mankind recognizing its mistakes and making the appropriate changes to correct them.

Two Paths is divided into two parts. Part 1 concerns the prophecies and possible events of 2012, and reveals vast amounts of information contained in no other book. It tells why we must act swiftly; we have very little time remaining to solve the world's problems before everything comes crashing down on us. Part 1 also reveals the possibility of ancient prophecies of this devastation coming to life before our eyes. This book refers to scientific data and recorded history as most of its evidence.

When I began writing this book, I didn't have any intentions or thoughts of profiting from it. The book was written with the intent of showing the country's people how to permanently fix the economy and pay off a home for every American adult, in retrospect, for free. I also didn't have any plans to include the prophecies of 2012. The book was to contain only information on the world's problems and their solutions. I had reached a point in my life where I could no longer sit idly by and watch the planet being trashed and the economy fail. I didn't see anyone stepping forward to make the necessary changes in the country's views, and I decided the time had come to get the job done myself. I've always had the desire to prepare for the future and have been interested in prophecy most of my life. I have researched the prophecies of 2012 for many years, but it wasn't until recently that I discovered the outcome of this time period will depend on mankind's actions in the next few years. This belief is mirrored in recent ultimatums given to the world from Maya elder Don Alejandro Cirilo Perez Oxlaj, head of the National Council of Elders of Guatemala (see chapter 6).

While researching the possible events of 2012, I found that many civilizations throughout history have passed down prophecies of this date. After correlating data and calculating probabilities, I decided that it was my obligation to pass on the *credible* information I discovered. I had proven to myself that not only is there a high probability that worldwide destruction will occur in or before 2013, but the extent of the devastation will depend on the changes we make in the next few years, which is the premise of this book.

This book's first chapters provide scientific evidence that prove Earth's magnetic fields are presently decreasing and could soon lead to a pole reversal of the planet, which would cause global destruction beyond imagination. They also provide verification that pole shifts of Earth have occurred at cyclic intervals in the past, and many ancient civilizations have passed down writings and prophecies of these re-occurring dates, after witnessing the almost complete destruction of at least four previous worlds.

Chapter 4: The Bible Codes explores the *verified* existence of computer-generated codes that have been found in the Bible's book of Genesis, which pertain to many recorded historic events and also contain prophecies of 2012. Thirty-two of these findings are equivalent to discovering information about thirty-two of our most recent presidents encoded in the Declaration of Independence, such as their names, cities and dates of birth, and death, among other facts!

Chapter 8: The Lost Book of Nostradamus reveals prophecies of 2012 that are currently being deciphered from drawings made hundreds of years ago. The book was discovered in 1994 at the Italian National Library in Rome and is now being called "The Lost Book of Nostradamus." The book contains prophetic drawings of future events and the Great Galactic Alignment rather than Nostradamus' well-known quatrains and verses.

In these drawings, Nostradamus informs us of a possible savior of the planet, the "One Male," written in English, an English speaking "king" who will possibly determine the outcome of the future. In the chapters ahead, you'll read about President Obama (and evidence indicating that he is Nostradamus' One Male), the government's role in the upcoming events leading to 2012 and the two possible paths facing our nation.

Upon nearing completion of Part 2 on solving the country's problems, and after spending more time researching 2012, I learned that the Hopi Indians are waiting for the emergence of a white man they call "Pahana," or the "True White Brother." The Hopi say that he won't be greedy like the other white men and will bring a great new plan of living to the world in the end of days. If the new plan is accepted, the world will experience peace for a thousand years; if the plan is rejected, destruction will follow. The Hopi say that Pahana will be identified by his *red cloak* and will bring with him the symbols and the missing piece to the sacred tablets. After learning about the prophecy, I suspected that a man drawn with long hair and carrying the weight of the world on his shoulders in one of Nostradamus' Lost Book images (see drawing on rear cover) is indeed Pahana. It wasn't until later that I was hit by the realization that if the man depicted in Nostradamus' drawing was indeed Pahana, he *must* be drawn wearing a *red cloak* or robe, which I quickly verified!

Part 2 of this book concerns the world's problems and their causes, and reveals radical ideas for solving these issues. Problems with our financial systems and economy, housing costs, lack of medical and dental care, the country's drug problem, crime, unemployment, deficits in education, over-population, terrorism, and the trashing of our planet all have logical solutions.

Chapter 12: Housing shows that by implementing the plans in this book, we could pay off a home for the average American adult and looking back five years from now, we would find that it was done for free! This would be a $13 trillion achievement! Our economy and our attitudes would soar! How could such a feat be accomplished without any cost to the country's people? *Please* read this book's chapter on housing! This plan is not an option, but *must* be implemented to repair our economy and our perspectives!

Enacting ideas presented in Chapter 14: Our Country's Drug Problem would shut down all drug trafficking and gangs, resulting in the elimination of 90% of the country's crime and would also stop trillions of dollars from flowing over our borders. Past government administrations have attempted to prevail in the war against drugs, but have failed drastically. With the odds stacked in opposition to us, how can we possibly succeed? Please read this book's chapter on drugs! We *can* gain control of our country's drug problem and quickly eliminate it, *without* using the "tough guy approach," which hasn't gotten us anywhere!

Implementing the radical ideas proposed in Part 2 could save the planet from being completely trashed by mankind (we've already almost finished the job) and save Earth from the 2012 cleansing it requires. Enacting changes regarding our country's views, morals, and ideals could result in the elimination of all poverty, wars, and terrorism throughout the world.

Everyone should envision a world where everybody is content and the major worries we face today don't exist, such as housing and health care expenses. We should imagine the best possible future for people. A Utopia of happiness and fulfillment with extra time for family and hobbies, and no place for homelessness, unemployment, hunger, despair, crime, or violence. Could this world be possible? Absolutely!

We possess everything we need to accomplish these visions. We have sufficient housing across the United States for everyone. In fact, according to the U.S. Census Bureau, we have a housing *surplus* (How can this be true, when 643,067 Americans are homeless?). We have enough food to feed everyone across the country, and we're feeding other countries as well (But many Americans, including children, go hungry!). We have enough resources for everyone in the United States. The only thing stopping us is *greed!*

Americans must realize materialism, greed, and selfishness have no place in a modern intelligent society! In today's society, the "American Dream" has become harder and harder to attain, and the gap between the rich and the poor becomes wider each day. In order to repair the underlying fabric of our society, greed must be erased!

The need to address problems in our country and around the world has never before reached such a critical point. Social, political, economic, and environmental problems in other countries now affect us more than at any time in the past, with poverty firmly planted as the roots of all our world's problems. Population growth, dwindling resources, and the circumstances of many impoverished nations need to be addressed and corrected immediately! The world's population has exceeded its ability to take care of itself. Our resources are being exhausted by Americans as well as all nations who glamorize our country's way of life, and it will only worsen as lesser developed countries become more prosperous.

There's plenty of wilderness left on Earth, but for how long? Situations in regions of Asia have become extremely serious. Almost all of the rain forests have vanished in several countries now, including Thailand and the Philippines. The Indonesian islands and New Guinea are now under serious threats due to China's huge consumption boom. Only 20% of the world's ancient forests remain! An area the size of a football field disappears *every two seconds*. The Amazon is shrinking; it's losing an area the size of Switzerland every year. In the last 300 years, we've lost half of Earth's forests. Earlier periods of loss cover the temperate forests of Europe and Northern America. We're now seeing losses of the tropical rain forests at a much quicker rate than ever before. Six thousand years ago, Europe was almost all forest. Now the only pristine forest that remains is the little forest Bialowieza, which is now being threatened from over-logging.

There are many species of animals in danger of extinction, such as the Amur leopard in Russia, where only 30 still exist in the wild. In Central America, frogs are threatened; the Golden Toad is now extinct. We're destroying ecosystems that will eventually lead to our own demise. We must save humanity from the folly of destroying the wilderness, the environment, and our wildlife.

The United States must now lead the way to repair the world rather than showing the world how to destroy it, as we have in the past. We must return to nature, before nature forces us to do so. Our country needs completely new views on housing, the economy, health care reform, our country's drug problem, and many other problems; new views supplied in the chapters to follow. Most of the ideas are radical, but that's what we require! After we repair our country's problems, other countries will see our successes and follow our lead. The ideas in this book may not be perfect, but will give a firm foundation for others to build upon. We need changes now, which will eventually lead to world peace, before world events lead us to self-destruction!

PART 1
THE 2012 PHENOMENON
INTRODUCTION

Many different cultures in ancient history had an interest in the date December 21, 2012. It corresponds to Hopi myths, Maya codices and calendars, graphs of the I-Ching, Aztec writings, Egyptian hieroglyphs, and relates to prophecies of Nostradamus, Roman oracles, and one of the most documented psychics of recent times, Edgar Cayce.

Recent discoveries concerning the "Bible codes" also refer to this date. Scholars were very skeptical upon first hearing that codes exist in the Bible's text, but after performing extensive research on the subject, many have no doubt that coded information does exist in Genesis, the first book of the Bible, given to Moses by God. People around the world need to understand how computers find codices in the Bible, the information they contain, and that someone encoded them into the Bible's text. The current debate on the Bible codes isn't whether or not coded information is contained in the Bible. Its existence is a proven fact. The raging debate now concerns whether the occurrence of the coded information found is merely coincidental, or if the data was intentionally placed there by someone. This book provides evidence that indicates the existence of the Bible codes is not just a coincidence and shows that it isn't just a twist of fate that many ancient cultures were concerned with the date of December 21, 2012.

In a nutshell, the prophecies of 2012 are based upon historic knowledge of cyclic "apocalypses" that reoccur about every 5,125 years (some calculate 5,160 years, others say 5,200). Four of these apocalypses have occurred in the last 25,800 years, each resulting in the beginning of a new world. The fifth of these rare reoccurring cycles is about to take place! On December 21, 2012, at 10 a.m. GMT, the climax of the Great Galactic Alignment will occur. Understanding exactly what this alignment is and how it comes about is essential to comprehend the possible outcomes for our planet at that time.

The Great Galactic Alignment will occur as the December solstice Sun aligns with the Galactic equator of the Milky Way Galaxy, the Dark Rift, and the black hole at the center of our galaxy. Galactic astrologer Raymond Mardyks was the first to discuss this alignment as one of the factors contributing to the astrology of 2012. Mardyks is recognized as having coined the phrase "Galactic Alignment" in relationship to Maya calendar dates and was the first to suggest an end date of 2012.

In 1987, José Arguelles brought worldwide attention to 2012 as the end point of the Maya 13th b'ak'tun cycle. In *The Mayan Factor*, José states that August 16, 1987, will mark the beginning of a 25 year harmonic convergence "phase shift" that will culminate to "Galactic synchronization" in 2012. He believes that this 25 year period will be a time of cleansing, which will lead us to a new era of humanity. Many people agree with this "cleansing" theory and believe that mankind's actions in the next few years will determine the extent of the cleansing the planet will require.

John Major Jenkins is also one of the main pioneers in the field of 2012 research. Based on the calendar systems used by the Maya, Jenkins asserts the end of their calendar was meant to coincide with the winter solstice on December 21, 2012. In his book *Maya Cosmogenesis 2012,* Jenkins reveals that we're now in the fifth and final Maya "b'ak'tun" cycle of the latest 25,800-year "procession of the equinoxes cycle," and believes this portends major changes for Earth.

To better understand the cycle of the "procession of the equinoxes" and the Great Galactic Alignment, it must be known that ancient cultures recognized four major dates within each year. These are the two solstices—when days are at their longest and shortest—and the two equinoxes—when the lengths of the day and night are equal. One solstice takes place in midsummer on the longest day of the year; the other occurring in December on the shortest day of the year. As the December solstice approaches, the Sun appears lower in the sky each day until it stops its apparent descent and pauses for three days before beginning to rise higher in the sky leading to the next mid-summer solstice. These three days of the winter solstice are the darkest days of the year. When the winter solstice ends (three days later), the Sun appears to experience rebirth on December 25, Christmas day. Christianity celebrates this day as the birth date of Jesus.

The two equinoxes, when the lengths of the day and night are equal, are also on opposite ends of our calendar year. The autumn equinox symbolizes "harvest" and the spring equinox signifies "promise." Ancient cultures knew when these dates were approaching by noting which stars were on the horizon at sunrise and sunset, and their relative placement to the Sun. If you watched for hundreds of years, it would become apparent that the stars were moving slightly out of position each year. This slight movement of the stars and constellations across the sky over hundreds and thousands of years is called the "procession" of the equinoxes.

The Great Galactic Alignment occurs as a result of this procession of the equinoxes and occurs only once every 25,800 years! The procession is caused by Earth wobbling very slowly on its axis and shifts the visual position of the equinoxes and solstices in the sky one degree every 71.5 years (See Fig. 1). Greek astronomer Hipparchus is widely acknowledged as the discoverer of the procession of the equinoxes, yet the ancient Maya and Egyptians were also aware of it.

In December 2012, Earth completes this *rare* procession cycle. When I say rare, I mean rare! Take a moment and think about how long 25,800 years is! Going back to the time of Jesus was only 2,000 years ago. The fact that this alignment will occur during our lifetime is mind-boggling! In order to fully understand the magnitude of this alignment, we need to include other factors such as the Dark Rift.

The Dark Rift is a dark cloud consisting of interstellar dust that runs along the Milky Way's Galactic equator from its center northward past the constellation of Aquila, and lies in the place where the December solstice Sun will rise in 2012. The Maya called the Dark

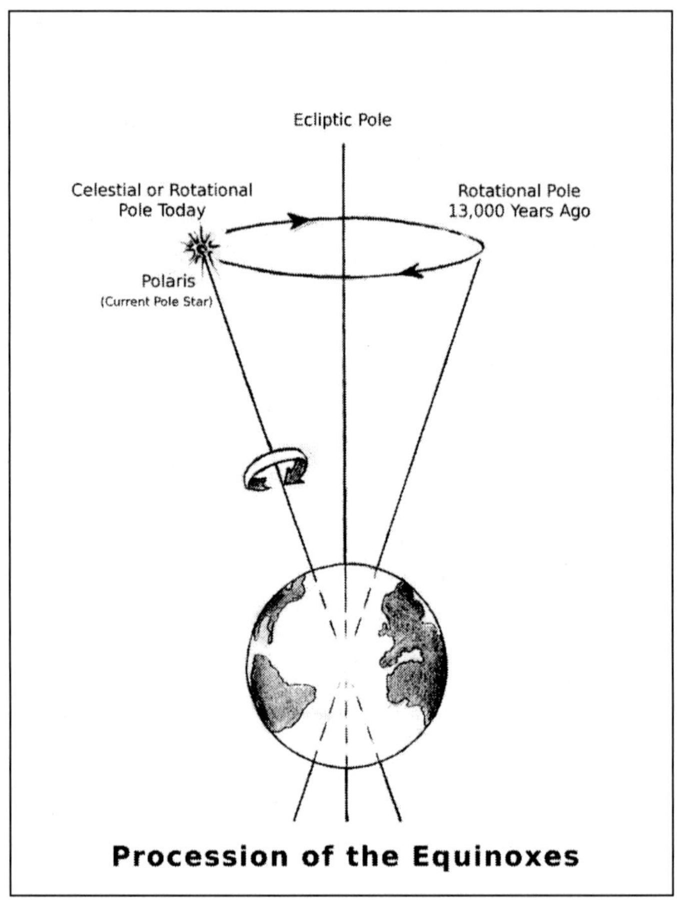

Fig. 1. As Earth spins on its axis (noted by the ribbon arrow), it wobbles, causing its rotational axis pole to rotate around the Ecliptic pole over a 25,800 year period. This amount of time would be required to witness the completion of one cycle of the slow movement of the constellations of the zodiac through the night skies. Drawing by Bruce Burtenshaw

Rift the "Black Road or Xibalba be" and believed it to be evil. Thus, in Maya astrology terms, we can describe the Galactic Alignment as the alignment of the December solstice Sun, the Galactic equator, and the Dark Rift. The Maya's captivation with the "evil" Black Road that *leads* to the upcoming Galactic Alignment becomes very apparent if you look at their Long Count calendar. Its end date corresponds to our date of December 21, 2012!

In December of 2012, we will see the Sun rise in the center of the Milky Way galaxy, and the Dark Rift cloud will appear behind the Sun. Our black hole, which is centered in the middle of the Milky Way galaxy, will also be in direct alignment with the three.

Yes, you read that correctly, our black hole. Most people don't have a clue that our Milky Way Galaxy rotates around a newly discovered black hole. Just a few years ago, while studying a faraway galaxy, scientists found this distant galaxy's center contained a black hole, and that the galaxy's stars seemed to be rotating around it! Upon studying other galaxies, scientists found that a black hole exists in the center of every galaxy studied. Using this newly acquired knowledge, they found that our galaxy, the Milky Way, also rotates around a massive black hole!

At this time, scientists don't know if the black holes at the center of all galaxies studied have anything to do with their formation, but we do know they exist. Hubble's law on the expansion of space tells us that the Universe is uniformly expanding. This universal expansion was predicted in "General Relativity" by Alexander Friedman in 1922, well before Hubble made his analysis and observations. This tells us the "center of the Universe" is a misconception, and that the Big Bang didn't occur at a central point. This would suggest to me that all galaxies in the Universe were born from their black holes!

Einstein's theory of general relativity predicted the existence of black holes, objects so dense they tear and distort the fabric of space time. A black hole is an extremely massive object that creates a very large dimple in the fabric of space time. They are formed when large amounts of matter are crammed into a very tiny space. All of Earth's mass would have to be forced into a space less than an inch across to turn into a black hole. Some black holes are believed to be caused by massive stars that have gone supernova. When this occurs, the core of the star collapses into its center, and the force of the implosion is so great that the matter can't stop itself and it falls into a black hole. In my opinion, black holes are created in many ways and are linked to the formation of all galaxies.

The fact that the Sun reverses its magnetic poles every eleven years further complicates the Galactic Alignment scenario. The last time its poles reversed was in the first quarter of 2001, and the cycle is set to reoccur in December 2012! As the winter solstice approaches, the Sun's poles will reverse. Many changes will result from this pole shift.

NASA predicts that as the Sun's poles reverse, and as it reaches the end of its current eleven year sunspot cycle, super solar storms and bursts will erupt from the Sun.[1] These eruptions could be up to 70% bigger than any in recorded history.[2] NASA also forecasts solar flares will increase in frequency and magnitude as we near the 2012 alignment, and we could see solar flares and bursts erupting *further* from the Sun than we've ever seen, with some possibly hitting Earth. Scientist Mausumi Dikpati at the National Center of Atmospheric Research in Boulder, Colorado, stated "The next sunspot cycle will be 30% to 50% stronger than the previous one."[8] Both she and colleague David Hathaway believe that solar flare activity, which reaches its eleven year cyclic peak in 2012, "will be a doozey!" Dikpati forecasts these solar maximums will occur in 2012, but Hathaway predicted that they will arrive in 2010 or 2011.[8]

This isn't the first time solar flare activity may possibly reach such a peak. Scientists have found evidence of past solar bursts hitting and burning Earth's surface. A related article in the magazine *New Scientist*, covered a meeting of the American Astrological Society, where a team of astronomers studying Sun-like stars found that most of these stars seem to produce a super flare about once every hundred years.[3] These Sun-like stars occasionally become as much as ten times brighter for periods of hours or days. Astronomers have no idea why our own sun is so stable. They say that perhaps the Sun does have massive flares that could cause extinction, but only every 5,000 years or so when its magnetic field reverses, causing global destruction with no surviving eyewitness accounts. Once before, in Noah's day, civilizations were destroyed by floods. Many ancient prophecies, including the Bible's chapters, say the planet will be destroyed again, this time by fire. Solar flares hitting Earth could definitely destroy one third of the planet.

Scientists have also discovered Earth's magnetic field has been steadily decreasing for the last several years, faster than if the magnetic field had just been turned off (which is discussed in the next chapter). The field will continue to decrease until we near the Galactic Alignment's end, whereupon Earth's magnetic field will slowly increase until it returns to its normal strength. Earth's magnetic field typically deflects harmful radiation from the Sun and cosmic rays from outer space. As Earth's field weakens, we will be hit by more radiation, and Earth's atmosphere will absorb more heat than usual. Global warming has been affected by mankind, but this cosmic alignment is also a factor. Earth's magnetic fields definitely seem to be more stressed recently. According to the National Earthquake Information Service of the U.S. Geological Survey, earthquakes grew from *one* severe quake from 1890 to 1999, to *765* from 2000 to 2004![4] The frequency and amplitude of earthquakes has steadily grown since then, with quakes in 2009 and 2010 becoming common occurrences.

Knowing that Earth's magnetic field is decreasing as we near the Galactic Alignment is important for several reasons. First, with a weakened magnetic field, our planet will be hit by more solar radiation. Second, as our magnetic field decreases and as the Sun reverses its poles, we could experience another effect. Since opposite poles attract each other, the magnetic poles of Earth and the Sun are now at their most unstable points. During the Sun's pole shift, its magnetic field will have the tendency to pull Earth with it, causing a pole shift of the planet or "reversal" of Earth's north and south poles!

With Earth's magnetic balance unstable, being hit by massive solar flares and clouds of plasma particles from the Sun could also cause a pole reversal of the planet. These theories are explored in Patrick Geryl and Gino Ratinckx's book *The Orion Prophecy*. In their book, they reveal scientific evidence that shows when a bolt of lightning strikes a magnet, a reversal of the magnetic poles takes place. On a larger scale, Earth is a magnet with north and south poles. What "bolt of lightning" could affect our magnetic state? Solar flares from the Sun. Chaotic outbursts of these sunspots catapult immense clouds of plasma into space. As shockwaves of particles and radiation reach Earth during an "out-of-balance state," a pole shift of Earth could occur.

In the book *The Earth under Fire*, astronomer Paul LaViolette writes, "Field flips have been accomplished experimentally by shooting large quantities of loaded particles into a strong bipolar magnet. These particles are then caught in the magnetic fields and cause a 'ring-stream' in them. At a certain moment, the stream speeds up to such an extent that the field of a magnet reverses completely." Scientists and astronomers know that the particles of a solar storm can compress Earth's magnetic field and temporarily speed up its power. In order for the Sun's solar particles to overpower Earth's magnetic fields, a solar flare many times bigger than has ever been recorded would be needed. NASA predicts this may happen in December of 2012!

Scientists have discovered that pole shifts of the planet have happened many times in the past and occur at cyclic intervals. Einstein first suggested the possibility of pole shifts in 1955. New studies from Princeton University reveal that our planet's poles have previously shifted many times.[5] Paleomagnetic evidence shows that prior pole shifts of the planet have resulted in worldwide destruction. Most pole reversals are believed to be caused by cycles of the magnetic fields of the Sun.

Many people believe that the physical orientation of Earth won't change during a pole shift. They believe a reversal of the magnetic poles inside the planet will occur without any physical changes to the planet's surface, and that this change will take place slowly. Modern day psychics and ancient prophecies don't concur with this theory! Many of the chapters in this book include prophecies of Earth physically turning upside down during an out-of-balance state, resulting in the reversal of Earth's rotation, all of which will happen instantaneously. The Bible's Book of Revelation states, "The stars of Heaven will fall from the skies, even as a fig tree casteth her untimely figs, when she is shaken of a mighty wind." If you were to see the stars fall from the sky, wouldn't you realize that the stars weren't actually falling? You would realize that the planet was rotating, making it appear as if they were. Correlating the speed of falling figs being ripped off their branches by high winds before they've ripened, to that of the stars falling from the sky, isn't hard. It would happen quickly. Edgar Cayce predicted the Great Lakes would empty into the Gulf of Mexico. When the next pole reversal occurs, there will be a physical change in the poles' locations, and the reversal will happen instantaneously, causing major havoc to the planet's crust.

Scientists also talk of the possibility of Earth being hit by a "Galactic super wave," a blizzard of cosmic radiation with destructive capabilities similar to that of radiation from nuclear explosions. These super waves originate from the center of the galaxy and could disrupt Earth's electromagnetic field, possibly resulting in a pole shift of the planet. Scientists have recently found evidence showing some type of Galactic super wave emanated from the center of our galaxy 13,000 years ago, roughly half the cycle of the Great Galactic Alignment, which may have wiped out most larger animals and reptiles. Physicist Paul LaViolette also wrote of galactic super waves with recurring cycles of 13,000 years emanating from our galaxy's center. He states that one is now overdue!

Other possible causes of previous and future reversals of Earth's poles include Earth being hit by a comet or large asteroid during an "out-of-balance state." Many ancient prophecies that concern 2012 speak of Earth being hit by fire from the heavens, falling stars, and other descriptions reminiscent of comets and asteroids. The Book of Revelation speaks of a comet called Wormwood slamming into our planet in the end of days. Prophecies of the Hopi Indians foretell of global nuclear war during this same time period. Could impacts from the explosions of the world's nuclear arsenal cause a pole shift of the planet while it's in an un-balanced state? Could mankind cause the pole reversal?

Regardless of what causes Earth's pole shift, if the shift occurs, gravitational and magnetic forces would cause destruction to the planet's surface beyond imagination. Global earthquakes with magnitudes unlike anything ever recorded would rock every continent, causing colossal tidal waves that would destroy all shorelines. Mountains would crumble, complete land masses would disappear into the oceans, and new lands could appear from beneath the seas. Cities would be leveled, flooded, and destroyed by tsunamis and high atmospheric winds. All the conveniences of modern life such as electricity, running water, available food and supplies, medical help, and transportation would cease to exist; society itself would disintegrate. All the comforts of living we now possess would vanish.

On a lighter note, new age interpretations of this transition time state that the world and its inhabitants will undergo positive spiritual transformations rather than an Armageddon, and that 2012 will mark the beginning of a new age of thinking and living, not the end of civilization as we know it. This would represent a global consciousness shift, where materialistic attitudes will change rather than the physical world. If this change in materialistic attitudes is to occur, our society has a lot of work to do! Other interpretations of the transition include transformations of the soul into higher dimensions of existence, where our present world comes to an end. If this were the case, all righteous people would have nothing to worry about. This idea sounds nice, and many people are counting on this occurring, but we shouldn't. We can't promote the attitude that if the world falls apart, it's okay, because as long as we're righteous, we'll be saved. Everyone needs to get involved in solving the world's problems with the goal of saving not only ourselves, but also the world and all its creations from impending doom!

Before proceeding further, I would like to divulge a few things I discovered long ago. Over the years, I've read many books on Nostradamus' prophecies (Michel de Nostradame), including several from authors Erica Cheetham and John Hogue. Nostradamus has been one of my biggest heroes for the last 30 years. His ability to foresee the future has never been matched by anyone throughout history. Hundreds of years ago, he predicted the world's first Antichrist by name, Napoleon, and foretold of his conquests. He predicted the world's second Antichrist, Hitler. Nostradamus called him Hister and predicted not only the year of the rise of the Nazis, but also the year of their fall. Hitler even attempted to use Nostradamus's predictions to prolong his reign of terror.

Back in 1990, after studying Nostradamus' quatrains for many years, I informed my friends and family that we would be fighting the Third World War against Arabs. No one took me seriously, stating that Middle East countries wouldn't stand a chance against us in a war. I told them New York City, Nostradamus' "new city at 45°," would be attacked by Arab nations, possibly with nuclear weapons. No one believed me.

Nostradamus also predicted the world's third Antichrist, by name, "Mabus." Since the early 1980s, I've been hearing, "Who is Mabus?" I've read this name many times. I've seen all the shows on Nostradamus and have heard many people talk about Mabus. All of the television specials that I have seen on Nostradamus throughout the years have spoken of Mabus, but no one has deciphered Mabus' true identity! I've known Mabus' identity since the early '90s.

Seeing the name "mabus" in small letters may allow a few of you to realize his identity. Usually the name is shown as a proper noun with the first letter shown as a capital letter, written as "Mabus." Actually, the capital letter should go on the other end. Put the word "mabuS" up to a mirror. What does it read? It says "Sudam"! Yes, Saddam (pronounced Sudam or Sadam) is the third Antichrist! Many scholars try to create an anagram or decipher some meaning from the word mabus, which only complicates translation of the word. We need to do nothing to the word mabus, except look at its mirror image. It's just that simple! Saddam's war started our current global conflict. This shows that we're well on the way to the end of days!

Nostradamus wrote:

Mabus will soon die and there will come a dreadful destruction of people and animals,
Sudden vengeance will be revealed, a hundred hands, thirst and hunger, when the comet passes.

Mabus is now dead. They hung him in Iraq. We now await the dreadful destruction of people and animals, thirst and hunger, when the comet passes. "The dreadful destruction of people and animals," sounds like devastation on a biblical proportion and could only be a pole shift of Earth, nuclear war, or Earth being hit by an asteroid, comet, or solar flares. The phrase "when the comet passes" could speak of the newly discovered comet McNaught, which was visible just before Saddam was executed on December 30, 2006, and in the next few weeks became the brightest comet in many decades, even brighter than Halley's Comet. Several of this book's chapters contain information concerning the recently discovered asteroid Apophis. This asteroid will pass very close to Earth in 2029 (its next passes are in 2013 and 2021), and it could also be Nostradamus' "comet."

Chapter 8: The Lost Book of Nostradamus doesn't contain deciphering of vague quatrains written by Nostradamus. These quatrains could be easily applied to many historical events. Instead of quatrains, historians are studying what is being called "The Lost Book of Nostradamus," a book filled with visionary drawings, seven of which directly pertain to our generation and the Galactic Alignment. This book was recently found in a library in Rome, exactly at the moment that its creator wanted it to be discovered! This is very intriguing, since the author of the Bible Codes recently allowed us to discover the codes existence.

My interests in Nostradamus' prophecies peaked in the late '80s to the mid-90s, after discovering Mabus' identity and seeing that the prophecies concerning the United States fighting Arabs in the Third World War were coming true. About this time, an episode of Unsolved Mysteries aired on TV that *really* got me interested in prophecies of the upcoming apocalypse.[6] They talked about a girl who had dreams constantly from the age of about twelve years until she was an adult, where wise men dressed in white robes came to her and told her of an upcoming apocalypse that would occur after the turn of the century.

The young woman was asked by the wise men to draw a future map of the United States, which would show land changes caused by this apocalypse, and she was given visions of how this map should appear. The show talked of her drawing this map over the years, refining it here and there upon instructions from the wise men in her dreams, until it was finally finished. Relatives and family members verified what the girl had experienced over the years, and they showed drawings of her earliest maps, which slowly progressed into more detailed versions. Her finished map was very frightening! Lower California, most of Nevada and Utah, along with other areas in the region were missing! The Pacific Ocean now bordered the bottom of Idaho. Massive changes had also occurred around the Mississippi River. It was drawn several hundred miles wider than its present width. New York City and surrounding areas were gone. Much of the East Coast had also changed, and most of Florida was missing.

Then Unsolved Mysteries showed a boy's story. This boy, who at the time the show aired was an adult, was raised across the country from the girl and had equivalent dreams with the same wise men appearing in white robes, and the same request was made of the boy to draw a future map of the United States! His map would also show the massive land changes to occur after the turn of the century. He too was asked to warn people of the upcoming land changes.

Comparisons were shown between both of their earlier maps, and both maps appeared similar. Copies of the final drafts were then compared by overlapping the two images, with both drawings having been finished in explicit detail. Both maps were indistinguishable! Destroyed coastlines on the two maps were identical! In both drawings the Mississippi River appeared to have been widened, all the way from the Great Lakes to the Gulf of Mexico (which correlates to Chapter 2: Prophecies of Edgar Cayce)!

What are the chances of two people growing up in different areas of the country and having the same apocalyptic dreams, being given the same information, visions, and images, and being given identical requests? Absolutely non-existent! First of all, decades ago no one knew anything about the possibility of an Earth pole shift, let alone that the shift would cause massive geographic changes and what these changes would be. The fact that both had created the same map blew my mind! It probably blew their minds also, because the story ended with them meeting and eventually getting married. You must understand both of these people started their maps as innocent children!

If you go online and search the Internet for "future map of the United States," several maps can be found, most of them appearing similar to the maps shown on Unsolved Mysteries. My favorite map, by far, is Stan Deyo's map.[7] Stan interpolated his map by calculating expected water intrusion based upon Hopi prophecies and not upon his own visions. It shows *exactly* what you would expect to see, particularly in the Snake River Basin in southern Idaho, which shows up as a crescent shape above where the Great Salt Lake in Utah now lays. This basin is shown as one of the new borders of the Pacific Ocean! This map is incredible! *Don't miss it!* Stan's map can be seen at the web-site listed in the notes.[7]

Many possibilities of the future exist, but there will be only one true future. If a person could truly see the future, he or she wouldn't see billions of its possibilities. They would see only one future. According to ancient prophecies, it would seem that all outcomes of the future result from at least two foremost possibilities. Many of the following chapters include information on these two possibilities.

There must be a turning point; one critical moment, where the decision of one man will change the course of human history. When this point will occur and who will make the decision that determines mankind's fate remains to be seen.

The Hopi Indians say that our fate will be determined by the True White Brother and his two great and intelligent helpers, for if they fail, destruction will follow. According to Nostradamus, the people who help determine mankind's fate will be the True White Brother and the "One Male" (written in English in one of his seven drawings).

How did so many diverse cultures from different parts of the world that lived in various times, formulate the exact same prophecies and "end of days" scenario? How could so many ancient cultures have foreseen Earth turning upside down, causing super earthquakes around the globe, and solar storms and flares hitting and burning the planet? They have knowledge of these predicted events because pole shifts of Earth have happened previously. Scientists now know that Earth has experienced many pole shifts in its history. Many ancient civilizations have been almost completely wiped out by previous pole shifts. Ancient prophecies of these events have been passed down for thousands of years as warnings to us. Psychics and prophets warn of these Earth changing events and also give warnings of comets, asteroids, solar flares, and nuclear war that could annihilate Earth.

According to many ancient prophecies, mankind will determine its own fate. If today's actions determine the future, we need to drastically change the world's views and abandon our destructive ways. We must stop destroying the planet and return to the path where we co-exist peacefully with nature and each other. With the approaching deadline of December 2012, we must begin many trans-formations, *immediately*!

If 2012 arrives and passes without any physical destruction to the planet, we may never know if the changes we made actually stopped the destruction of the world, or if devastation of the planet would have never occurred had we not made the changes, but we will have at least saved the world from self-destruction and pre-served the planet for our children and future generations. The rea-son all of these prophecies have been given to us is to open our eyes, so that we might make the appropriate changes necessary to save the world and its inhabitants from extinction. Prophets of the past who had the ability to see the future would have also seen the chang-es they made by giving us their prophecies.

Regardless of what transpires in 2012, the world requires major changes, now! Immediate deadlines need to be established. Scientists warn we will soon reach a tipping point, where the destruction of our planet will be beyond repair. The time has now come for com-plete decisive action, before we reach this point of no return!

After gaining new awareness from reading the next chapters on 2012, most people should agree that there is a good possibility that these predictions will be fulfilled. Many people studying ancient pro-phecies, myself included, believe that in the end God or a higher power will decide our fate based upon our actions or lack thereof in the next few years. It's *our* responsibility to ensure the world follows the correct path to create paradise on Earth, rather than the possible extinction of mankind!

1

EARTH'S DECREASING MAGNETIC FIELD

Most people are oblivious to the fact that our planet is constantly bombarded by deadly cosmic radiation. The only thing that protects us from this radiation is Earth's magnetosphere, an invisible force field that shields the planet. Earth's magnetosphere is crucial to our existence and deflects cosmic radiation that causes genetic mutation and global warming. New scientific evidence indicates this vital shield is weakening.

Earth is like a large magnet. Its magnetic fields emit from the South Pole and re-enter at the North Pole, forming a shield around the planet. Superheated particles travel through our solar system called "solar wind" and hit Earth's magnetic shield at speeds of up to one million miles per hour. Particles that impact Earth at its poles are more likely to break through its protective barrier because of the weaker magnetic fields in these regions. We now have stations that monitor solar activity and radiation. During high activity, airplane flights over the poles are prohibited due to the possibility of exposure to harmful levels of radiation.

Off the coast of Brazil in the Atlantic lies a region known by scientists as the South Atlantic Anomaly.[1] Over three million square miles and growing, this area of Earth's magnetic field has decreased in strength so much that it has actually *reversed* its magnetic polarity and is now *attracting* cosmic radiation normally deflected by Earth's magnetic field! Every day more and more cosmic radiation reaches our planet's surface here. This is scientific proof that Earth's magnetic field is changing and decreasing in strength!

This correlates with Professor Gary Glatzmaier's studies at the University of California, Santa Cruz. Gary created a remarkable computer model of Earth's magnetic field in which each year in time of his model equals 100,000 years of simulated time.[2] With his supercomputer, he observed how Earth's magnetic field evolved over the millennia. Around 36,000 years into the simulation, Glatzmaier's models showed that certain areas of Earth's magnetic field began to decrease in strength. In fact, these areas progressively decreased in strength to the point where the field disappeared completely! Soon after the field vanished, Earth's magnetic poles switched entirely! The north magnetic pole spontaneously became the south due to complex magnetic processes within Earth's core. His models also show that there was a decline in the magnetic field strength of our planet before and after these reversals. The fact that Earth's magnetic fields are presently weakening in the South Atlantic to the point where they are reversing, now attracting cosmic radiation instead of repelling it, would suggest that the magnetic poles of our planet are now preparing to flip!

Ancient clay pots tell us a lot about the strength of Earth's magnetic field hundreds of years ago. Clay contains tiny particles of a magnetic-based material called magnetite. When clay is fired at high temperatures, the magnetite align with Earth's magnetic field like little compass needles and are locked in place when the clay cools, recording the exact strength and direction of the field when the pot was made. By testing clay pots from 400 years ago, scientists have found that Earth's magnetic field strength has decreased 10% when comparing an old clay pot to a new clay pot.[3]

Scientists then wondered how much of this decrease occurred recently. Upon studying the South Atlantic Anomaly and many lava flows throughout the world, they've discovered that the biggest reduction of Earth's magnetic field has occurred within the last few years!

Professor Jeremy Bloxham states it would take 15,000 years for Earth's magnetic field to disappear if we hit "the turn off switch."[4]

Recent calculations indicate that if Earth's magnetic field strength continues to decrease at the current rate, no field would remain in 1,500 years. This tells us that our planet's magnetic field is decreasing *ten times* faster than if we had just turned it off completely! An outside force is definitely weakening Earth's magnetic field.

Scientists have now found concrete evidence in Hawaii's lava flows that prove previous pole shifts of Earth have occurred.[5] As in clay pots, lava flows act as history's recorders by documenting the changes of Earth's magnetic fields over time. Magnetite are also present inside the cooling lava, and they line up with Earth's magnetic field in a north-south alignment, like tiny compass needles, recording both the strength and direction of Earth's magnetic fields. Predictably, lava flows that have formed since the planet's last pole shift all have magnetite flowing in one direction, and previous flows have magnetite flowing in the opposite direction. By dating lava flows and analyzing the magnetite, we can determine when pole shifts of Earth have occurred. Samples of lava taken within the last 700,000 years show their field aligns with today's magnetic north, but older samples show the magnetic particles are reversed! After analyzing thousands of lava samples, geophysicists discovered that our planet's magnetic field has reversed many times in the last 20 million years. Samples also show that on both sides of these reversals there are periods of dramatically reduced field strengths, which is precisely the same thing we're seeing right now. It's no longer a question of *if* there has ever been a pole shift of the planet, but rather *when* it will reoccur.

Scientists are very disturbed about new developments concerning the South Atlantic Anomaly, and in 2011, the European Space Agency will launch SWARM, large satellite arrays whose missions will be to generate accurate and up to date maps of Earth's magnetosphere and predict its future activity.[6] Professor Nils Olson of the Danish National Space Center is working on this mission to identify new areas where Earth's poles are reversing and detecting changes to predict when the next pole shift might occur.[7] Once these satellites are operational, we'll find many more areas of our planet where the magnetic fields are weakening, collapsing, and reversing.

Many of this book's 2012 chapters contain prophecies of Earth losing its balance and turning upside down in the end of days. Scientists have discovered not only that Earth's magnetic field strength is weakening, but it has done so many times before and has lead to many previous pole shifts of the planet. Earth's magnetic field will continue to weaken until we pass the Galactic Alignment.

At any time between now and the Alignment, Earth could be hit by an asteroid, comet, solar flares, or particle clouds of cosmic radiation, any of which could cause another pole shift of Earth. Many ancient civilizations have survived previous pole shifts of the planet and passed down knowledge of their destructive cycles. Others have inherited ancient prophecies of devastation that are set to occur in our time and have given us warnings of these events, which must be heeded in order to change the future. Will we listen, or will we continue to follow our current path to self-destruction? After reading this book, and after calculating and comprehending the probabilities, hopefully you will agree that mankind must change its ways now, or face the destruction of the world as we know it!

2

PROPHECIES OF EDGAR CAYCE

Edgar Cayce was the most gifted psychic of the century, and possibly the most renowned prophet in all of recorded history; his ability to acquire knowledge "from the cosmos" was absolutely amazing! Edgar would go into trances where he said that he was able to tap into the eternal consciousness of the Universe. In his trances, he gave 14,306 readings, all of which are archived and catalogued at the Association for Research and Enlightenment in Virginia Beach, Virginia.[1] This is the largest collection of psychic material collected from any single source and covers subjects ranging from undiscovered scientific knowledge to prophecies of future events.

As a child, Edgar was surprised to find that others didn't have his psychic abilities. He saw auras around people that changed in color, shape, and intensity depending upon the individual's emotional state. He learned to see and sense people's moods by studying auras and knew when people were lying by seeing ugly changes in their auras' appearance. Edgar had many psychic abilities, including the ability to memorize entire books by sleeping on them.

In 1900, at the age of 23, Cayce developed a severe case of laryngitis. Unable to speak for about a year, he decided to seek out help. He visited Dr. Al Lane, a homeopathic psychic, who recommended self-induced hypnosis. On March 30, 1901, lying on a couch, Edgar went into his first self-imposed trance. While in the trance, and in his normal voice, Cayce unexpectedly described his symptoms and explained what needed to be done to cure his ailment! After waking, Edgar had no memory of anything he had said during the trance. Soon, the knowledge of his healing abilities spread throughout the country and he began giving readings. At the beginning of the readings, Edgar was given the name, location, and descriptions of the client's ailments. He immediately responded with a diagnosis and prescribed the cure.

Cayce could also look at a person and instantly see his or her illness. He could read the human body of his subject as if he was an x-ray machine and used accurate medical terminology in his diagnoses.

In 1905, Cayce told surgeons to fix George Dalton's badly broken leg by inserting a nail into the break. George had been told he would never walk again, but he did, thanks to Cayce's insight. This was a historical moment in medical history; the first time that a nail was used to fix a broken bone.

In the summer of 1911, doctors told Cayce that his wife Gertrude would die of tuberculosis. However, she followed her husband's recommendations for treatment and quickly recovered. The New York Times raved about Cayce, stating, "His language is usually of the best, and his psychological terms and description of the nervous anatomy would do credit to any professor of any nervous anatomy, and there is no faltering in his speech and all his statements are clear and concise, while in his normal state he is an illiterate man, especially along the line of medicine, surgery, or pharmacy of which he knows nothing."[2]

All Cayce needed to know to give a reading on someone was their name and location. As soon as he opened his eyes after a reading, he forgot everything that he had stated during the trance.

When asked a question about the outcome of a horse race or the stock market, he would answer. As clients got rich off his answers, Cayce began to get unexplainable migraine headaches. He discovered that selfish purposes made him sick, and he quit giving readings. In 1912, he moved to Selma, Alabama, where he worked as a photographer.

The TV show Unsolved Mysteries aired a segment about Edgar Cayce back in the 1980s. The show spoke of a young girl whose doctors had informed her family that she would need a leg amputation due to an open wound on her leg that had become very infected. While in a trance, Cayce instructed the girl's parents to travel south to a small town and find a particular drugstore. He predicted that on a back shelf behind other bottles, the family would find a bottle labeled "Oil of Smoke." They were then told to put this ointment on the girl's wound.

Upon first searching for the medicine, it couldn't be found, so the family sent Cayce correspondence regarding the problem. Cayce went into another trance, where he told them to look again and gave more precise directions. Using the additional information, they found the bottle and soon applied the ointment to the girl's wound. As Cayce predicted, the ointment cured the infection and saved the girl's leg.

Cayce again demonstrated his insight for healing when his son, Hugh Lynn Cayce, badly burned his face and eyes after accidentally dropping a match into a can of camera flash powder. Doctors told him he would never see again. While in a trance, Cayce instructed them to rinse Hugh's eyes with a concoction including the active ingredient sulfuric acid! Doctors told him this would worsen the condition, but Edgar said that if that's what he said to do, then to get it done! After following Edgar's recommendations, within weeks Hugh's vision was good as new.

Edgar then decided to help people again, but made it a rule that his wife would be the only one to ask questions. She would act as a filter against selfish motivations to prevent her husband from falling into illness as he had in his hometown.

In the 1920s, the United States expanded with rapid change. Corporations formed and the industrial boom began. Edgar gave many readings for many people on many subjects. It didn't matter whether you were rich or poor, no one was charged for these readings. Cayce relied on donations only. He gave many readings for people inquiring about the future, including prospectors looking for oil. Some of the most remarkable readings Edgar gave were geophysical oil readings, where he was correct on an almost foot by foot break-down of the geophysical conditions for a particular site. Thomas Edison gained information from Cayce on the nature of electricity.

In 1925, before the stock market crash of 1929, he was asked by a client, "How would business progress?" While in a trance, Cayce stated, "In the adverse forces that will come then in 1929, care should be taken lest this without the more discretion in small things be taken from the entity."[2] Cayce had seen the stock market crash of 1929 four years before it happened! He predicted that recovery would start in the spring of 1933, and it did.

In 1935, he predicted there would be an alliance between the Germans, Austrians, and Japanese, and he gave the beginning date of World War II and said that the new order of peace would be established in 1945, which it was.

Edgar said his information came from the subconscious minds of the people that he was reading and the eternal consciousness of mankind. He stated there is no future or past; it's all occurring simultaneously. He said time is an illusion that has purpose. Cayce also said that the future is changeable.

Cayce is also mentioned in the Bible codes. Since you haven't read this book's Bible code chapter yet (that is if you're reading the chapters in sequence), I'll just give you the information found by Fabrice Bect using Bible codes 2000 software. Edgar Cayce was a great man, but the Bible codes found make him seem "evil." The codes read, "Edgar Cayce, proud of spirit, to speak evil, to practice wicked works," and "fire of E. Cayce, his father is Satan, the sin of necromancy/sorcery."[3] Edgar gave many readings for selfish people looking for monetary gain, which he found made him ill. He knew that his powers could be used for good or evil, and it's evident that he did both. He's a hero for many people. Most people don't see him as an evil man, even after reading the Bible codes. Cayce may have made mistakes, but he did far more good in his life than bad.

Edgar also spoke of earth changes that will occur shortly after the turn of the century. In his trances, he stated there will be a change in the direction of Earth's rotation, and a pole shift of the planet will occur. He said most of Japan will sink into the ocean, and there will be major changes on the east and west coasts of the United States, as well as the central areas around the Mississippi River. Europe will change "as in the twinkling of an eye," and the Great Lakes will empty into the Gulf of Mexico. Cayce said that signs within the interior of our planet will warn us of the coming of the pole shift, and there will be major earth changes that will increase in activity from 1958 to 1998. He stated:

When there is the first breaking up of some conditions in the South Sea (China and Japan) and those as apparent in the sinking or rising of that that's almost opposite same, or in the Mediterranean, and the Etna area, then we many know it has begun.

The greater portion of Japan must go into the sea. The upper portion of Europe will be changed as in the twinkling of an eye.

Watch New York, Connecticut and the like. Many portions of the East Coast would be disturbed, as many portions of the West Coast, as well as the Central portion of the United States.

The earth will be broken up in the western portion of America. Los Angeles, San Francisco, most of these will be among those that will be destroyed before New York, or New York City itself, will in the main disappear. This will be another generation though, here; while the southern portions of Carolina, Georgia, these will disappear. This will be much sooner. The waters of the Great Lakes will empty into the Gulf of Mexico.

There will be upheavals in the Arctic and Antarctic that will make for the eruption of volcanoes in the torrid areas, and this will begin in those periods from '58 to '98. There will then be the shifting of the poles so that where there have been those of a frigid or semi-tropical will become the more tropical, and moss and fern will grow.[2]

If there are greater activities in Vesuvius or Pelee, then the southern coast of California and the areas between Salt Lake and the southern portions of Nevada, we may expect, within the three months following same, inundation by the earthquakes. But these are to be more in the Southern than the Northern Hemisphere.

As to conditions in the geography of the world, of the country—changes here are gradually coming about. No wonder, then, that the entity feels the need, the necessity for change of central location. In the next few years land will appear in the Atlantic as well as in the Pacific. And what is the coast line now of many a land will be the bed of the ocean. Even many battle fields of the present will be ocean, will be the seas, the bays, the lands over which The New World Order will carry on their trade as one with another.

Cayce's prediction concerning "the shifting of Earth's poles" is very interesting. In the early 1900s, they didn't know that pole shifts of the planet have previously taken place! Edgar's predictions don't tell us exactly when Earth's poles will shift, but does give us some information on sequential events.

Cayce predicted that a violent surge in the amount of storms and earthquakes will occur just before the end of days. In the last ten years, hurricane activity has peaked and an increasing amount of earthquakes have rocked the globe. In 1999, German researchers recorded over 200 earthquakes in only seven months above the Arctic Circle. Edgar said this would lead to eruptions of volcanoes in "the torrid areas." Earth's Torrid Zone is the area of Earth's surface between the Tropic of Cancer and the Tropic of Capricorn and is divided by the equator. After we see volcanic activity taking place at either Vesuvius or Pelee, we should anticipate seeing major changes in the west coast of the United States (within three months). We can also expect changes in the southern hemisphere and Europe to be a lot more drastic than what we may see on the North American continent. Witnessing anything worse than the Great Lakes emptying into the Gulf of Mexico as the planet's poles shift is hard to imagine.

After giving over 14,000 readings while in his trance state, Edgar Cayce died. He predicted the date of his burial on January 5, 1945, and was correct. With complete libraries dedicated to him, Edgar Cayce was definitely the world's most renowned psychic. His predictions of the upcoming Earth pole shift are very detailed, clear, and unmistakable in their meanings. Nothing needs to be deciphered, just comprehended. He also stated the future is not set in stone. Cayce's prophecies were meant to prepare us for the possibility of an upcoming apocalypse and possibly avert disaster by changing our ways. Let us heed his warnings!

3

PROPHECIES OF THE

HOPI INDIANS

Most of the Hopi Indians who live on "Turtle Island" (what the Hopi call the United States of America) live at the "Four Corners," the land where New Mexico, Utah, Arizona, and Colorado meet. The Hopi are a very spiritual tribe and have passed down prophecies through oral tradition for thousands of years. Their prophecies tell of an apocalypse that will come in the end of days. The Hopi Indians believe that the extent of the devastation caused by this apocalypse will be determined by mankind's actions in the next few years.

Ancient Hopi prophecies predicted that white men would arrive from far away and attempt to conquer their lands and lead their people into evil ways. The Hopi were told by the Creator, the Great Spirit Maasau, that if they held onto their ancient religion and didn't respond with violence, their land and people would be saved, and that their home would become the center of the emergence of the "True Spirit." The Hopi were also told that they would lead the reconstruction of the new world.

In 1963, Frank Waters compiled a list of all known Hopi prophecies in his book *The Book of the Hopi*. In his book, he writes about the prophecies of White Feather.[1] In the summer of 1958, Reverend David Young was driving down a desert highway and stopped to pick up an old man walking alongside the road. The old man told the Reverend that his name was White Feather, and that he was a Hopi of the ancient Bear Clan. He said he would be dying soon and had no one to receive and pass on his ancient wisdom. He had traveled to the North, the South, and the East to find and meet with other Hopis and didn't know if he could make it back home to tell of what he had learned before he died.

White Feather said time was growing short, and that his people are awaiting Pahana, the "True White Brother." He said that Pahana will not be like the white men we know now, who are cruel and greedy. Pahana will bring with him the symbols and the missing piece to the sacred tablets. White Feather also said the fourth world shall end soon and the fifth world will begin. He also told Reverend David Young of nine signs the Hopi were to watch for. At the end of these nine signs there would be an apocalypse.

<u>The Nine Signs of the Apocalypse</u>

The first sign: "We were told of the coming of white-skinned men like Pahana, but not living like Pahana, men who take the land that is not theirs, and men who strike their enemies down with thunder."

The second sign: "Our lands will see the coming of spinning wheels filled with voices. In his youth my father saw this coming with his own eyes, the white man bringing their families in covered wagons."

The third sign: "A strange beast like Buffalo but with great long horns will overrun the land in large numbers. This White Feather saw with his own eyes, the coming of white man's cattle."

The fourth sign: "The land will be crisscrossed with snakes of iron."

The fifth sign: "Our land will be crisscrossed by a giant spider's web."

The sixth sign: "Our land will be crisscrossed with rivers of stone that make pictures in the sun."

The seventh sign: "You will hear of the sea turning black, and many living things dying because of it."

The eighth sign: "You will see many youth wear their hair long like my people, who will come and join our tribal nations to learn their wisdom and ways."

The ninth and last sign: "You will hear of a dwelling place in the heavens above Earth that shall fall with a great crash. It will appear as a blue falling star. Very soon after this the ceremonies of my people will cease."

The Nine Signs: An Interpretation for Today

As you read about the nine signs, visions appear in your mind. Most of the signs are easily read; a few may seem ambiguous until they're given historical context by subsequent prophecies. The first sign's "thunder" that strikes down enemies surely refers to guns used in the conquest of the Hopi's land. The second and third signs are deciphered by White Feather above. In the fourth sign, the crisscrossed snakes of iron are obviously railroad tracks. The fifth sign, a prediction of "crisscrossed spider's web," means electric and telephone lines. In the sixth sign, the rivers of stone that make pictures in the sun are clearly roads and highways, which cause mirages in the heat waves above the pavement. The seventh sign speaks of oil spill disasters in the oceans, the black oil killing many living things on the shores and in the oceans. The eighth sign is definitely the "hippie" movement, where youth started growing their hair long, revolting against a consumerist society and wanting to return to nature for a more spiritual way of life. The meaning of the ninth and last sign is not as immediately clear as the preceding prophecies. Only after reading it a few times did it hit me! The dwelling place in the heavens above Earth must be the space station, which fell from the skies in 1979. According to Australian eyewitnesses, the space station appeared to be burning blue as it burned up in our atmosphere, the "blue falling star"!

Following his enumeration of the nine signs, White Feather then said, "These are the signs great destruction is coming. The world shall rock to and fro. White men shall battle against other people in other lands with those who possess the first light of wisdom. There will be many columns of smoke and fire such as White Feather has seen the white men make in the deserts not far from here. These will come and cause disease and great dying. Many of my people, understanding the prophecies, shall be safe. Those who stay and live in places of my people also shall be safe. Then there will be much to rebuild."

Hopi prophecies state World War III will be started by the people who "first received the light." This is China, Palestine, India, and Africa.

Hopi prophecies such as "no grass will grow for many years, causing a disease no man can cure," along with "many columns of smoke and fire such as White Feather has seen the white men make in the deserts not far from here," surely refer to nuclear missile testing and their mushroom clouds that White Feather and other Hopi witnessed in the nearby desert. Radiation poisoning is the disease that no man can cure.

Other Hopi prophecies say the United States will be destroyed by "gourds of ashes" that fall to the ground and boil the rivers and burn the earth. Turtle Island (the United States) will turn over, and "the oceans will join hands and meet the sky." Turtle Island "turning over and the world rocking to and fro" is again the pole shift of Earth! The Hopi called this imminent condition "Koyaanisqatsi," which means "world out-of-balance, a state of life that calls for another way."

The Hopi are waiting for Pahana, the True White Brother, who will bring with him two intelligent and powerful helpers. Together, these three will show the people of Earth a great new life plan that will lead to everlasting peace. The Hopi say that if the True White Brother and his helpers succeed, we will have peace on Earth for a thousand years, and Earth will be blessed with an abundance of life and food. If Pahana and his helpers fail, terrible evil will befall the world, and many people shall die. Those who are saved will share everything equally. All races will intermarry, use one common tongue and exist as one family.

Hopi prophecies state that one of Pahana's two great and powerful helpers will have a sign of a swastika (a symbol of *masculine* purity) and the sign of the Sun. Obviously, Pahana's great and powerful male helper is the astrological sun sign of Leo, whose ruling planet is the Sun. The "sign of the Sun" is Leo and refers to the most powerful man in the world, our Leo president, President Barack Obama! The second great helper will have the sign of a Celtic cross with red lines between the arms of the cross (representing *female* life blood). After researching the top 50 influential women of the world, I found that either Hillary Clinton or Oprah Winfrey is the most likely woman to be Pahana's second helper. The second great helper is a woman, who will have the sun sign of a Celtic cross, which is a *cross with a circle.* Oprah Winfrey is an Aquarius, whose ruling planet is Uranus. The sign (or glyph) of Uranus is *a cross with a circle.* Its cross also has two lines connected to the horizontal line of the cross, which reminds me of the letter "H" as in the word "helper." Hillary Clinton is the sign of Scorpio, whose ruling planet is Pluto. The sign (or glyph) of Pluto is a capital "P" with an underline, but has an alternate glyph that is *sometimes* used, which is *a cross with a circle* and a "U" shape connected to the cross. The True White Brother's two intelligent and powerful helpers are President Obama and possibly Oprah Winfrey or Hillary Clinton.

Upon first learning of Pahana, I wondered if President Obama might be the True White Brother, despite the fact that he is African American. After researching the name Pahana, which means "lost or true white brother"[3] and after discovering that Nostradamus depicts Pahana as a long-haired white man in one of his drawings (of which I elaborate in a moment and in Chapter 8: Lost Book of Nostradamus), I dismissed the notion. President Obama is also depicted in one of the lost book drawings *along with Pahana*, which indicates he isn't the True White Brother.

Upon discussing the True White Brother and his identity with my wife, she commented that Pahana could be Al Gore. After all, he is bringing a message of major importance to the world. Bringing a problem to people's attention is far from supplying solutions to the problem! Al Gore is not the True White Brother, because Pahana will *not* be greedy like the other white men. Since Al Gore stopped doing mainstream politics, his personal fortune has climbed from $1.9 million to an estimated $96 million![2] Gore said it was "certainly not true" that he would become a "carbon billionaire" and that the idea came from global warming skeptics.[2]

He stated, "I am *proud* to put my money where my mouth is for the past 30 years, and though that is not the majority of my business activities, I absolutely believe in investing in accordance with my beliefs and my values."[2]

During a hearing for clean energy legislation, Gore was questioned by Republican Congresswoman Marsha Blackburn about his investments. She asked, "The legislation that we are discussing here today, is that something that you are going to personally benefit from?"[2]

Al Gore replied, "I believe that the transition to a green economy is good for our economy and good for all of us, and I have invested in it." In a heated debate Gore said, "If you believe that the reason I have been working on this issue for 30 years is because of *greed*, you don't know me."[2]

Gore said he was proud of his record of investing in green technology, and that he is not greedy, but global warming critics aren't convinced. Marc Morano of climatedepot.com stated "Al Gore wants to become the first carbon billionaire and he is poised to do it. As much as Gore's made now, it is going to be a piker league compared to what he is going to make in five years if all these new carbon trading mandates go through."[2] Greed and pride are two of the seven deadly sins. Pahana wouldn't posses either of these traits.

The charitable True White Brother is not Al Gore, but is a common American white man who is depicted in one of Nostradamus's drawings that shows the current situation of the world (see fig. 6). The Hopi say that the True White Brother will be identified by his red cloak, and we should also look for the coming of a person wearing a red hat. In the drawing, a long-haired man *in a red cloak* is shown carrying the weight of the world on his shoulders. Pahana would definitely be carrying the weight of the world on his shoulders. If he fails in bringing his new plan to the world, destruction will follow! Neither the Hopi's description of Pahana (who will not be greedy like the other white men) nor Nostradamus' drawing of Pahana resemble Al Gore.

The Hopi say that Pahana will be our last hope to change the views of the country's people and convince them to revert to a path where greed is no longer a desired trait. This change in the country's views was predicted and recorded long ago. Near Oraibi, Arizona, an ancient Hopi carving on a large rock has survived *for thousands of years* (see fig. 2). Known as Prophecy Rock, the carving shows two

Fig. 2. This is an exact drawing of the carving on Hopi Prophecy Rock show-ing mankind's possible two paths of the future.

possible timelines of the future. The Hopi's Great Spirit is shown standing to the left, laying down his weapons and holding onto a timeline that is read in thousands of years. At the top of the timeline, there is a box signifying the coming of white men. Two separate timelines, which represent the two possibilities of the future, extend from the box. The upper timeline signifies white man's path of sci-entific achievements, which leads to a chaotic and horribly hard fu-ture. The lower timeline signifies a much easier path leading to para-dise, the choice of living in harmony with nature as Hopi traditions encourage. A cross below the box indicates the time of the coming of Christianity. Four stick figures on the top road indicate the past four worlds that were destroyed. There is a line drawn between the two timelines at a certain point, which indicates the last chance for man-kind to return to the bottom path. If the True White Brother and his helpers fail, mankind will continue on the upper path, the hard road.

If they succeed in implementing a great new life plan and people change their ways and return to the bottom path, Earth will be saved from destruction and we will have everlasting peace.

The Hopi are not the only Native American Indians who see two possible futures. Navajo, Hano, and other Native American peoples believe the final cleansing of Earth began in the '90s, when five brother planets aligned themselves and guided in energies to cleanse Earth. They say that between this time and December 2012, all living things will be purged. If mankind's energy does not align with the transformation of the Cosmos, our destruction will follow. The world is currently experiencing this "cleansing period." The extent of the cleansing required will be determined by mankind's actions between now and December 21, 2012.

Obviously, there is a critical turning point that will lead us down one of two paths. Will we be intelligent enough to find this point and make the correct choice? Only time will tell. Wouldn't you agree that we must take this turn *immediately* and follow the Hopi's lower path to peace and harmony? Taking the upper path to nuclear destruction and the annihilation of Earth and its inhabitants doesn't sound like much fun. We *can* live in harmony with the planet and still use new technologies, but technologies *must* be used in harmony with Earth!

Mankind has been caught in a reoccurring "time warp" for many thousands of years, where four previous advanced worlds on Earth were destroyed, possibly by higher powers (saving the planet from mankind before we could cause the destruction of our previous worlds?). Are higher powers now trying to awaken us to the fact that we are headed in the same direction? If we hear their plights, will we listen? Will our world be the fifth to be destroyed and forced to make a new beginning? Think of everything that could be lost! We must travel to other stars and colonize their inhabitable planets, not revert back to ancient times where we wonder what stars are!

The thought of this beautiful world and all its creations being destroyed by our own hands makes me absolutely sick. Earth has existed for billions of years, and we have trashed it in less than a century! The world must change its ways now, before it is too late!

4

THE BIBLE CODES

In the 16th century, religious mystics first began searching the five books of Moses, the first part of the Old Testament, for coded prophecies of the future. A century later, Sir Isaac Newton spent most of his life searching for codes in the Bible, but apparently the codes' author didn't want the codes to be revealed until the proper time—our time.

Around the beginning of World War II, a pioneer code researcher named Chaim Ber Michoel Dov Weismandel again stirred up interest in deciphering the codes when he claimed that he had found basic word patterns in the books.[5]

In August of 1994, the scientific world was shocked by a paper that was published in a leading scientific journal, *Statistical Science*.[1] The article was written by Eliyahu Rips, a respected professor at the Hebrew University of Jerusalem and co-authored by physicist Doron Witztum and Yoav Rosenberg.[5] Rips had created the world's first Bible code computer program. Using ELS skip codes, or equal distant letter sequencing skip codes, Rips had found the names, birth dates, and death dates of 32 famous rabbis encoded in the Bible's text! He had found a highly accurate code in the book of Genesis that included words, phrases, names, dates, and complete sentences that are related to and are in close proximity of each other.

This is how ELS skip codes work. First, a skip code length is chosen. For example, a person may desire to select every tenth character from a text. He or she would start by choosing and writing down any character in a text, whether it's a letter, number, or punctuation mark. The individual would then pick and write down every tenth character. Or let's say a person desires to use a skip code length of 12 and picks every 12th character. No matter how many characters are skipped before selecting the next character, the same number of characters is skipped each time. The chosen letters, numbers, and punctuation marks are then consecutively combined to form words and sentences.

Computers use Bible code search programs to find related information in close proximity to each other by forming graphs filled with the text from the book of Genesis. The closer related information is found to each other, the higher the probability of it not being just a coincidence. The easiest way to visualize how these related words and sentences were first found is as follows: As an example, I'll use a skip code of ten. Visualize a large square graph containing 100 squares. The graph would be 10 squares wide by 10 squares tall. The graph could be longer, we just need to see that when using a skip code of ten, the graph would be ten squares wide. Once filled with characters (letters, numbers, and punctuation) from a text, this graph looks like a word search puzzle, so many letters (or characters) wide, by so many letters tall.

Eliyahu Rips did just this. He took all the characters from the original Hebrew text, the book of Genesis, the first of the Five Books of Moses given to Moses by God, and in sequential order filled his graph with these characters, excluding spaces. Just as in a word search puzzle, words, phrases, names, dates, and complete sentences appeared horizontally, vertically, and diagonally!

What would you think if you obtained a copy of the original Hebrew text of the book of Genesis, the first book of the Holy Bible, chose one of the small chapters, and upon selecting every 12th character of the text, your complete name was spelled out? What if you then selected every 8th character from the same text, and adding the letters together revealed your city of birth? Next, by picking every 17th character, you find your exact birth date. Upon picking every 5th character, you find your father's name. Choosing every 27th character, again from the same text, reveals your city of death, and every 21st character, reveals the date of your death! What would you think? Using this method, along with the text from the original Hebrew book of Genesis, Bible code researchers have found all this same information on not only one person, but on 32 famous rabbis that didn't yet exist when the book was written!

The next step in understanding the nature of the codes' complexity is to visualize how the codes were created. As an illustration, let's imagine that we desire to construct a graph and encode the information "President Barack Obama, first African American president, McCain will lose" in an ELS skip code length of eight. Using a sheet of graph paper (graph paper contains equal squares that completely cover the paper's surface area) and beginning with any upper-left square, we would insert the letter "P" (the first letter of the word President) in that square. Then counting eight squares to the right, we would insert the letter "r" into this box, then counting eight more squares to the right, the letter "e" would be placed in that box. This sequence is continued until all the letters of the words "President Barack Obama" are used.

Next, we want the words "first African American president" to appear *in the same area* as the words "President Barack Obama," so we would write the words "first African American president" with a different ELS skip code length; let's say seven. Again, starting at any upper top left box, we would insert the first letter of our phrase, "f", into that box. Then counting seven boxes to the right, the letter "i" would be added, and again counting seven more boxes to the right, we would write the letter "r." We would then continue counting and inserting each consecutive letter into every seventh box, finally finishing with the letter "t."

We would then encode the phrase "McCain will lose" at a different skip code length, perhaps eleven, using the same method and inserting the letters in close proximity of the other two phrases. Once we finished inserting the phrase "McCain will lose" in every eleventh box, all of the "secret" information will be clumped together in the small graph!

Next, we would go through and fill in all the empty boxes with characters, but not just any characters. We are writing a book. The letters, numbers, and punctuation inserted, when combined with the previous information we put in the boxes, must make complete sentences! The more information we put in the same area, the harder it will be to make complete sentences that make sense. This is the reason why finding multiple pieces of information encoded in the same area of any text, which are related to each other, is highly unlikely! Also, it must be noted that many of the rabbi's names that were found contain uncommon letters such as "z," making the author find words for sentences that contain the letter z. If one of your skip codes inserted an "h" next to a "z," you might have to make up a word, such as some strange name, possibly "Alzhia." This is why the book of Genesis has so many weird names in it! For example, Genesis 4: 20-24 reads as follows:

20. And A'dah bare Ja'bal; he was the father of such as dwell in tents, and of such as have cattle.

21. And his brother's name was Jubal; he was the father of all such as handles the harp and organ.

22. And Zil'lah, she also bare Tu'bal-cain, an instructor of every artificer in brass and iron; and the sister of Tu'bal-cain, was Na'a-mah.

23. And La'mech said unto his wives, A'dah and Zil'lah' hear my voice; ye wives of La'mech, hearken unto my speech: for I have slain a man to my wounding, and a young man to my hurt.

24. If Cain shall be avenged seven-fold, truly La'mech seventy and seven-fold.

Genesis rambles on and on with people's names and random speech patterns such as "I have slain a man to my wounding, and a young man to my hurt." Is this just poor translation from the original Hebrew text, or were the words created to fit and fill in the empty boxes in a graph? Some of the chapters contain dozens upon dozens of names, like chapter 11, which includes 68 strange names in 22 verses! Some of the information given on these people is completely meaningless and seems like trivial and insignificant information for a history book written by God.

I may be incorrect, and all this information may be relevant, but the fact remains that Genesis is encoded with tons of information, and whoever created the book must have encrypted it exactly as I have presented it above. After inserting their secret data into the graph, they would have then needed to fill in all the empty boxes with their history information. The more hidden data they packed into one area, the harder it would have been to make fluent sentences with their history information while still making sense, and the more weird names they would have been forced to use to combine the letters.

Harold Gans, former *Senior* Crypto-logical Mathematician for the National Security Agency of the United States Government Department of Defense was a skeptic of the Bible code theory.[5] Having 28 years of experience cracking codes for the Department of Defense, Gans knew that it was completely possible to do an ELS skip code search on any book and find words and phrases. His wife told him that he should check into the codes and verify whether they were credible or not, but he declined, saying it was all a bunch of garbage. After a year and a half, his wife talked him into researching the codes validity. She commented that if he didn't want to attempt to prove whether Rips' findings were valid or not, why didn't he prove that the codes found were merely coincidental? He said, "That, I can do!"[4]

So, Harold Gans set out to prove that anything the Bible code researchers were finding was purely coincidental. He proved himself wrong. He actually proved to himself that the Bible codes existed, and that they were *not* just a coincidence! He performed what he called "the cities experiment." Gans searched for names of the cities where the 32 famous rabbis found were born and had died. He found the names of the cities of birth and death, of all 32 famous rabbis, in close proximity to the rabbis' names, birth dates, and death dates! Some also include other information!

The History Channel aired a special where they talked about the Bible codes.[4] One of their examples of the 32 rabbis was Moshe Ben Maimon Maimonides. Can you imagine selecting every 10th letter out of the book of Genesis and coming up with this rabbi's name? How many books would you need to search in order to find this name? Other information found on the rabbi, in close proximity of each other, includes his city of birth, Avraham, his birth date of 1204, death date of 1287, and something extra, his father's name, Rambam!

If you preformed an ELS search on the Bible and came up with your full name, the city's name in which you were born (and would die), your birth date (and projected death date), and your father's name, all in close proximity, wouldn't you be a firm believer in the Bible codes? Not only did Rips find all this information on one rabbi, he found this data on 32 rabbis! The possibility of this is unimaginable; billions upon trillions to one! This would be comparable to finding the same amount of information on the first 32 Presidents of the United States encoded in the Declaration of Independence! Can you imagine finding President Ronald Reagan's name along with the names of the cities and dates of his birth and death encoded in the Declaration of Independence? Absolutely unbelievable!

Harold Gans said this concerning the comparison between Nostradamus' quatrains and the Bible code findings, "The fact is that the Bible code is completely scientific and mathematical, Nostradamus is simply subjective and is ambiguous. The Bible code can be evaluated mathematically and scientifically, there is no subjectivity involved, there is no ambiguity involved, you calculate probabilities and as mathematical accuracy, either it's valid, or it's not valid. It's not a matter of opinion, it's a matter of fact!"

Moshe Shak, author of the book *The Bible Code Breakthrough*, said "Nostradamus created his own verses; all his predictions are his own codes. The Bible codes are divine, they were created by God."[5] Moshe is a firm believer in the Bible codes. He found not only his name in the codes, but in close proximity discovered his family matrices. He found the first and last names of his family going back 11 generations! He also found his birth date. The possibility of retrieving this information from any other book would be nonexistent.

The Book of Genesis is very short. It's absolutely amazing that groupings of words concerning the 32 rabbi's history have been found in such a small book, but these findings are only the beginning. One of the more interesting word groupings found is as follows. The example is given as if you had found it yourself. Remember, these are actual findings that can be verified by anyone purchasing an online Bible code program and a copy of the original Hebrew text of the book of Genesis.

Let's imagine you choose a chapter and decide to use an ELS skip code length of 15. Upon inserting all of the characters from the chapter's text into your squares, you start searching for words horizontally, vertically, and diagonally. Suddenly, you see the word "Hitler." Wouldn't you agree that this could be feasible? What are the odds, one hundred to one? So you circle the word Hitler, which you found running vertically (up and down), and continue searching. You then see the word "Berlin" running horizontally at the top! Wow, that's weird! Imagine finding the words Hitler and Berlin in the same small chapter! So you circle the word Berlin and continue onward, thinking to yourself what are the chances of that happening, a thousand to one?

Next, you find *the phrase* "Nazi and enemy" a few lines underneath Berlin, also running horizontally. "Holy Moses!" you cry. This is really weird. Finding the words Hitler, Berlin, and Nazi and enemy in close proximity of each other! Wow! What are the probabilities of that happening, a hundred thousand to one? Unbelievable! You continue searching, but don't find any other words. You then make another graph, 12 letters wide, *using the same exact characters*. You start searching these characters that are now in rows of 12 instead of 15, as in your previous graph. To your disbelief, you then find still another associated word, "Auschwitz," and your mind jumps to Hitler's extermination of the Jews. You then see an additional related word written horizontally above Auschwitz, the word "extermination." Now your mind is definitely blown away. You continue on after circling the other words, thinking you must have exhausted your chances on finding any other hidden words that relate to Hitler. You were wrong. Staring at you is the word "Eichmann," Hitler's henchman! In complete disbelief and utterly awed, you circle the word, thinking what are the chances of this, a billion to one? So you continue. Suddenly, two more words pop out, the words "slaughter," and "oven." In one small chapter, by picking every 12th and 15th letter, you have found the words Hitler, Berlin, Nazi and enemy, slaughter, extermination, oven, Eichmann, and Auschwitz! This is absolutely unbelievable! Who made this word search puzzle, you or a higher power? Can you even imagine achieving these results?

Well, these are actual findings. All the above words were found in one small chapter of Moses' book, Genesis. The information discovered about Hitler wasn't found using the exact number of letters skipped in the example above, but all the words were found in the same area using various ELS skip code numbers. The chance of this occurring is actually more than a trillion to one, but yet the first small book of Moses contains dozens and dozens of these prophecies!

If you've ever created a word search puzzle, you would know that you insert your main key words that are associated with each other, running vertically, horizontally, or diagonally, and then you fill in all the blank spaces with random letters. If you tried making a word search puzzle where all the words had a common theme and used *all random* letters for your graph, the possibility of finding even a few short words would be slim.

Selecting every 15th letter from a chapter is very random. Try it. Take any book and open it to any chapter. Write down every character (in sequential order) in a graph 15 squares wide by as many lines of 15 letters long that it takes to finish the chapter. Now try to find words, any words. Then make a second graph 12 digits wide using the exact same characters, and see if you can find any words or dates that relate to the words or dates you found in the first graph. Can you imagine getting any results such as the Hitler example above? Absolutely impossible! Now try compounding these results to be equivalent to *all* the findings that have been found in the book of Genesis!

Here's another one of my favorites; this one can also be seen on the History Channel's Bible code special.[5] The following example shows codices that were found in close proximity to each other in the text of the book of Genesis. In the middle of the graph, running vertically top to bottom, are the words "Twin Towers Bin Laden." The upper left corner reads "I will name you." In the lower left corner it says "cursed is Bin Laden." At the top right, three words, one above the other, read "terror, incident, and destruction." In the lower right corner is written "revenge belongs to the Messiah." Other words found relative to each other and in close proximity include "ground zero, the twin, towers, ground, and they fell upon their faces." These lines need no explanation. The most incredible aspect about these matrices is that the words "terror" and "incident" are encrypted in an ELS skip code length of two! This is the smallest skip pattern of any graph in Genesis! The chances of finding these 9/11 prophecies in any book are 1 in 10 to the 34th power!

There is also a prophecy written about the Pentagon. Four words, one above the other, read "plane, crash, secondary, and target," and to the side, running vertically, it says "Pentagon." In the same small area of the chapter we find the word "airplane," and underneath this word are the words "attack" and "twin towers." On the right side running vertically is the word "twice," and on the left side the word "Muslim."

Another chapter of Genesis contains more prophecies of the Twin Tower disaster. The words "twin" and "towers" are encoded next to each other, and to the right it reads "in the end of days." Two other chapters include the words "in the end of days." One reads "world war, in the end of days," and the second "atomic holocaust, in the end of days."

Many more of our country's saddest days are prophesied in Moses' book. One such prophecy reads horizontally across the top of the graph, "His name is Timothy," and to the right, running vertically, is Timothy's last name, "McVeigh." On the left side, running vertically, the prophecy reads "day 19," and in the middle, three lines read, one on top of the other, "in the morning, he ambushed, he pounced." Most of us remember the morning of April 19, 1995, when Timothy McVeigh blew up the Murrah Federal Building in Oklahoma City.

Here is another related prophecy that has been found. Do you remember the guy back east that hid in the trunk of a car and shot innocent people through the trunk's enlarged keyhole? He used a rifle. The prophecy reads "John Lee, days of fear, from that upon his left hand, with his right finger, Washington, killed." John Lee's days of fear terrorized Washington. His rifle sat upon his left hand, and his right finger pulled the trigger, killing innocent people.

Another prophecy from one of Moses' chapters reads "Eric, Dylan, Trench Coat Mafia Massacre, April, in cold blood." On April 20, 1999, seniors Eric David Harris and Dylan Bennet Klebold of Columbine High School in Columbine, Colorado killed 13 people and wounded 21 others. Harris and Klebold were members of a group that called themselves the "Trenchcoat Mafia,"[7] which was verified by Harris' father, in a recorded phone call to 911 that he made on April 20, 1999. What are the chances of these three killers being named in the Bible, along with descriptions, locations, and dates of their crimes? Incredible, absolutely incredible!

There are also many prophecies of well-known assassinations. Using information from the Bible codes, the assassination of Prime Minister Rabin was actually predicted before it occurred. Michael Drosnin found matrices in the Bible codes concerning Prime Minister Rabin's assassination and warned people that he would be killed. Within two years, he was assassinated. The assassination of Anwar Sadat is also revealed in the Bible codes. In a small area of one chapter it reads "Sadat, 1981, shot, eighth of Tishri, Chaled." Sadat was shot on the eighth of Tishri (October), 1981. Chaled was the name of Sadat's killer.

The following is a public statement made by Harold Gans, retired Senior Crypto-logical Mathematician for the United States Department of Defense, who spent twenty-eight years decrypting codes for the government and is now working as an independent mathematical consultant.[2] Public statements from Eliyahu Rips and Doron Witztum follow Gans' statement, after which this chapter reveals the most intriguing and troubling Bible code matrices found!

<u>Public Statement by Harold Gans:</u>
I have reviewed the book "The Bible Code" by M. Drosnin.

1. The book states that codes were found in the book of Genesis by Doron Witztum and Eliyahu Rips. An experiment was performed using scientific protocols specified by independent reviewers. The results of the experiment provided extremely strong statistical evidence for the existence of the encoding of great Jewish sages' names and dates of birth and death in the Hebrew text of the book of Genesis. This is all true.

2. The book states that I undertook an independent evaluation of the Witztum-Rips experiment. I duplicated their experiment and provided corroboration of their results. This is correct.

3. The book states that I also performed a new experiment, using

the same methodology of the Witztum and Rips, in which I found that the sages' names were also encoded in Genesis with their respective cities of birth and death. The statistical results obtained were even stronger than that obtained for the first experiment. This is all true.

4. The book also indicates that in spite of concerted efforts by many, no fatal mathematical flaw has been uncovered in the Witztum-Rips experiment. This too, is correct.

5. The book states that the codes in the Torah can be used to predict future events. This is absolutely unfounded. There is no scientific or mathematical basis for such a statement, and the reasoning used to come to such a conclusion in the book is logically flawed. While it is true that some historical events have been shown to be encoded in the Book of Genesis in certain configurations, it is absolutely not true that every similar configuration of "encoded" words necessarily represents a potential historical event. In fact, quite the opposite is true; most such configurations will be quite random and are expected to occur in any text of sufficient length.

Mr. Drosnin states that his "prediction" of the assassination of Prime Minister Rabin is "proof" that the "Bible Code" can be used to predict the future. A single success, regardless of how spectacular, or even several such "successful" predictions proves absolutely nothing unless the predictions are made and evaluated under carefully controlled conditions. Any respectable scientist knows that "anecdotal" evidence never proves anything.

6. A plethora of books have appeared over the last several months, concerning the codes. Unless the work is reviewed by qualified scientists or mathematicians, the reader accepts such a book at his own risk.

7. After exhaustive analysis, I have reached the conclusion that the only information that can be derived from the codes discovered in Genesis is that they exist, and the probability that their mere coincidence is vanishingly small.   Harold Gans 1997.

The following is a public statement made by Eliyahu Rips, professor at the University in Jerusalem.[2]

<u>Public Statement by Eliyahu Rips:</u>
I have seen Michael Drosnin's book "The Bible Code."

1. There is indeed serious scientific research being conducted with regard to the Bible Codes.

2. While I did meet and talk to Mr. Drosnin, I did not do joint work with him.

3. I do not support Mr. Drosnin's work on the Codes, nor the conclusions he derives.

4. There is an impression that I was involved in finding the code related to Prime Minister Rabin's assassination. This is not true.

5. However, I did witness, in 1994, Mr. Drosnin finding a tableau about Prime Minister Rabin, which now appears on the cover of his book.

6. For me, it was a catalyst to ask whether we can, from a scientific point of view, attempt to use the Codes to predict future events. After much thought, my categorical answer is no. *All attempts to extract messages from Torah codes, or to make predictions based on them, are futile and are of no value. This is not only my own opinion, but the opinion of every scientist who has been involved in serious Codes research.

7. The only conclusion that can be drawn from the scientific research regarding the Torah codes is that they exist and they are not a mere coincidence.

8. Mr. Drosnin's book fails to point out that the leading figure in Codes research is Doron Witztum. Therefore, I think it is appropriate that Mr. Witztum should make a statement about the research and answer any questions.

*For the Balance: "The scientific research carried out by Doron Witztum, Yoav Rosenberg, and myself shows that there is a code in the book of Genesis. Details of events that took place thousands of years after the Bible was written are enclosed in the Bible. In a few cases, details of events have been found in the Bible before they happened. My colleague, Doron Witztum, found the exact date that the first SCUD missiles would be launched against Israel, weeks before the Gulf War started. Michael Drosnin found a prediction of the Rabin assassination encoded in the Bible and showed it to me more than a year before the Prime Minister was killed."   Eliyahu Rips '97

The following is physicist Doron Witztum's public statement on his research.[5]

<u>Public Statement by Doron Witztum:</u>

People often ask why, over the last 12 years, I have spent so much time in the field of hidden codes in the Torah, instead of my original field of interest—modern physics and general relativity. The discovery we have made concerning hidden patterns in the Torah is ultimately much more far-reaching and significant. The repercussions of our discovery touch on the very nature of human existence. It can be looked at as the same feeling Robinson Crusoe had when he first discovered the tracks in the sand, that he wasn't alone on the island.

A. We have called this press conference as the researchers who did the original research on the topic of hidden codes. We will be focusing on three issues:

1) How, using standard scientific and statistical tools, we found that details of ancient and modern history are encoded in the original Hebrew text of the Torah.

2) To discuss the many books and works that have been published related to this field that have no scientific basis, and are therefore meaningless.

3) As the researchers, we will explain why it is impossible to use codes to predict the future.

B. A brief overview of the development of codes research.

1. According to mystical sources in Jewish tradition, the Torah can be read and understood on many levels, including the level of a "hidden text." It is composed of words spelled out by skipping equal numbers of letters through the original Hebrew text. We call this phenomenon ELS- Equidistant Letter Sequences. The problem with measuring the significance of what we find is that ELSs will certainly appear in any text, and any word may appear many times at many skip distances.

2. Twelve years ago, I developed a method to see if this hidden text could be scientifically and objectively validated. The idea is as

follows: It is a natural property of any text that words that are conceptually related are likely to appear in the same area of the text. Therefore we decided to see if the ELSs of related words also tends to appear in the same area of the text of the Torah. In order for the convergence of two ELSs to be considered successful, we developed two criteria.

a) A close proximity of two ELSs.

b) That the ELSs that appear are ELSs with a relatively short skip distances between the letters, compared to other ELSs of that word.

*For example: hammer and anvil.

3. Professor Eliyahu Rips developed the mathematical system for measuring the statistical significance of the results. Yoav Rosenberg took Eliyahu's ideas and developed an appropriate computer program to carry out these experiments.

4. In 1986, an extensive experiment was conducted which checked the overall tendency of convergence of a large list of pairs of words: names of famous personalities and their dates of birth and death. The experiment succeeded. A paper describing the results was sent to a scientific publication, and this became the beginning point of a rigorous six year process of review and analysis until it was finally published. Several referees checked the work and asked for further testing. One of these involved re-running the experiment with a completely fresh set of data, and also checking other control texts. This was done and the research passed all tests with very highly significant results. The article was finally published by Statistical Science in 1994.

5. Harold Gans, formerly a Senior Crypto-logical Mathematician at the U.S. Department of Defense, conducted an independent experiment to test the phenomenon that we discovered, using a different set of data. His experiment also succeeded with highly significant results. He sent his paper for publication to a scientific journal. Their response was, "This phenomenon has already been scientifically established, so your work is just another example of the phenomenon."

6. We have conducted seven other experiments that are available as pre-prints.

7. At present, I am completing a book that gives a true view of this fantastic phenomenon, and that will describe not only the ten experiments I mentioned, but also many other successful experiments which reveal a vast spectrum of subjects, ancient and modern.

C. Our comments on the book of Michael Drosnin, and other similar books that have been published.

1. On the one hand, we are happy to see publicity for the phenomenon of Torah codes.

2. On the other hand, there is a danger that the entire credibility of codes research will be destroyed. Mr. Drosnin's work employs no scientific methodology. No distinction is made between statistically valid codes, and accidental appearances, which can be found in any book. For example, Drosnin's "code" of the comet Shoemaker Levy crashing into Jupiter is statistically meaningless. Such a code can be found by accident in 1 out of any 3 books checked!

3. What is the danger of research done with no scientific parameters? For example, we know that the field of health involves systematic rigorous testing of new medicines. If someone freely distributes a medicine that has undergone no scientific testing, there are two areas of damage:

a) The credibility of useful and helpful medicines will be severely compromised.

b) People may end up using useless medicines in place of helpful ones. In codes research, we are dealing with a similar situation:

c) The credibility of serious codes research will be compromised by amateurs whose "discoveries" are scientifically meaningless.

d) People will exploit the Torah to present all kinds of counterfeit proofs, by finding "hidden messages," that bolster their ideology.

We have a very important and valuable phenomenon that has been discovered. It's a scientific discovery that can really help us get a better understanding of the nature of our existence. Rather than have it watered down with people's personal exploitation or misunderstanding, we should be investing more in serious research and understanding of the phenomenon.

In summary, one who wishes to show legitimate examples of Torah codes should at least follow two basic rules:

e) Use mathematical tools that can provide a level of statistical measurement between the minimal occurrences of ELSs.

f) Use an objectively chosen list of words to look for: I will now show an example of what I mean by an objective list. This example has never been shown before publicly.

The process is to take one central word, find its minimal occurrence in the text, and then construct a tableau based on it. In this case, our topic is the death camp Auschwitz. We take an objectively chosen list of related words. In this case, we are looking for the names of the sub-camps that comprised the Auschwitz complex. We make a tableau based on the words "of Auschwitz." With our tableau set, the computer will systematically look throughout the text for a minimal occurrence of each of the sub-camps. Any one of these words can appear anywhere in the text of Genesis. We find something very unexpected—that they consistently appear in the area of the words "of Auschwitz."

D. The Future: Mr. Drosnin's book is based on a false claim. It is impossible to use Torah codes to predict the future.

I, myself, as the original researcher of the phenomenon of Torah codes investigated thoroughly the question of predicting the future. I reached the conclusion that it is impossible. I saw this through experimentation and also as a simple point of logic. There are several reasons why it's impossible. I will give the most basic reason. In general, we always have difficulty understanding a text where we don't have any syntax or punctuation. In the plain Hebrew text of the Torah, without punctuation, I could easily read the Ten Command-ments as telling me to steal and murder. There's a verse that describes Moses being commanded to bring incense. I could easily read it as a commandment to use drugs. All we have is a few isolated encoded words of a hidden text. Maybe we're missing some very critical words. It's literally impossible to learn a coherent story out of the juxtaposition of a few words that may be somehow related.

Additionally, just like there is a code that Rabin will be assassi-nated, I also found a code saying that Churchill will be assassinated! Figure 3. "Churchill will be assassinated."

Even regarding past events, there are ELSs of words that appear near each other that have no relation to each other. It is therefore unwise, and one could say irresponsible, to make "predictions" based on ELSs of words appearing near each other.

In summary, we see that predicting the future is impossible. We see that by publicizing books and works of examples of codes that have no scientific basis, it ruins the integrity of serious research. And finally, we see that the scientific phenomenon of Torah codes is a real one, and is one that deserves serious attention.   Doron Witztum – Physicist - Jerusalem College of Technology June 4, 1997.

It's hard for me to believe that the Bible codes were discovered over 15 years ago, and most people aren't aware of their existence. I don't believe anyone I know has any knowledge on the codes, unless this information came from me. This makes me wonder how many people don't know they exist.

Here are a few more examples of matrices found, as seen on the History Channel's Bible Code special.[4] One tableau, discovered by Doron Witztum, *before the event actually occurred*, reads "fire, missile, Hussein, war, on 3rd Shevat." Saddam Hussein fired his first SCUD missile on January 18, 1991, which is the 3rd of Shevat in their calendar.

Another tableau, with all its words reading horizontally, one above the other and in phrases, reads "axis powers, alliance of evil, 5705 (1945 in our equivalent year), they did not prevail." The alliance of evil and the axis powers are obviously Japan and Germany, and they didn't prevail.

Another reads "Who is he? President, Watergate, but he will be kicked out." This tableau obviously talks about President Nixon and the Watergate scandal where he was impeached. A closely related tableau reads, "Clinton, nation against impeachment." And another reads "Clinton," and off the letter "i" in Clinton, running horizontally is the word "impeachment," and underneath impeachment is the phrase "hidden secret lover of maid servant."

There are also two tableaux predicting natural disasters that are unmistakable in their meaning. The first one reads "Floyd, hurricane, September, USA, 5760 (1999 in our calendar year), evacuation." This is a prophecy of hurricane Floyd, which hit the United States in September of 1999. In the second tableau are the words "Kobe, Japan, the big one, 1995" with the words "fire and earthquake" written beneath the city's name.

Codes in two more books of Genesis talk of Saddam Hussein. One reads "Saddam, Hussein, 2003, who will be destroyed" and another that reads "has been, captured, humiliated, they hated him, Saddam."

Some graphs show names of scientists and their discoveries. In tightly formed graphs, we find the words "Edison, light bulb, electricity" followed by "Newton, gravity" and "Einstein, science, he overturned present reality."

Two more interesting tableaux read, "Shakespeare, Macbeth, Hamlet, presented on stage," along with "Wright Brothers, airplane," and "Napoleon, Elba, Waterloo, France."

Other graphs describe our history, such as "American, Revolution, 1776," as well as "the depression, 1929, stocks, economic collapse," and "world war, Germany, England, Japan, United States, Russia, France." Another reads "atomic holocaust, Japan, 1945" and an additional one reads "November 7, 2009, Gore, Bush."

One of my favorites starts at the bottom, reading upwards until it splits into several directions, "spaceship, Columbia, consumed by fire."

Many Bible codes are revealed in websites on the Internet that people have discovered using Bible code search programs.[3] In each instance, the people discovering the codes show where they found the codes in the original Hebrew Bible text and include all ELS information. The most interesting codes were discovered by Juan from Spain, who goes by the name LOrd KyrON, and Fabrice Bect from France.[3] These two have discovered more Bible code prophecies that have come true after they found them, than anyone else I've researched. Their tableaux read "for the fireplace of Yellowstone, they were cast into the lake of fire" and "Yellowstone, this place appeared dead." Another reads "Yellowstone, Volcano, the mound, descend, this place died in appearance." Still another reads "Yellowstone, the day of the Lord is near in the valley of decision, the Sun and the Moon become black, and the stars withdrew their shining, they shall be devoured as stubble fully dry," and another "Yellowstone, threat, menace, the mountain threatens, Volcano, hill, mound." Many more words are found, including "Yellowstone, Volcano, accumulate, Etna, fire, choking, asphyxia, burning, darkness, toxic, ashes, cinders."

The descriptions of the "dead appearance" of Yellowstone are very interesting, since most of Yellowstone Park remains burnt from the fires years ago during the government's "let it burn naturally" policy. Scientists say that if Yellowstone's super volcano did erupt, everything could be cooked within a 200 mile radius. Wow! My family lives about 100 miles away from Yellowstone!

The two tableaux I saved for last, which can also be seen on the History Channel's Bible Code special, relate to the future events of 2012.[5] Though Rips, Gans, and Witztum say they don't believe that anyone should attempt to use the codes to predict the future, it's obvious to me that had the appropriate codes been found before certain events happened, history might have been changed. The author of the Bible codes knows the future. No matter how many possibilities of the future exist, there will be only one true future. The author of the Bible codes would also know the possible outcomes of any change that could, would, or will occur that affects the future, thus knowing our true future. Both of these last two tableaux describe the same event, but each contains a different outcome.

The first tableau gives us information on one of the two possibilities of the future. In the center, reading horizontally is the word "Earth," and underneath Earth is the word "annihilated." Below this is written the year "5772," which is our calendar year 2012. To the side of these three lines is the word "comet." This tableau states that Earth will be annihilated by a comet in the year 2012, the consequence of mankind continuing to travel down its current path of self-destruction. The Bible's Book of Revelation tells us of a large star that will fall from the sky in the end of days, and the star will be called "Wormwood." Almost all of this book's chapters on 2012 contain scenarios of Earth being hit by a comet in 2012, but as shown in other chapters, this future can be changed. Prophecies from all cultures seem to convey the same message. We have a choice in determining which future is ours. We owe it to ourselves to make the right choice.

The second tableau, which tells of the opposite outcome, gives us hope. It describes the reward for changing our current path of greed and destruction of the planet, to a path where we care for all the people of the world and live in harmony with Earth. On the right, reading top to bottom is the word "comet," which appears *exactly* in the same position as the previous tableau! The next words are *also* in the same positions as the first tableau, which read "Earth annihilated 2012," but rather than reading "annihilated," it reads "it will be crumbled," and below that is the phrase "I will tear to pieces," and *again* at the bottom is "2012." This should give us all hope. The word "annihilated" has been replaced with "I will tear to pieces" and "it will be crumbled"! This hits you like a ton of bricks! The author of the book of Genesis and the creator of the Bible Codes, God, or whoever is the author, will stop the comet of 2012 from annihilating Earth, if we choose the right path and quit destroying our planet!

LOrd KyrON and Fabrice Bect have also discovered many Bible codes concerning an asteroid or a comet strike. These codes read "An impact of a great rock, a coming of a mountain of rock, a death of fire, and a word I give; at any time a star shall light up the water, Atlantic Ocean, comet, meteor, impact, great wave, the repercussion of the impact will make noise, fire of the comet, earthquake, to judge, O Lord to whom vengeance belong, O God to whom vengeance belongs show yourself, vengeance belongs to Jesus." Other coded matrices found seem to describe the same scenario. "The planetoid body will return, stone, rock, spin, he will shatter, the judge has return, on the seventh day, threaten, wail, Learmonth, Observatory, watchtower, expectant, pull, affect, influence, impact, comet, Wormwood, warning, pandemonium."

Most of these descriptions remind me of the asteroid Apophis, which was recently discovered by astronomers at NASA and will pass closely by Earth several times in the coming years (unless it actually hits Earth). It's astounding to read the words Learmonth, observatory, and Wormwood, because scientists have based operations at Learmonth Observatory in Australia to watch the skies for earthbound asteroids and comets. Fittingly, the name of the project is Wormwood!

Other codes actually speak of Apophis, such as "Apophis, asteroid, I smote you with blasting, Wormwood, ambusher, asteroid, ancient, prophecies, object, shattered, percussion, thundering, noisy, terrified, burnt-up, obliterate, desolation, comet impact, from space, the end of man, Apophis, asteroid, Apophis arose alas!, the one smiting you is a judgment."

This "judgment" will obviously be based on the actions we're taking today. Other codes contain the date 2012, making me wonder if there will actually be two or more comet or asteroid impacts in that year (and perhaps causing a pole shift), one possibly hitting Canada. These codes read "2012, comet, stone-like, planetary wanderer, fragmentary, scatter-gun, Earth annihilated, smitten, Canada, ultimate, terrifying, lethal, axis, tilting, tipping, eradication."

Other codes discovered concerning 2012 read, "2012, impact, extinction, human, cosmic plan, Messiah, year 2012, comet, premature death, from impact, God, year 2012, God." Still another code speaks of solar flares, "stove of the dead, I will send to all men, guilt, holocaust, day of judgment, solar flare."

Another tableau warns of an event that happened in 2010. It reads "great, earthquake, L.A., Calif., in 5770 (2010 in our calendar year)." Los Angeles encountered an earthquake on March 16, 2010. Nearby Baja California's quake on April 4, 2010, was a 7.2 magnitude!

After comprehending the mathematical possibilities of finding relevant information encoded in the texts of the Bible, can you see how anyone could refute the existence of the Bible codes? The History Channel showed one man who disputes the codes existence, Professor Brendan McKay.[5] He states that many such word clusters can be found in any book of sufficient length.

To prove his point, Professor McKay showed matrices that he found using an ELS skip code program on the book *Moby Dick*, which supposedly describes the assassination of Martin Luther King, Jr. and John F. Kennedy. McKay's matrice for Martin Luther King's assassination are "mlk, tenn, gun." If you found these three "words," would you think of them as descriptions of Martin Luther King, Jr.'s assassination? The letters "mlk" supposedly stand for Martin Luther King, Jr. and "tenn" means Tennessee, where he was shot. Mckay's matrice for Kennedy's assassination reads "kennedy, in cars, shot." These graphs show very little information, no dates or names of places and contain words with very common letters. Also, the length of the book *Moby Dick* (written in English) doesn't compare with the small length of the book of Genesis (written in ancient Hebrew).

Brendan didn't find even one of *Moby Dick's* chapters that contain loads of information on our history. He didn't find any dates that correspond with any event or name that he found. He didn't find even one rabbi's name, let alone 32 names of famous rabbis, their cities of birth and death, along with their birth dates and death dates. He didn't find any graphs showing events in our history, or any information even slightly close to the information found in the book of Genesis! When opponents of the Bible codes find *any* matrices containing information on historical events in any book, which include names, dates, and specific descriptions of the event and find dozens of these graphs, then everyone will admit that the existence of the Bible codes may be a random occurrence. This will never happen.

Harold Gans, former Senior Mathematical Cryptologist for the United States Defense Department, stated "I do have a response to Brendan McKay and his work, I have a paper, a 64-page paper, which addresses all of the scientific issues that Brendan McKay raises, and it can be found on the World Wide Web, and downloaded from the Internet."[4] Author Moshe Shak stated "I challenge Brendan McKay to follow my procedures, my methodology, and come up with anywhere near what I have done. He will not be able to."[4]

Many people agree that there are three possibilities of how the codes could have been encrypted into the book of Genesis. The first possibility envisions a human being traveling from the future to the past, who gave our ancestors the coded books that would eventually warn us of our impending destruction. Time travel is possible, which is being proven using the formula "speed = distance/ time," we just don't yet have the knowledge to "change distance." In space travel, speed, which is the speed of light, remains constant *in outer space* (the speed of light slows as it travels through substances). Thus, if the speed of light remains the same and distance changes, so does time. If we change "distance," we can change time! Einstein said that if we travel away from Earth at almost the speed of light for one year and then turn around and return to Earth at the same speed, when we reach Earth everyone we knew would be long dead! Space travel does affect time!

The second possibility of how the codes were encrypted is alien intervention. This would require the "alien" to "change distance" while traveling through outer space. Years ago, people would have said this would be impossible, because knowing that nothing can travel in space faster than the speed of light, and knowing that the nearest sun to ours is well beyond our reach even traveling at the speed of light, tells us that we couldn't reach the nearest star in our lifetime. New theories on "warp speed" are intriguing; theories of space travel, where we shrink space in front of us and expand space behind us, thus changing "distance." With this theory, we wouldn't need to travel faster than the speed of light. Instead of traveling to a distant point in space at the speed of light, we would bring that distant point in space to us! This technology is still hundreds of years in the future for us, but it's possible that intelligent beings out there somewhere are using it right now!

A third possibility of how the codes were encrypted into the book of Genesis is that they came from God (it's written that Moses received the book of Genesis from God). Either a human being from the future, or an intelligent being from another world could have played the role of God, or God himself encrypted the book. Why would anyone encrypt codes into the text of Genesis? Because the author wants to warn us of possible future events and prove to us that prophecy of the future is not only feasible, but is a fact! Someone wants to make us aware of the seriousness of the plights of our fellow man and the world around us. Someone wants us to implement the necessary changes to solve the world's problems and stop trashing the planet, or our civilization as we know it will be destroyed. If we can't change our current path of self-destruction, someone will change it for us! That someone could be God. If so, God didn't encode the prophecies into the Bible's text for us to be awed and frightened or to show off His power. God put these codes in the book of Genesis, first, in order for us to see that prophecy of the future is possible, and second, so that we would be able to see the possibilities of the future and make changes to follow the correct path.

Before closing this chapter, I'd like to add one last bit of information that surfaced recently. I stated in the first of this chapter that names and descriptions in Genesis' genealogy seem to ramble on and on with meaningless and trivial data for a history book written by God. I thought that the chapters *must* have tons of encoded information hidden in them. I was so convinced of this that I made a list of the names given in Genesis 5, showing descendents from Adam through Noah. I tried making sense of the list, thinking that there was a deeper meaning or code embedded in the names, but was unsuccessful in deciphering anything. I recently discovered several sites on the Internet that made total sense of the names! The first website I found had postings from Fabrice Bect, Bible code researcher, and the second was by Dr. Chuck Missler, author of *Cosmic Codes*.[6] After verifying their research and translations, I found several more sites with the same translations.

It's been found that translating the Hebrew names into English, and adding the interpretations together, forms a complete meaningful sentence! God is truly amazing! Here is the gospel encoded within the genealogy of Genesis:

Hebrew Name:	English translation:
Adam	man
Seth	appointed
Enosh	mortal
Kenan	sorrow
Mahalalel	the blessed God
Jared	shall come down
Enoch	teaching
Methuselah	his death shall bring
Lamech	the despairing
Noah	rest and comfort

Adding the translated words together reads, "Man (was) appointed mortal sorrow; (but) the blessed God shall come down teaching (that) his death shall bring the despairing rest and comfort." Absolutely amazing!

After accumulating and correlating all the information that I have compiled in this book's 2012 chapters, I'm a firm believer that there are two paths we may follow, each leading to opposing outcomes of the future. One path will direct us to self-destruction and the complete annihilation of Earth, where few people will survive. The second path will guide humanity to world peace and living in harmony with the planet for a thousand years. It's our responsibility to choose the correct path *before* December 21, 2012!

People need to acknowledge that the Bible code prophecies do exist, and the information contained in them is not just random chance. We must realize that foreseeing of the future is possible, and we must listen to these prophecies and other sources of ancient wisdom that are included in this book's 2012 chapters and act upon them immediately! Please help me convey this information to the world; we are surely approaching what could be the end of days!

5

OUR LADY AND THE CHILDREN

OF FATIMA

Most people have never heard of the Children of Fatima or the events of Fatima, Portugal, which were officially declared "worthy of belief" by the Catholic Church. This will become one of the most widely recognized miracles that deal directly with the end of days and confirms the fact that the world must immediately change its "evil" ways, or face destruction of civilization as we know it, which is the premise of this book.

"Our Lady of Fatima" is the title given to the Blessed Virgin Mary in honor of her manifestation to three shepherd children tending sheep at Fatima, Portugal. She first appeared before Lucia Santos and her younger cousins, siblings Jacinta and Francisco Marto, on the 13th of May in 1917 and returned on the 13th for the next five months. In these visions, the apparition specifically identified herself to the three as the "Lady of the Rosary." Lucia, the eldest of the three children, later became a nun and devoted her life to God through the Catholic Church.

On Sunday, May 13, 1917, the three children were tending sheep at the Cova da Iria near their home in Fatima. Ten–year old Lucia later described seeing a woman cloaked in white "brighter than the Sun, shedding rays of light clearer and stronger than a crystal ball filled with the most sparkling water and pierced by the burning rays of the Sun."3

According to Lucia, throughout the progression of Mary's six appearances, the Lady confided secrets to the children along with other important messages. The collection of divine revelations and descriptions of visions is now known as "The Three Secrets of Fatima." The children were given prophecies that told of a horrible end to the world if people didn't return to a path of righteousness, a fore-warning echoed by myself, the Hopi, Nostradamus, and others.

On July 13, 1917, on Mary's third visit, Mary fulfilled her promise to reveal how mankind had sinned, how they might be redeemed, and what the terrible outcomes of the future might be if we continue to offend God. She gave them three secrets to be revealed at specific times according to the divine plan.

In the first secret revealed by Mary, the children were shown visions of what would happen if mankind continued its evil ways. They saw visions of fire: both land and people were burning and melting. Lucia recalled:

Our Lady showed us a great sea of fire, which seemed to be under the Earth. Plunged into the fire were demons and souls in human form, like transparent burning embers, all blackened or burnished bronze, amid shrieks and groans of pain and despair.[3]

In my opinion, the "sea of fire" describes the horror of people being burnt by blast waves emanating from nuclear explosions (see Chapter 22: Nuclear Power and Nuclear Weapons), the result if mankind continued its evil ways.

Lucia knew people would expect proof that the three children were actually receiving revelations from Mary. She asked the Lady to help her and her cousins to convince people they were telling the truth. Mary promised a miracle for the last of her appearances on the 13th of October so that all could believe and examine their own actions.

The miracle was to occur at noon, and it didn't take long for the crowd gathered at the Cova da Iria to reach 70,000 people. Numerous reporters and photographers comprised the crowd, while the Pope and other high-ranking Church officials waited by a podium near the center of the mob. From horizon to horizon, people huddled under umbrellas, as it rained heavily. About noon the rain stopped and the Sun shone visibly behind a mask of clouds, allowing everyone to view the Sun without discomfort.

The noon deadline came and passed, and after about an hour the members of the crowd became noticeably restless. The Pope rose and began to tell the congregation to disperse and go home. Exactly at this moment, people started crying out, "Look at the Sun!" Onlookers watched, stunned, as the Sun began to change colors and rotate like a fire wheel! Some reported seeing the Sun fall from the sky, race toward Earth and return to its normal position in the sky only moments before it would have slammed into Earth. For others, the Sun zigzagged. This phenomenon was witnessed by over 70,000 people in the crowd below, as well as by people up to 40 kilometers away. The event was soon to be dubbed "The Miracle of the Sun."[1]

Columnist Avelino de Almeida of *O S'eculo*, Portugal's most influential newspaper, reported:

Before the astonished eyes of the crowd, the Sun trembled, made sudden incredible movements outside all cosmic laws, the Sun danced according to the typical expression of the people.[1]

Similarly, eye specialist Dr. Domingos Pinto Coelho of the newspaper *Ordem* wrote:

The Sun, at one moment surrounded with scarlet flame, at another aureoled in yellow and deep blue, seemed to be in an exceeding fast and whirling movement, at times appearing to be loosened from the sky and to be approaching Earth, strongly radiating heat.[2]

After the Sun returned to its normal position, color, and brightness, heavy clouds again filled the skies, and the rain resumed. Over 70,000 people, including the Pope, had witnessed a true miracle and were eager to hear the Blessed Virgin Mary's prophecies and mandates.

Mary then told Lucia that the people should now believe in Her messages, and that the prevailing war (World War I) would soon end, but a worse war would break out during the pontificate of Pius XI if atheism continued, and people did not cease to offend God. In 1917, Pope Pius did not yet exist.

Of course, people didn't stop offending God, and in November of 1917, communism was born in the former Soviet Union. Soviets soon believed Lenin was the Anti-Christ. He told people that there was no God, installed a secular government and destroyed all churches and religious articles. Lenin's goal in the Russian Revolution was to destroy all organs of self-administration and all other parties and social organizations, except his own.

The Blessed Virgin Mary then told Lucia:

When you see the night illuminated by an unknown light, know it is a great sign given to you by God that He is about to punish the world for its crimes, by means of war, famine and persecutions of the Church. To prevent this, I shall come to ask for the consecration of Russia to my Immaculate Heart (the "consecration" of Russia refers to the complete conversion of Russia to the one "true Church" created by Christ, the Catholic Church) *and the communion of reparation on the first Saturdays* (performing Church activities on the first Sundays of each month such as prayer, meditation, receiving Communion, and going to Confession). *If my requests are heeded, Russia will be converted, and there will be peace. If not, she will spread her errors throughout the world, causing wars and persecutions of the Catholic Church. The good will be martyred, the Holy Father will have much to suffer, and various nations will be annihilated. In the end, my Immaculate Heart will triumph. The Holy Father will consecrate Russia to me, and she shall be converted, and a period of peace will be granted for the world.*

Twelve years later in 1929, Lucia reported to the town's people that Mary returned to her, again asking for the consecration of Russia to her Immaculate Heart.

On January 25, 1938, Lucia saw the blood red "fire in the skies event" that was seen throughout Europe and into Russia, the ominous sign of war Mary had previously predicted, the great sign given by God that He is about to punish the world for its crimes, by means of war, famine and persecutions of the Church. We now know that these ominous series of light patterns that illuminated the skies over Europe were aurora displays caused by solar maximums that occurred that year. Soon, as predicted, World War II started.

In 1943, upon becoming ill, Lucia wrote down the three secrets. She sealed them in an envelope and left instructions for it to remain sealed until 1960 when their meanings would be better understood. As we now know, Soviet nuclear armament in Cuba began in the 1960s and led to the intensification of the Cold War tensions between the Soviet Union and the United States.

Pope John Paul II may have known the third secret for decades, but didn't realize he was part of the secrets until 1981. Sister Lucia wrote:

The Blessed Virgin Mary showed us a bishop dressed in white, we had the impression that it was the Holy Father; the Holy Father passed through a big city half in ruins, having reached the top of the mountain, he and the other religious figures are slain by bursts of bullets and arrows.

On May 13, 1981, *exactly* 64 years after Mary's first appearance in Fatima, 2,000 people lined the Vatican square for an address and witnessed the attempted assassination of Pope John Paul II. Bullets barely missed Pope John Paul II's vital organs; the Pope believed the Blessed Virgin Mary guided the bullets' paths around them. As he recuperated for three weeks, he asked for all the information on Fatima and re-examined the secrets. One year later, after a Catholic priest tried to stab him, the Pope finally decided it was time to consecrate Russia. He wrote letters to all the bishops inviting them to join him. In March of 1984, the Vatican granted consecration to Russia, and soon after Sister Lucia received word from Mary and informed the Holy Father that Heaven had accepted the consecration.

Shortly after this, Mikhail Gorbachev took power of the Soviet Union and met with the Pope and Sister Lucia. They told Gorbachev of the events of Fatima and of the prophecies given to Lucia and convinced Gorbachev that unless something was done quickly, the world would be plunged into a nuclear holocaust and many nations would be annihilated.

Mikhail Gorbachev's insight soon led to the Soviet Union's collapse and religious practices were reestablished. In 1989 the Berlin wall came down, and the threat of nuclear annihilation almost vanished. The Blessed Virgin Mary had apparently revealed the second secret (the possibility of nuclear war between the United States and the Soviet Union) to Sister Lucia in order to save the world from nuclear annihilation!

The Blessed Mother Mary predicted this outcome. She previously said that in the end, Her Immaculate Heart would triumph, the Holy Father would consecrate Russia to Her, and that Russia shall be converted. Mary also said a period of peace will be granted for the world after this occurs. *This period of peace has now passed!*

It is very noteworthy that the Soviet Union was established after the Russian Revolution of 1917, when Czar Nicholas II was overthrown and forced to sign his abdication on March 15, 1917.[4] In this same year, the Communist Party took power, and the Blessed Virgin Mary visited the children of Fatima to ensure the communist's eventual downfall!

The Vatican held the third secret until June 26, 2000, despite Lucia's directions that it be revealed after 1960. In 1960, rather than releasing it, the Vatican released a statement claiming the world "was not quite ready for it yet."[3]

It has been alleged that Cardinals Bertone and Ratzinger engaged in a cover-up of a one-page document from the Blessed Virgin Mary, which contains information about the apocalypse and a great apostasy.[3]

On June 26, 2000, the Vatican finally released the third secret. To this day, many still believe the Vatican has not yet disclosed the full secret due to the chaos it may cause. This third secret reveals Lucia's vision of yet another possible annihilation scenario, due to occur in the near future. The text released by the Vatican, the Lady's Third Secret of Fatima read:

At the left of Our Lady and a little above, we saw an angel with a flaming sword in his left hand, flashing, it gave out flames that looked as though they would set the world on fire; but they died out in contact with the splendor that Our Lady radiated towards him from her right hand; pointing to Earth with his right hand, the angel called out in a loud voice, penance, penance, penance.

We can easily apply a modern interpretation of these dated words. Earth will soon be threatened by bursts of fire coming toward it, either in the form of solar flares, a galactic super wave, an asteroid, or a comet. If mankind heeds the Blessed Virgin Mary's warnings and changes its evil ways, the destruction of Earth will be prevented. The solar flare (or other threat) will be absorbed or destroyed by "contact with the splendor that Our Lady will radiate."[3] Does this scenario sound familiar?

In the Bible codes, God also shows us two possible versions of the future that hinge on mankind's actions. The Bible codes speak of a comet annihilating Earth in the matrices "2012, comet, Earth annihilated." The flashing, flaming sword described above could be a comet or an asteroid. It's also very possible that in 2012 Earth will be threatened by solar flares and *later* by a comet, super wave, or an asteroid. This book's next chapter on the Maya and Egyptians introduces a known asteroid called Apophis, which was discovered in 2004 and could soon annihilate Earth. Apophis has an elongated shape, and as it spins past us in coming years, its "flashing" will be visible to the naked eye. Apophis is likely to pass uncomfortably close to Earth and could cause the sort of damage that the ancient Egyptians experienced. Their writings speak of "The Destroyer," an orbiting heavenly body that devastated Egypt 3,600 years ago. The Egyptians say that the Destroyer (discussed in detail in later chapters) passed very close to Earth and described it as a giant ball of fire!

Sister Lucia's prophecies state there will be either terrible worldwide annihilations or world peace depending on individual choices in the coming years. The people of this planet can only hope for divine intervention and protection from the extreme solar flare, asteroid, or wandering comet, if we take responsibility for our collective fate. Let's decide to make the necessary changes today so that we can assure our survival and lasting peace for tomorrow!

6

PROPHECIES OF THE MAYA AND THE EGYPTIANS

The Maya, one of the most intriguing civilizations of the new world, inhabited lands that are now Guatemala, Belize, El Salvador, Honduras, and parts of Mexico. Many ancestors of the original Maya* civilization still live and continue to speak ancient Mayan.

The Maya were excellent astronomers and kept track of the solar and lunar years as well as eclipses and cycles of the planets. Many of their buildings and monuments were designed and precisely positioned to correspond with known astronomical cycles.

The Maya were very obsessed with time, their calendars, and astronomical cycles. Maya astronomers, using only the naked eye, carefully recorded their observations and passed down these notations of planetary positions and reoccurring astronomical cycles (which were also recorded in their codices) through countless generations over thousands of years. They were able to calculate planetary positions, eclipses, and alignments of heavenly bodies thousands of years into the future. The Maya used this knowledge to make their prognostications. They knew that many past events will reoccur at their corresponding later dates.

One of their most astounding predictions was the prophecy that white skinned bearded gods would come to them on March 5, 1519. On this date, Cortez and his conquistadors arrived on their shores!

*Note on Maya terminology: I observe protocol of Maya scholars, in which the word "Mayan" is used only in reference to the spoken language of the Maya.

The fact that this prediction was made hundreds of years previous to it becoming recorded history shows us that Maya predictions can be pegged to an *exact date!*

The Maya's interest in time, or chronology, led them to develop a high degree of sophistication in mathematics. Their number system is based on the number 20 rather than our familiar base 10. Using dots and bars that represent numbers, their mathematical system is capable of quickly calculating large numbers. The ancient Maya were also familiar with the concept of "zero," which didn't appear in western civilization until the 12th century.

The greatest tools used by the ancient Maya to map time were their calendars (See Fig. 3). The Tzolkin and the Haab, which are their two main calendars, are more accurate than the calendar we use today. The Maya calculated the seasonal year to be an equivalent of 365.2420 days. Contemporary science calculates it at 365.2422 days. Such precision in ancient days required years of calculating data and relatively sophisticated mathematics.

The Maya and Aztec calendars are greatly documented and completely understood, consisting of several spherical cycles with outer gears that can be synchronized and interlocked to produce more extensive time cycles. In their calendar system, 20 days equal an "uinal," 18 uinals (360 days) equal a "tun," 20 tuns (7,200 days) equal a k'atun, and 20 k'atuns (144,000 days) equal a b'ak'tun. Thirteen b'ak'tuns are equivalent to 5,125 years. The Maya date of December 21, 2012, would be written as 13.0.0.0.0., or 13 b'ak'tuns, 0 k'atuns, 0 tuns, 0 uinals, and 0 days since the day of the last creation (and the beginning of the current creation). The deity Itzamna supposedly brought the knowledge of this calendar system to the ancient Maya. This Maya date represents a countdown to zero from 13 b'ak'tuns, a countdown of 5,125 years that ends exactly on our calendar date of December 21, 2012!

These calendars, which include cycles of the moon, contain cycles of 260, 365, and 360 days. The Tzolkin, the most important calendar, contains 260 days and is combined with another calendar known as the "Haab," which contains 365 days. These two calendars form a synchronized cycle lasting 52 Haabs (See Fig. 3) called the "calendar round."

The 360 day year, which is made up of 18 months of 20 days each, is used in a system called the Long Count. The Long Count calendar, used to track longer periods of time, is based upon the number of elapsed days since a specific recorded date of great significance. Using the Long Count calendar, the Maya had a perfect system for recording events in a linear relationship to one another. They found that natural cycles reoccurred with the repetition of various cycles of the calendar and were able to make divinations associ-

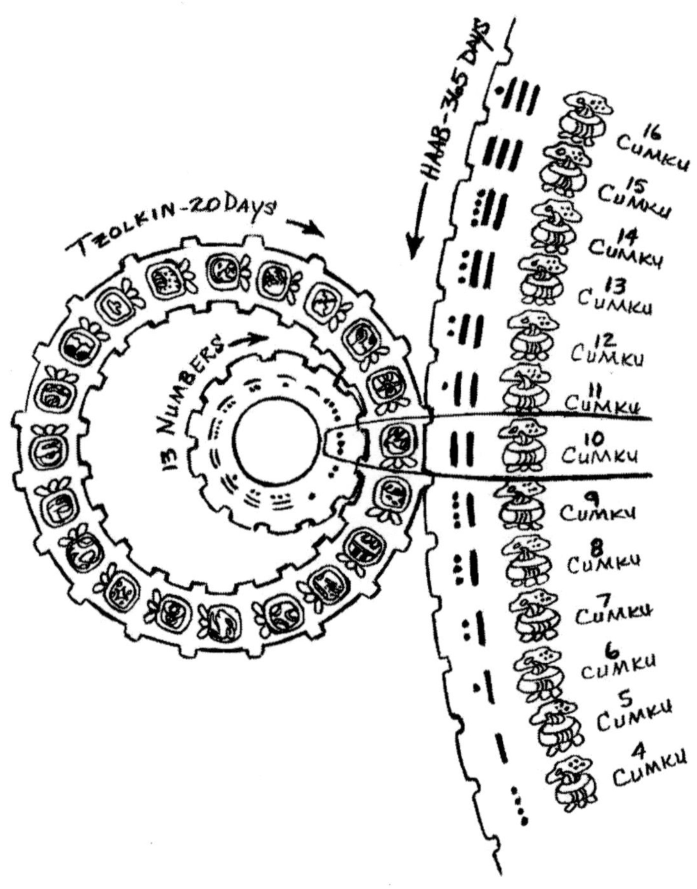

Fig. 3. This drawing shows the Calendar Round, its interlocking gears, and the gear's movements. Drawing by Bruce Burtenshaw

ated with certain configurations. They knew that future events would be influenced by the same things that occurred in its corresponding previous cyclic dates. A cyclical interpretation is included in Maya creation accounts that tell of previous worlds destroyed by the gods. The Aztec, as well as the Maya and Hopi, believe four different creations preceded the present world, each destroyed by a different cataclysm. Plato's Atlantis is believed to have been destroyed by one of the four cataclysms. How many more cleansings of the planet will mankind require before we finally understand why they are occurring? God or a higher power could have prevented the previous cleansings of Earth, but they were obviously required. The last cataclysmic cycle came to an end 13 b'ak'tuns or 5,125 years ago, which is equivalent to one cycle of the Long Count calendar. Descriptions of the cataclysm that occurred on this date are revealed in a moment.

In his book *The Maya Factor*, José Arguelles was the first to show that since the Tzolkin is made of 260 kin (or days), and the 13th b'ak'tun cycle is made of 260 k'atuns, the 13th b'ak'tun cycle is therefore a harmonic of the Tzolkin, being precisely 7,200 times its size. Five of these 13 b'ak'tun cycles equal the length of one cycle of the procession of the equinoxes!

In 1957, Maya researcher Maud Worcestor Makemson wrote, "The completion of a Great Period of 13 b'ak'tuns would have been of the utmost significance to the Maya."[2] These Long Count cycles were definitely of great significance. They lasted 5,125 years each, and all four ended in cataclysms! The Maya fittingly call the last day of the 13th b'ak'tun "creation day." The end date of the previous Long Count calendar of 3114 B.C. (the year 2012 minus 5,125 years, which also accounts for the year 0) would have definitely had great significance to the Maya. Evidence of a major catastrophe has been discovered that dates the event to about this time period.

In his book *Beyond 2012; Catastrophe or Awakening*, Geoff Stray writes of an article that concerns this cataclysm. In this 1999 article called "Mountain of the Ark" that was published in the London *Daily Express*, Egyptologist David Rohl revealed evidence showing that the 11 foot deep layer of silt found by Sir Leonard Woolley, originally

Fig. 4. The Aztec Calendar Stone, or Sunstone, is a twelve foot carving made in 1479 AD during the reign of Axayacatl, only a few decades before the arrival of the Spanish. The stone is on display at the National Museum of Anthropology in Mexico City.

thought to be evidence of the Great Flood in Sumerian legends called the *Epic of Gilgamesh* (in which the original Noah was called Utnap- ishtim), could be carbon dated to around 3100 B.C.[3] This gives us evidence that the biblical flood of Noah's day occurred around the start of the 13th b'ak'tun cycle! According to Maya researcher Joseph Goodman's statement in 1897 (*over 110 years ago!*), the current Long Count calendar's beginning date was August 11, 3114 B.C. and the calendar's end date is December 21, 2012![1] Several other sources give us the same date for the end of the current Long Count cycle, in- cluding the Maya manuscript called the Dresden Codex (which is discussed shortly) and the Aztec Calendar Stone.

The ancient Aztec Calendar Stone (see Fig.4) is a rounded stone carving almost 12 feet in diameter that represents the cyclical nature of Aztec cosmology. A mutilated deity is carved into the center of the stone and is surrounded by symbols that represent the four previous worlds and the present age, whose symbol fittingly means "motion and earthquake." A triangle at the top of the stone points to the inscribed date of doomsday, which is our calendar date of December 21, 2012!

Another important Maya calendar was dedicated to the Venus cycle, which the Maya calculated with extreme accuracy. Six pages of the Dresden Codex are devoted to the accurate calculation of the helical rising of Venus. Various theories exist as to why Venus cycles were important to the Maya. They plotted its orbit far into the future and associated its looping patterns with past events in order to predict future reoccurrences. The Maya also knew that Venus aligns exactly with the Sun and Earth just before the end of the current 13th b'ak'tun in 2012!

The Maya were the first people of the New World to keep historical records. Most of their writings were carved on stone monuments called "stele" and recorded mainly their knowledge of astrological events and calendar dates. They also wrote manuscripts on tree bark. Most of these manuscripts, called "codices," were burned by Spanish monks in 1521, because they were seen as works of the devil. Four of the codices survived, one of which is called the Dresden Codex. It was written on 74 pages of tree bark in about 1200 A.D. and is believed to be the oldest surviving Maya manuscript. Cortez seized the manuscript from the Maya and presented it to the King of Spain. Thereafter the book made its way around Europe and ended up in the museum in Dresden. The book begins with prognostication pages, which helped the Maya plan their day to day schedules. The book also contains 74 pages of highly accurate astronomical calculations. Deciphering of the last page of the Dresden Codex warns of a future apocalypse, a reoccurring cycle that had almost wiped out all past civilizations.

There is only one inscription in the Codex that directly mentions the end of the current 13th b'ak'tun, which corresponds to December 21, 2012. Tortuguero Monument 6, which was partially destroyed, has been translated by Maya scholar David Stewart to read, "The 13th b'ak'tun will be finished on four Ajaw, the third of Uniiw, ____ will occur."[4] The information of what will occur on this date is missing, but if we refer to the drawings on page 74 of the Dresden Codex manuscripts (see Fig. 5), we see what the ancient Maya expected to occur on this date. Four calendar symbols are drawn at the top that represent the ending date of the Great Maya Time Cycle. The codex shows Maya astronomers calculated that an apocalypse will occur after 13 cycles of the Long Count have elapsed. The countdown end date reads 0 Katuns, 0 Tuns, 0 Uinals and 0 Kins, or December 21, 2012. Two eclipses are depicted on the page. One represents the eclipse of Venus against the Sun that will occur in 2012 and will not reoccur for another 100 years, and the other represents the eclipse of the Sun against the galactic center of the Milky Way in December 2012. Drawings of gods and serpents pouring water upon mankind are also shown on the hieroglyphs. Other deciphered symbols say that at this time, Earth will turn upside down and massive earthquakes and tidal waves will hit all of the planet's continents.

Fig. 5. This is a photo of Page 74 of the Dresden Codex showing the prophesied event of 2012. Photo credits go to Akademische Druck –u. Verlagsanstait –Graz –Austria, copyright 1975-2004.

In 1966, after studying these hieroglyphs and the Maya calendar system, Michael D. Coe declared in his book *The Maya* that Armageddon will overtake the people of the world and all its creations on the final day of the 13th b'ak'tun, thus annihilating Earth.

It's obvious to me that knowledge of these cataclysmic cycles has been passed down for almost 10,000 years from the previous two Maya civilizations, four civilizations almost having been completely annihilated by apocalyptic events. A reoccurring astrological event would need to happen at least twice after its original occurrence before anyone could know that it was indeed a reoccurring cyclic event. This makes me believe that the Maya couldn't have known that the first two cataclysms were actually reoccurring cycles until the destruction of their third civilization. After witnessing the almost complete annihilation of four previous civilizations, wouldn't you think that passing down this information to future generations would be of great importance to the Maya people? The Maya have been waiting for 2012 for almost 5,125 years (some say 5,160 years, this figure being one-fifth of 25,800 years; others say 5,200 years; it would also make sense that the procession of the equinoxes cycle is actually 25,625 or 26,000 years)! Regardless of the actual start date of our present world, or the actual length of these cycles, the Maya have brought our attention to the date of December 21, 2012 *and* the date of March 31, 2013!

Maya elder Don Alejandro Cirilo Perez Oxlaj, head of the National Council of Elders in Guatemala, has been sent by the council to warn the world of impending doom that could occur (in 2013?). He stated:

Now let's speak about the future. We, the traditional Maya elders, and all indigenous peoples in the world, meditate on the future. We don't think only for today, the present, we think for tomorrow for our children, grand children, and future generations. We see a dark shadow approaching, a shadow that will cause a lot of harm. It is the great contamination. All this is due to manâs creation. We are digging our own graves. Wars are being transported to other countries; they reason in their speeches it is on behalf of freedom, but the result is more slavery. They speak that it will bring new development, but the result is more hunger for the underdeveloped countries. If we continue like this, the time will come when there are no more soldiers to form battalions. The Maya National Council of Elders of Guatemala asks all nations of the world – their governors and the governed ones – to put a stop to the contamination; and to the big and small enterprises, to find alternatives. We don't want any more wars, no more death, no more nuclear testing, no more chemicals, because the warming up of the planet is unbearable to Mother Earth. If we don't change, sooner or later, she will strike back with millions of lives lost. Don also stated: *You and I may meet again in another dimension after the year Zero. The year Zero is the word of the Maya. On March 31, 2013 the Sun will be hidden for a period of 60-70 hours and this is when we shall enter the period of the Fifth Sun. Then will you realize that what the Maya speak are facts and not false preaching.*[5]

The fated date of March 31, 2013 is very disturbing. It may be a very bad day, knowing that members of the National Council of Elders of Guatemala have foreseen an event where a "dark shadow of contamination" will darken the Sun for 60-70 hours. This is reminiscent of the Book of Revelation, where it is stated that the Sun will become black as sackcloth. Could it be possible that this is the day of our planet's pole shift? Will Earth be hit by solar flares, or a galactic super wave of cosmic debris that will be belched from our black hole at the center of the Milky Way Galaxy? We should have more credence in this date being the date of the apocalypse rather than the end date of December 21, 2012.

The Egyptians, as well as the Maya, prophesied a future apocalypse that is to occur in 2012. The Egyptian *Book of the Dead*, originally called *The Book of Coming Out by Day*, a document designed to ease the Egyptians' transformation to the afterlife, describes the coming of a great reoccurring global catastrophe that took place thousands of years before the rise of ancient Egypt.

This disaster happened last when Venus made a looping pattern around Orion in 9782 B.C. Text in the Book of the Dead tells us that when this reoccurs, it will be the year of the next great cataclysm. Researchers say this will occur in 2012! The chapter also states "after the destruction, the Old Lion turned around." The "Old Lion" is thought to be Earth. This could also be a reference to the Sphinx, previously the figure of a lion whose head was later transformed into an Egyptian king's head. Either way, the Old Lion is "turned around" after the destruction, indicating a pole reversal of Earth!

The Kolbrin Bible, rediscovered in the last few decades, also speaks of the coming apocalypse. This 3,600 year old Egyptian Bible is separated into 12 books. The first six were written by ancient Egyptians, and the remaining books were written by Celtic priests. According to the Kolbrin Bible, the extraterrestrial force that will cause the pole shift is not the Sun, but a celestial body called "The Destroyer." The book says the Destroyer will not hit Earth, but will pass close enough to cause global devastation. The book also states the Destroyer has passed by Earth many times before. One of its passes was 3,600 years ago, which caused complete destruction of Egypt. The text states:

MAN: 3:1 *Men forget the days of the Destroyer. Only the wise know where it went and that it will return in its appointed hour.*[8]

MAN: 3:2 *It raged across the Heavens in the days of wrath, and this was its likeness: It was as a billowing cloud of smoke enwrapped in a ruddy glow, not distinguishable in joint or limb. Its mouth was an abyss from which came flame, smoke, and hot cinders.*

MAN: 3:3 *When ages pass, certain laws operate upon the stars in the Heavens. Their ways change; there is movement and restlessness, they are no longer constant and a great light appears redly in the skies.*[8]

MAN: 3:4 *When blood drops upon the Earth, the Destroyer will appear, and mountains will open up and belch forth fire and ashes. Trees will be destroyed and all living things engulfed. Waters will be swallowed up by the land, and seas will boil.*

MAN: 3:5 *The Heavens will burn brightly and redly; there will be a copper hue over the face of the land, followed by a day of darkness. A new moon will appear and break up and fall.*

MAN: 3:6 *The people will scatter in madness. They will hear the trumpet and battle cry of the Destroyer and will seek refuge within dens in the Earth. Terror will eat away their hearts, and their courage will flow from them like water from a broken pitcher. They will be eaten up in the flames of wrath and consumed by the breath of the Destroyer.*[8]

MAN: 3:7 *Thus it was in the Days of Heavenly Wrath, which have gone, and thus it will be in the Days of Doom when it comes again. The times of its coming and going are known unto the wise. These are the signs and times which shall precede the Destroyer's return: A hundred and ten generations shall pass into the West, and nations will rise and fall. Men will fly in the air as birds and swim in the seas as fishes. Men will talk peace one with another; hypocrisy and deceit shall have their day. Women will be as men and men as women; passion will be a plaything of man.*

MAN: 5:1 *The Doom shape, called the Destroyer, in Egypt, was seen in all the lands thereabouts. In color, it was bright and fiery; in appearance, changing and unstable. It twisted about itself like a coil, like water bubbling into a pool from an underground supply, and all men agree it was a most fearsome sight. It was not a great comet or a loosened star, being more like a fiery body of flame.*[8]

This fiery body of flame reminds me of the descriptions in the Third Secret of Fatima, where Mary may stop the "flame" from hitting Earth!

The Kolbrin Bible Chapter 3:7 verse above speaks of the great 3,600 year cycle. "110 generations shall pass into the West and nations will rise and fall. Men will fly on the air as birds and birds fly and swim in the seas as fishes." Obviously these are descriptions of airplanes and submarines. Each Egyptian generation equals about 33 years. Thirty-three times 110 is about 3,600, which is equivalent to the great cycle number! We could see the Destroyer return at any time!

Could the Destroyer be a planet, comet, or an asteroid? Unstable, bright, and fiery sounds like an asteroid. Many people believe this object is Planet X, a 10th planet with an orbit of 3,600 years. Could this be the comet described in the Bible codes that could annihilate Earth in 2012? Is this Wormwood, a falling star that will hit Earth as described in the Book of Revelation?

The fact that the Destroyer will not hit Earth, but will pass close enough to cause global devastation, is very interesting. On June 19, 2004, an asteroid was discovered by Roy A. Tucker, David J. Tholen, and Fabrizio Bernardi who were working with the NASA funded University of Hawaii Asteroid Survey at the Kitt Peak National Observatory in Arizona.[6] The asteroid was named Apophis for the snake like Egyptian god of chaos and darkness, which is intriguing, since this asteroid may indeed be the Destroyer that caused the Egyptians chaos!

Apophis will pass by Earth in 2013, 2021, and again in 2029, when it will pass as close as 18,300 miles from Earth and will be visible to the naked eye. Flashing alternations will be observed; these visual effects will be created by the spinning of the asteroid and are due to tidal forces caused by Earth's gravitational fields. This sounds eerily like the descriptions of the spinning and flashing light that were given by the people who witnessed the events of Egypt 3,600 years ago and of Fatima, Portugal, in 1917! According to NASA, in its 2029 pass, the asteroid Apophis will enter a "keyhole" that could set up a trajectory orbit where Apophis would slam into Earth in 2036!

It's noteworthy to mention that the Moon is 240,000 miles from Earth. Depending on where the Moon is situated during Apophis' approach (in reference to Earth), Apophis could slam into the Moon and cause a major shower of debris to hit Earth (as Egyptian prophecies state will occur in the next pass of the Destroyer)!

As Apophis passes Earth in 2013, Arecibo radar will detect the asteroid's direction of rotation. Determining whether it's a retrograde or a pro-grade rotator will give us information on impact probability. If the comet is a retrograde rotator, impact probability will be much higher. Also, the "keyhole" can't be calculated now and can only be determined in retrospect, that is, after the comet passes through it!

Many things could alter the asteroid's projected course. The gravitational pull or impacts of other asteroids or heavenly bodies could alter its course in the coming years. Also, we must take into consideration the Yarkovsky Effect, which occurs when orbiting objects pass through the solar system and absorb solar radiation from the Sun and then re-radiate it causing slight orbital changes. On December 25, 2004, it was estimated that the probability of Apophis hitting Earth would be 1 in 42, and if the asteroid did hit Earth, the impact would release 110,000 times the energy of the Hiroshima bomb. Most scientists agree 2029 will be the last possible year to intervene if a mission is to be launched to change the asteroid's course.

If the asteroid doesn't hit us, will it pass near enough to cause global devastation? If Apophis comes too close to Earth in 2029 and 2036, it could be torn into fragments by Earth's gravitational field (depending upon its density and composition), as was the Shoemaker Levy 9 comet when it came too close to Jupiter in July 1994. We could be hit by its fragments in 2029 and in 2036!

Earth could also be hit by a comet with very little notice. Unlike asteroids, comets don't have reoccurring orbits and can appear out of nowhere. Anytime between now and 2013, a comet could slip out from around the backside of the Sun and slam into our planet with only a two week notice. We learned a lot from the Shoemaker Levy 9 comet that impacted Jupiter in 1994. As the comet approached Jupiter, the planet's gravitational field ripped the comet apart. The original comet's size was estimated to be up to 3 miles wide, before it was torn in 21 separate fragments. The first of these 21 fragments impacted Jupiter on July 16th, causing a large dark spot 6,000 km wide, which was visible from Earth. The largest piece, fragment G, caused the most damage and impacted on July 18th, causing a dark spot 12,000 km wide, which is the diameter of Earth! Plumes were seen erupting from Jupiter and were *larger* than Earth itself! These images made us realize how much power was unleashed by these collisions. The impact of fragment G alone was estimated to have released the energy equivalent to 6,000,000 megatons of TNT. That's 600 times the world's nuclear arsenal! If an asteroid or comet over 1 mile wide slammed into Earth, our planet would be absolutely annihilated. In a near miss scenario, Earth's gravitational forces could tear an asteroid or comet into pieces before impact, and Earth may only be hit by smaller fragments. One very interesting item caught my eye concerning the fragment impacts from the Shoemaker Levy 9 comet. Many of the impacts formed large crescent shapes on Jupiter's surface, possibly a reference of the crescent shapes in several of Nostradamus' drawings that relate to our times. The Bible codes also speak of a comet or asteroid splitting into pieces before it impacts Earth.

There is one last bit of information that should be revealed, which concerns the dozens of ancient Maya pyramids in Central America and the Egyptian pyramids of Giza. Many people have fascinations with these pyramids. How and why they were built are questions mostly unanswered today. Robert Bauval, a construction engineer who has spent most of his life in the Middle East and Africa, found a very distinctive pattern linking the pyramids of Giza with the stars that form the constellation Orion's belt. Of the three pyramids of Giza, the two large pyramids run parallel to the equator on a diagonal line, and the smallest of the three pyramids is slightly offset from this line. The positions of the three pyramids replicate the exact positions and sizes of the three stars that make up the belt of Orion. The two larger bright stars form a diagonal line and the smallest third star is slightly offset! Bauval also discovered that the four narrow shafts that are built into the great pyramid of Giza's structure, each only 8 inches wide and running diagonally from the chamber upwards to the surface of the pyramid, align with various important stars in the skies, one of which happens to be one of the stars of Orion's belt! This gives us verification that the positioning and size of the great Pyramids of Giza are a direct representation of the stars of Orion's belt!

Due to the effects of the procession of the equinoxes, the stars of Orion's belt will be located on the celestial equator in December 2012, after which the constellation will again start its southward trek and continue its cycle until it aligns with the Galactic equator during the next Galactic Alignment. The constellation of Orion was of great significance to the Egyptians. It would rise just before the flooding of the Nile, which was very important for their agricultural methods. The size and placement of the great pyramids of Giza are not only representations of the bright stars of Orion's belt as Bauval believed, but that they also signify the importance of Orion's cosmic position during a reoccurring cataclysmic apocalypse, where the

Egyptians watched the destruction of three previous civilizations! It's also possible that the Egyptians and Maya were trying to give us additional information with their pyramids on how to survive the upcoming apocalypse of the Galactic Alignment.

The structure of the pyramid itself may be the answer. If you were to build a structure strong enough to endure the elements of an Earth pole shift, what physical shape for a building would hold up best? A pyramid! High winds and flood waters would be forced to circulate upward and around the sides of a pyramid structure and would exert even downward pressure onto the structure. This pressure, pushing down on the sides of the pyramid, would be absorbed and handled by the opposing angled 45° sides of the pyramid, unlike the sides of a square building, where force would push the walls head-on and collapse them. It's possible the Egyptian and Maya pyramids were built to withstand the forces of nature during a pole shift of Earth!

Until recently it was believed that the pyramids were built as tombs for Egyptian royalty. We now know this isn't true. The pyramids were actually living quarters with plumbing and ventilation systems. The pyramids may have been built as large bunker shelters for the kings and queens, since the structures were strong enough to withstand cataclysmic destruction!

The Maya and the Egyptians accumulated mass amounts of knowledge regarding planetary positions and reoccurring astronomical events. They knew of the upcoming Galactic Alignment and its alignment of Earth, Venus, the Sun, the Milky Way's equator, and the Dark Rift. They were also aware of previous apocalypses and repeated cycles of monumental events that were recorded in their history and passed down over countless centuries. These dire warnings concerning cosmic events that are set to reoccur in 2012 have reached you and me. What we do with this information is up to us.

Maya elder Don Alejandro Cirilo Perez Oxlaj, head of the National Council of Elders of Guatemala, has been sent as a messenger from the council of elders to warn the world that we must change the way we live and take care of Earth if we're to avert our self-destruction. This, again, is the premise of this book. Will we listen?

7

PROPHECIES OF THE ROMAN ORACLE: THE SIBYL

In the ancient world, the Roman Empire revered an oracle they called "The Sibyl."[1] The word "Sibyl" comes from the Greek word "sibylla," meaning "prophetess." She lived in a cave in Cumaea, around the sixth century B.C. The great Michelangelo painted her on the ceiling of the Sistine Chapel, and Plato wrote of her prophecies. She predicted the invasion of Italy by Hannibal, 700 years before it occurred, and she also predicted his defeat.[2] She prophesied the rise of Emperor Constantine and gave his name, 800 years before he was born. The Sibyl also predicted the fame of Socrates and Alexander the Great. One of her greatest prophecies stated a child would be born, who would start the Golden Age. Yes, the Cumaean Sibyl predicted Jesus' birth, 20 years before it happened.[2]

The Sibyl would pass into trances, where she gave divinations of the future. She said that the god Apollo would take over her body, whereupon she spoke utterances and prophecies, which were collected in a series of scrolls and kept in the Temple of Jupiter Capitolinus. They were considered to be the most important religious documents of ancient Rome. These scrolls were later compiled into books that are now called *The Sibylline Oracles*. Her prophecies, which are included in these books, state that in the distant future, there will be a great apocalypse. She predicted that the world would last for nine periods of 800 years each, the 10th period would begin about the year 2000 A.D., and it would be the last![2]

New archaeological discoveries suggest that the source of the

Sibyl's powers wasn't from God, but possibly hallucinogenic states brought on by volcanic gases that ran underneath her cave through underground fault lines.[2] Many other oracles throughout history have also lived in underground caves, where it's believed that they were also able to see future events due to the effects of volcanic gases. No matter how these trances were induced, or how they came about, it still remains a fact that she definitely had the ability to foresee the future.

The following is one of Sibyl's prophecies concerning the 10th generation, which began about the year 2000 and can be found in the Sibylline Oracles, book four. She wrote:

These things in the 10th generation shall come to pass. Earth shall be shaken by a great earthquake that throws many cities into the sea. There shall be war. Fire shall come, flashing forth from the heavens, and many cities will burn. Black ashes shall fill the great sky. Then know the anger of the gods.[2]

The great earthquake, accompanied by the sea devouring many cities, sounds reminiscently familiar to what would happen during a pole shift of Earth. Fire that comes "flashing from the heavens," which burn many cities, could possibly be nuclear war, a galactic super wave, an asteroid, comet fragments disintegrating into Earth's atmosphere, or massive solar flares hitting Earth. In the sentence, "Black ashes shall fill the great sky," the words "great sky" portray an image of global catastrophe, where the entire planet's atmosphere is filled with black ash.

We are presently in the Sibyl's 10th and final period. Her track record of fulfilled predictions speaks for itself. She foresaw many events of the future, including a cataclysm that will occur in our time. This information has been passed down to us so that we might listen to her warnings. Many civilizations have profited from heeding her prophecies. Will we?

8

THE LOST BOOK OF NOSTRADAMUS

While attending a book exhibition in 1994 at the Italian National Library in Rome, Italian journalist Enza Massa discovered a book now called "The Lost Book of Nostradamus."[1] Upon seeing the terrifying images on television of the Twin Towers burning in 2001, Enza was immediately reminded of one of the drawings in Nostradamus' book, a depiction of a tower with flames bursting out windows, openings, and the top of the tower.[2] She remembered distinct details in Nostradamus' drawing that showed the flames expanding in every direction, outwards, as if it were exploding, rather than just on fire. The book has since been studied by many scholars who are fascinated by the prophetic drawings it contains. The drawings allow better interpretation through visual conception, rather than the ambiguous and unclear interpretations of Nostradamus' well-known quatrains and verses. Deciphering the book tells us that its illustrations were meant to awaken mankind to the events that could occur in 2012.

Purchased in 1888, the book was listed in the manuscripts catalog as being the work of Michel de Nostradame, more commonly known as Nostradamus. He is also listed as the author on the title page. Scientific testing on the book has confirmed the paper used to create it was of the same type used in the 15th and 16th centuries, which dates the book's origin to Nostradamus' time.[1]

Today it is believed that the images were drawn by his eldest son Cesar Nostradame, with instructions from his father, since it's known that Nostradamus was not much of an artist. It's also believed that the book was hidden by the Catholic Church and feared by the Vatican, because it clearly contains images that relate to the church. In Nostradamus' day, recording prophecies of the future was seen as the work of the devil and was punishable by death. This forced Nostradamus to hide most of his prophecies and warnings in his quatrains and drawings.

The images drawn are of Nostradamus' future, but many are of our past and have already occurred. Seven consecutive drawings were specifically meant for our generation. This is supported not only by the fact that the images translate to the coming events of 2012, but that the author, Nostradamus, obviously did not want the book to be found until recently! He more than likely saw future images of his book being found and knew exactly what to do or what must occur in order to make the book appear when and where it did! The seven images reveal our current situation and possibilities of the future.

All seven images show "The Wheel of Time" at the top of each drawing. My interpretations of these images are slightly different from others who have deciphered the drawings. Some scholars interpret this wheel as "The Wheel of Life," which it's not. It's an *exact* drawing of the Wheel of Time! These drawings don't have as much to do with life as they do with time. The Wheel of Time signifies reoccurring events of time. As the wheel turns, each spoke eventually makes it back to a reoccurring cyclic point. It should be noted that the Hopi Indians believe in the Wheel of Time and its cyclical idea of time. Two of Nostradamus' seven images show the Wheel of Time *and* representations of Hopi prophecies, which is discussed further in a moment.

Time is often referred to as the Wheel of Time because the creations of the world manifest, remain for a time, and then dissolve. After the destruction, creation starts over again like a wheel in a cyclic motion. Nostradamus is trying to show us the significance of a major reoccurring cyclic event!

In six of the seven pictures, the wheels contain eight spokes that represent the Galactic Alignment of December 2012. These eight spokes consist of two overlapping crosses called the divine and the terrestrial crosses. These crosses will align in December 2012. This hasn't occurred for almost 13,000 years!

The terrestrial cross (or the mundane cross), which is viewed from the ground, is formed from intersecting lines created by the solstices and equinoxes. The horizontal line of this cross is created by picturing a line that extends from the winter solstice to the summer solstice, and the vertical line of the cross is created by visualizing a line that extends from the "Autumnal" equinox to the "Vernal" equinox in spring.

The divine cross is a cross in the sky that doesn't move and is formed by picturing a horizontal line running along the plane from the center of the Milky Way galaxy to its outer edges. The vertical line of the cross is formed by the elliptic between Sagittarius and Scorpio. This cross was also called "The Crossroads" by the Maya, or "The Sacred Tree." Both are excellent terminology, since during this alignment period the tree of life will be at a crossroad! Which path we choose will determine mankind's fate.

The elliptic between Sagittarius and Scorpio is also the center point of the celestial equator and is located where the Dark Rift lies. This is also the area in the sky where the 13th sign of the zodiac is found, the secret sign of Ophiuchus. Of the thirteen zodiacal constellations, which are constellations that contain the Sun during the course of the year, Ophiuchus is the only one not counted as an astrological sign. Its time cycle was known by ancient cultures to be unlucky and full of misfortune!

A separate illustration in the lost book also shows the Wheel of Time and seems to be a depiction of our current situation. The other seven sequential drawings that pertain to our times show future events that proceed from this image. The image shows the Wheel of Time drawn in the middle of the picture rather than at the top as in the other seven drawings (See Fig. 6). The wheel has a crank handle connected to its center, which is being controlled and turned by a higher power "from the heavens." This would indicate that a higher power, or God, controls the advancement of time and our destiny.

At the top of the wheel sits an hourglass, telling us that time is running out. A peacock is seen holding onto the hourglass as the wheel they sit on rotates, passing the hourglass (or time) from the

Fig. 6. This is a drawing of our current situation that is thought to have been originally drawn by Nostradamus' son Cesar Nostradame under guidance from his father. All nine drawings in this chapter were revitalized by artist Bruce Burtenshaw to exactly replicate poor quality originals, which can be viewed on the Internet by searching "Lost Book of Nostradamus."

"fair" peacock to the "foul" fowl sitting on the other side of the hourglass. This implies the passage of good to bad times. On the right side of the wheel, a lion, whose identity I believe to be President Barack Obama (who is the zodiacal sun sign of Leo, which in astrology is represented by a lion), rides the wheel as it turns. I will elaborate on Obama being Nostradamus' lion further in a moment. Mankind's fate seems to be hanging in the balance (possibly being determined by the lion, as indicated by the man shown hanging from the lion's tail) as the wheel (or Earth) turns upside down. The lion seems to control a noose around the neck of a religious symbolic figure and could signify turmoil within the Catholic Church in the end of days.

Behind the wheel, a futuristic city is drawn in the background with a harbor and skyscrapers that appear to be New York City, Nostradamus' "new city," and what appear to be two airplanes flying in the sky near the skyscrapers! All these images seem to be stacked on top of a stressed man with long hair, who is wearing a *red robe* and is drawn carrying the burden of the world's situation on his shoulders. The man's sandals have tread patterns on the bottom, which depicts modern day sandals. His red bathrobe also seems to be from recent times. It reminds me of the style of robe that many men wear today. An eagle and a religious cap sit on his right arm, signifying the man is an American who believes in God. The "blue bell" hanging around his neck, like a dog tag worn by modern man, could be a name tag, a clue to the man's name or identity.

The man in the *red robe* is the "True White Brother" that the Hopi are waiting for, who will emerge wearing a *red cloak* and will not be greedy like the other white men. He will bring a great new plan of life to the nation and the world. If the True White Brother and his two helpers fail, and the world's people don't welcome the new plan, we will follow a path to self-destruction. If the True White Brother succeeds and his plan is accepted, we will be rewarded with paradise for a thousand years.

The man in the red robe seems to be cleaning a large blue globe, Earth, with what I first assumed to be a broom, until I noted the broom's handle has a looping shape, indicating it's flexible and not rigid like a normal broom handle. Upon showing the drawing to my wife, it was instantly obvious to her that the object was not a broom, but a lion's tail! Confirmation of her correct observation and analysis occurred to me later, upon noticing that the tail and the lion are both painted with the same yellow ochre paint. This drawing shows that both the True White Brother and the lion (President Obama) will perform the "cleaning up" of our blue planet.

To the left of the man who is carrying the weight of the current situation of the world on his shoulders is another man with a sword at his side. He has a serpent wrapped around his neck and a cross on his pants. This symbolizes the evils (poverty, greed, selfishness, and hubristic pride) mankind and religion must expel from the world in order to change our outlook and save the planet from impending doom.

One aspect of this drawing is quite disturbing. The True White Brother is using the lion's tail to clean the planet. Where is lion's body? Could this mean that the President will be assassinated, removed from the picture, and the only thing remaining will be his "tale" or story? If he isn't assassinated, will someone replace him in the elections of 2012?

Chapter 10: President Obama reveals Bible codes on President Barack Obama's assassination. Is it possible that the one key turning point, for the two possible paths of the future that will determine the outcome of 2012, is whether or not his assassination takes place? The FBI has already thwarted several assassination attempts on his life, as discuss in Chapter 10. Will there be another assassination attempt? If the President is assassinated, will destruction follow?

The first of the seven sequential drawings relating to our times, which proceeds from the drawing of our current situation, shows the Wheel of Time at the top of the image, and its uppermost spoke is missing (see Fig. 7). All of the other illustrations contain a wheel with eight spokes. A true Wheel of Time is represented by a wheel with seven spokes, which reflect the Seven Great Ages.[4] Nostradamus is showing us the Wheel of Time here, clarifying the difference between the Wheel of Time and the alignment of the two crosses in the following drawings. Some scholars believe he is showing a progression of time; the two crosses haven't yet aligned.

Above the Wheel of Time is a wavy scroll. All of the seven images show drawings of scrolls. This made me wonder, "What is the significance of these scrolls?" I later realized there is an important feature of the scrolls in the last image, which I reveal during explanations of

Fig 7. The First of Seven Sequential Drawings

the seventh drawing. The Sun is drawn large and prominent in the middle of the picture, which shows it will play a major role in this sequence of drawings and in the events of 2012. Under the Sun, a lion sits on Earth, basking in the Sun's rays and wearing a red hat!

The obvious interpretation of the lion, since Nostradamus was an astrologer, is that it signifies the astrological sign of Leo. The sign of Leo runs from the 23rd of July to the 23rd of August and leads scholars to theorize that the drawing of the lion signifies this time period. I believe that the lion denotes this time period *as well as a person!* What I first noticed about the drawing is that the lion is wearing a red hat! If he wasn't wearing a hat, I would agree that the lion represents only a time period. The red hat comes into play in Hopi prophecies. The Hopi say that the True White Brother will be identified by his red cloak or red hat. We have both here in Nostradamus' drawings! In the previous image the True White Brother is depicted wearing a red robe and carrying the weight of the world's situation on his shoulders, and this drawing signifies the time of the True White Brother's "emergence" (between the 23rd of July and the 23rd of August) *and* possibly reveals his main helper's identity, our Leo leader, President Barack Obama!

Upon first seeing this image, I thought the lion wearing the red hat depicted our Leo president as the Hopi's True White Brother. Evidence presented above and in Chapter 3: Prophecies of the Hopi Indians, which shows that President Obama is one of Pahana's two great and intelligent helpers, made me dismiss the notion.

The second image (See Fig. 8) again shows a scroll at the top. It faces the same direction, but has fewer number rolls, indicating the unfolding of the story in each sequential image and leads to a final "peculiarity" in drawing seven, which is revealed in a moment. The Wheel of Time is shown below the scroll, now with eight spokes, and depicts the alignment of the crosses and the Galactic Alignment.

Under the wheel are three eclipses inside a V-shaped arrow. The bottom of the V is touching a drawing of the Moon. In 2012, three eclipses will occur. There will be a total eclipse of the Sun, an eclipse of Venus against the Sun, and the major eclipse, the Sun against the center of the Milky Way galaxy. One of Nostradamus' more famous quatrains also speaks of a great eclipse. He wrote:

There will be a solar eclipse more dark and gloomy than any since the creation of the world,
And it will be such that one will think the gravity of Earth has lost its natural movement,
And that it is to be plunged into the abyss of perpetual darkness."

This not only talks about the eclipse caused by the Galactic Alignment, but also speaks of the unbalanced state of Earth during the alignment.

Below the Moon, a crab is drawn approaching our spiral galaxy, the Milky Way. The crab represents the astrological sign of Cancer, which is ruled by the Moon and runs from June 22nd to July 22nd. This indicates the advancement of time through the sequence of images

Fig. 8. The Second of Seven Sequential Drawings

with the scorpion of Scorpio drawn in the next image. The drawing of the spiral galaxy is quite amazing. In Nostradamus' time, they didn't know our galaxy existed, let alone that it's a spiral galaxy!

The third drawing (See Fig. 9) again shows the Wheel of Time at the top, and below that is seen a tree being hit with a club. This obviously depicts the tree of life being hit and damaged, symbolizing the current damage being done to Earth by mankind and the further damage that will result in 2012. The tree also signifies "the sacred tree" of the Maya, a symbol for the divine cross, which plays a major role in the alignment of 2012. In the center of the drawing is a spiral "S" that symbolizes our spiral galaxy, the Milky Way, and is shown with a sword penetrating its center. The sword is held by a human's arm and directs us to the center of the Milky Way galaxy, where the Sun will align in 2012.

Towards the bottom, underneath the arm with the sword, is a scroll facing outward, which becomes significant in later images.

Underneath the scroll is a scorpion, a drawing of a lamb, and a

Fig. 9. The Third of Seven Sequential Drawings

golden rectangular box. The scorpion represents the astrological sign of Scorpio, which runs from October 24th to November 22nd and shows the progression of the drawings and time toward the December alignment. The lamb symbolizes Jesus, the end of times, or religion, which will play a major role in the outcome of 2012. The golden rectangular box at the bottom of the image is the "Golden rectangle."

The Golden rectangle has side lengths that correlate to the "Golden ratio," equivalent to approximately 1: 1.618 (phi). A unique characteristic of this rectangle is that when a square section is removed, the remaining area is another Golden rectangle, that is, with the same proportions as the first rectangle! Removing squares, when repeated infinitely, leads to approximation of the "Golden spiral," which appears as a spiral when graphed. The most obvious correlation to a spiral implied here would be another reference to our spiral galaxy, the Milky Way, and the upcoming Great Galactic Alignment, but a spiral galaxy has already been *clearly* drawn in the second image (with no interpretation necessary). Nostradamus knew that the Golden rectangle and the Golden ratio relate to spirals. He also knew that they have *direct* correlations to 2012!

Discoveries made by Dr. Sergey Smelyakov, a professor of mathematics at Kharkov University in Ukraine, imply that the Golden ratio (which he calls the Golden section) determines the movements of the asteroid belt and planetary orbits in the solar system and also controls cycles of solar activity. When Smelyakov applied the same phi harmonics to the Maya 13th b'ak'tun cycle, he found a phi spiral that if started at the beginning of the 13th b'ak'tun cycle, appears to spiral in on itself on December 21, 2012! He calls this point of time implosion the final "point of bifurcation."

Originally, Smelyakov's "Auric Time Scale" placed the completion point of the downward spiral toward the end of 2013. In Geoff Stray's book *Beyond 2012: Catastrophe or Awakening?*, Stray points out that Smelyakov had based his theory on a start date of August 6, 3113 B.C., which Smelyakov found in Jose Arguelles' book *The Mayan Factor*. In fact, the start date of the 13th b'ak'tun was actually August 11, 3114 B.C. After correcting the assumption that Arguelles' start date was a Gregorian historical date, calculations now show that the spiral's end date is December 21, 2012! Stray also points out that Smelyakov's sequential spiral bifurcation points better correlate to actual historical events after making corrections on the start date to read one year earlier. With Stray's calculations, one of the more recent spiral bifurcation point lands within days of the world's first atomic explosion in 1945!

Stray's computations show that the last major bifurcation point occurred on August 25, 2010. On this date, President Ahmadinejad of Iran was shown in pictures across media outlets with Iran's first unmanned aircraft capable of carrying atomic bombs over long distances. Ahmadinejad has publicly announced that he will destroy Israel soon after Iran gains a nuclear arsenal. Representatives from the United States told Israel not to worry, because it will be another year before Iran gains nuclear capability. It may be wise to prepare for our next bifurcation point, which Geoff Stray's graph shows to be July 15, 2011.

The next spiral bifurcation point will occur on January 31, 2012, which leads to *twenty-three* more bifurcation points between then and the last three minutes of the spiral's collapse on December 21, 2012, where the spiral will cycle an *infinite* number of times until it finally implodes!

The fourth image (See Fig.10) again shows the scrolls and the Wheel of Time at the top. Underneath the Wheel of Time is a king, known by many scholars as the "Lion King," a man who has a lion's paw as a hand, a crown, and an unruly long mane. He holds an open book with the tree of life on one page and writing on the other page. All of the writing on the second page is written in a foreign or un-known language, except two words in the middle of the page (See Fig.11), which clearly read in English, "One male." At the bottom of the image, rather than the scorpion (as in the previous image), an archer is shown with a bow and arrow and symbolizes the sign of Sagittarius, which runs from November 23rd to *December 21st!* Our timeline has now advanced, approaching December 21, 2012. In our view of the nighttime sky, the arrow of the archer Sagittarius is drawn back, and the arrow's tip precisely marks the middle of the Milky Way galaxy at the center point where the Sun will rise on December 21, 2012!

The Lion King, drawn gazing at the book, obviously plays a major role in the outcome of 2012. "One male," written in English on one of the book's pages, predicts that an English-speaking male will deter-mine what happens to the tree of life. The One Male and the Lion King (Leo President) is again President Obama, the one male who has enough power to bring big changes to the world. The king's long hair could also relate to Nostradamus' drawing of the True White Brother (drawn with long hair), who is also "One Male" that could change what happens to the tree of life. The drawing of the two fish (the symbol of Pisces) shows the advancing timeline of this image, which is toward December 21st, where the Great Age of Pisces ends.

The fifth image (See Fig.12) again shows the Wheel of Time and

Fig. 10. The Fourth of Seven Sequential Drawings

the scrolls. A woman, Mother Nature, is shown taking away an archer's bow and arrow. The blindfolded male, mankind (who is blind and can't see the destruction he is causing), must be awakened to reality. This image might also represent mankind receiving a sudden jolt of reality upon discovering and verifying the possibility of an asteroid or comet striking Earth! I say this because a crescent shape is drawn above the woman.

In 1994, the Shoemaker Levy 9 comet fractured into 21 fragments before slamming into the planet Jupiter and left many large crescent shaped spots on the planet's surface. This drawing of a crescent shape could be a depiction of such an impact. It could also symbolize some type of Islamic involvement, perhaps indicating the time-frame for a nuclear war in the Middle East.

At the bottom of the picture is a set of balancing scales, the symbol for the sign of Libra. Venus is Libra's ruling planet, indicating Venus' role in the upcoming alignment. It's possible that a heavenly body colliding with Venus propels debris that hits Earth, and this is what causes the pole shift of our planet. The scales also indicate our failing balance of Earth; its tipping point is coming closer.

Fig. 11. Exploded view of Drawing Four

In the drawing, there is nothing on the balancing scales weighing surfaces, but the balanced scales are starting to tip. A stag in the bottom left corner is known to signify Christ, rejuvenation, rebirth, and the continuation of time; it represents the upcoming start of the new world.

The sixth image (See Fig.13) contains the usual Wheel of Time with a scroll underneath it. Behind the scroll is a drawing of what many people believe to be a boat or an ark, suggestive of Noah's Ark. In Chapter 6: Prophecies of the Maya and Egyptians, I show evidence that Noah's flood occurred at the end of the previous Maya Long Count. This image could be a warning of a reoccurring apocalyptic

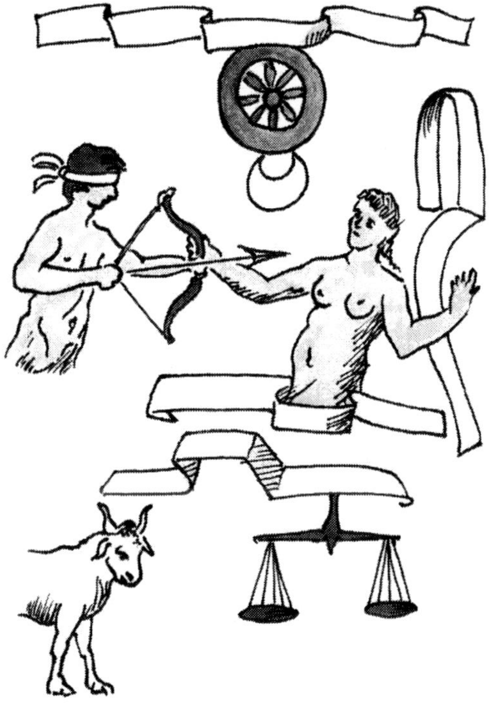

Fig. 12. The Fifth of Seven Sequential Drawings

disaster that will befall us in 2012. It could also be a curtain draped between two points. In the seventh and final image, the curtain or cloak has been raised, "revealing or unveiling" the final outcome. The word "apocalypse" means a disclosure to certain privileged persons of something hidden from the majority of mankind, "unveiling" or revealing something hidden, such as the apocalypse in the Bible's Book of Revelation. In the middle of the picture, we see Nostradamus reading the "Book of Life." Below him are drawings of what appear to be three women, who are separated from each other by a scroll. These women are understood by some scholars to be the Crone, the Mother, and the Maiden, who will soon *turn* the story (the scroll) *around* to create a new tale of the "Book of Life" that Nostradamus holds in his hands.

Some see the three women as the Greek "three fates" who weave time and destiny. Upon looking at the three figures at the bottom of

Fig. 13. The Sixth of Seven Sequential Drawings

the page, I see two women and one man with long hair who are separated by a scroll, or the story. Their significance is revealed in drawing number seven. The man with the long hair seems to have a "mullet" haircut (short hair in the front and long hair in the back). This would also relate to today's times.

In the seventh and final image (See Fig.14), the spokes of the Wheel of Time have shrunken and are fading away. Time has run out. Again, a stag is drawn at the bottom of the picture, known to represent Christ, rejuvenation, rebirth, and the continuation of time, and signifies the start of the new world. The two scrolls have reversed. I repeat. *The two scrolls have reversed!* The two scrolls have *turned around.* Don't these sentences ring a bell, or sound like anything I've been talking about the entire book? The scrolls have reversed means *the poles have reversed!* In the fifth illustration, the out-of-balance

Fig. 14. The Seventh and Final Drawing

scales are drawn connected to the two scrolls. The scrolls have now reversed in the seventh image and imply that Earth's out-of-balance state will lead to the "reversal of the scrolls," or the reversal of the poles! I wouldn't have discovered this had I not written "reversal of the poles" so many times in this book!

Nostradamus was a mathematician and a numerologist. In order to change the word "scrolls" to "poles," we need to transform the letters "sc" at the beginning of the word scrolls, to the letter "p" and are left with the remaining letter "r." In numerology, the letter "s" is equivalent to the number 19, and the letter "c" is equivalent to the number 3 (A= 1, B= 2, C= 3, D= 4, etc.). If we subtract "c" which equals 3, from "s" which equals 19, we come up with 16. The number 16 is equivalent to the letter "p." Thus, in numerology, the combination of the letters "sc" can be equivalent to the letter "p"! The resulting left over letter "r" stands for "reverse," or reversal, or the resulting (left over) "r" can be added to the word pole, meaning "polar," as in polar reversal!

In the center of the drawing, Nostradamus is shown holding an open book. The book's pages are blank. This tells us that at this point the future is not written. What happens from this point forward is up to us. At the bottom of the drawing, two women are facing a stag. Some believe they symbolize the Blessed Virgin Mary and the Crone, who will create our next chapters of life, as of now untitled and unwritten. Two distinctions I noticed about the drawing of the two women is that they are the same women as in the previous image except they are older, and the man is missing from the picture. Could this image be a prediction that mankind (or many of us) will be absent after Earth's poles reverse?

This is the story that Nostradamus has drawn for us, a warning from the past of events that *could* occur. Nostradamus knew that the future can be changed. Our actions from now until December 21, 2012 will determine what is written next in our book of life, a future of immense knowledge and happiness, or one of complete devastation.

Nostradamus is telling us that the future is up to us, and a higher power will prevent our destruction if mankind changes its current path to self-destruction. Many chapters in this book echo this scenario. Nostradamus believed we should receive the future we deserve, which is the reason he gave us his prophecies. There wouldn't be any purpose for his warnings had he seen only one terrible outcome of the future. He had faith in mankind and could see a future where we change our destructive ways and start taking care of the planet and its inhabitants. It's even a possibility that by giving us these prophecies and drawings of the Lost Book that Nostradamus himself has already changed the future! We must heed Nostradamus' warnings and make the necessary changes to avoid the destruction of mankind. Please help me pass the information contained in this book to others. We must fulfill Nostradamus' visions *of our successes*. Our future, the world, and all its creations depend upon it!

9

PROPHECIES OF THE

BOOK OF REVELATION

The discovery and verified existence of the Bible codes should show everyone that the Bible definitely contains prophecies of present times and warnings of an upcoming apocalypse. The Book of Genesis is not the only book in the Bible that reveals prophecies of the future. Prophecies are scattered throughout the books of the Bible, but the book most well-known for its predictions is the Book of Revelation, the last book of the New Testament. Its pages are filled with symbolism and images of beasts and monsters, signs of the end of days, and descriptions of the apocalypse itself. The meanings of the prophecies in the Book of Revelation aren't as clear as the information revealed in the Bible codes, but many of its verses are easily visualized.

Is Armageddon coming soon? Many people believe so, after witnessing increases in frequency and magnitude of earthquakes and hurricanes, global warming trends, terrorism, wars, and uncontrollable disease.[1] Was the Book of Revelation written as a wake-up call? It's one of many. It's not just a coincidence that numerous ancient prophecies from different times and areas of the world all predict the same events. In the Book of Revelation, which seems to echo these other ancient prophecies that describe God's plan for the end of days, it is written, "Blessed is the one who reads the words of these prophecies and blessed are those who take to heart what is written in them, for the time is near!"

Many Bible theologians believe the Book of Revelation and its

109

prophecies were written and intended for the struggling religious people in Roman times. They say the writings are symbolic and have either already occurred, or won't occur at all. First, the Bible codes in the book of Genesis were encoded and written in the same era as the Book of Revelation, and the Bible codes were definitely meant for our generation. Just because something was written in the times of Jesus, doesn't mean it was meant only for the people of His time period. If the Bible codes were encoded for our generation and the end of days, the Book of Revelation's end of days prophecies were meant for us also. Second, many of the book's verses describe one third of Earth being destroyed by fire from the heavens. One third of Earth's land and seas haven't been incinerated in the last 2,000 years. The prophecies also state the seas will turn red and all living creatures in them will die. That hasn't yet happened either. The book describes prophecies of events to occur in the end of days. Obviously the end of days has not yet occurred!

The Book of Revelation was written in the year 100 A.D. by Saint John the Divine, sometimes called John of Patmos. John was a Christian preacher who was condemned for his religious beliefs and exiled to the small island of Patmos. The book tells us of prophecies set to occur during the last days before Judgment Day and paints pictures of destruction on a magnitude mankind has never witnessed. God revealed these visions to John and commanded him to write them down. He was then instructed to present them to the seven churches.

In these visions, John saw God with a scroll in his right hand. The scroll had writing on both sides and was sealed with seven seals. John watches Jesus open these seals, presenting a countdown to the end of the world. As each seal is broken, a new disaster occurs; another sign that the end is near.

The first four seals, which are opened by Christ, reveal the four horsemen of the Apocalypse. The word apocalypse means "veil lifted, or disclosing something hidden from the general population." Each seal opened will cause destruction to the world, each in its own way.

The first horse, a white horse, signifies conquest and wars, which are obviously occurring today. It's very interesting that we're fighting wars in the Middle East, where the Bible first originated.

The second horse, a red horse with a rider carrying a set of balancing scales, is seen by some to represent terrorism, genocide, and the atrocities that now torment the world's inhabitants. The balancing scales could be a reference of the imbalances around us and Earth's balance (or lack thereof) in the end of days. Nostradamus also included drawings of balancing scales in his book of illustrations.

The third horse, a black horse, is said to signify death, famine, and hunger. We see this all around us in global warming, deforestation, mass starvation, and drought. Each year 25,000 square miles of land are swallowed up by desert sand, and it's only getting worse. The United States is presently feeding much of the world. If a major catastrophe happened that negatively affected our nation's agricultural productivity, many countries would suffer greatly.

The fourth horse, a pale horse, will bring cataclysmic death to the world. Most people believe this horse signifies plague. We see disease all around us, including AIDS, SARS, malaria, and the threat of biological warfare. In 1918, almost 100 million people were killed by the Spanish flu. We're now looking at a disease called H5N1, a mutated bird virus, which could easily kill 150 million people. Two Bible code matrices found on the subject read "H5N1 FLU, influenza, grippe, flu, inoculate, vaccinate, death, sick, pigeon, bird, pandemic, panic," and "SARS, inflammation, inflammatory, SARS, China, virus, mutate, pandemic, lung, lethal, kill, death, panic, incurable." As of now, the H5N1 avian virus hasn't mutated into a form that could devastate mankind, but seeing the word "mutate" in the matrices is scary!

When the fifth seal was opened, John saw under the altar the souls of those that were slain for the word of God and for the testimony which they held. And the souls cried, "How long, oh Lord, holy and true, dost Thou not judge and avenge our blood on them that dwell on the Earth?" And white robes were given unto every one of them, and it was said unto them, they should rest yet for a little season. This basically says that mankind will soon be judged and held accountable for our actions.

When the sixth seal was opened, the Bible states:

There was a great earthquake; and the Sun became black as sackcloth of hair, and the Moon became as blood; and the stars of Heaven fell to the Earth, even as a fig tree casteth her untimely figs, when she is shaken of a mighty wind. And the heavens split apart as a scroll when it is rolled together; and every mountain and island was moved out of their places. And the kings of Earth, and the great man, and the rich man, and the chief captains, and the mighty man, and every bondman, and every freeman, hid themselves in the dens and in the rocks of the mountains; and said to the mountains and the rocks, fall on us, and hide us from the face of him that sitteth on the throne, and from the wrath of the Lamb; for the great day of his wrath is come, and who shall be able to stand?

Obviously, this translates to a pole shift of Earth. Scientists don't really know how fast Earth would take to complete a pole shift, but if we are to imagine the stars falling from the sky (which is exactly what it would look like during a pole shift), the prophecy states that the stars would fall as quickly as figs falling from the tree in a heavy wind, so we should expect the shift to occur very rapidly. The Sun becoming black could indicate an eclipse or possibly the Sun being blocked out from all the debris in the atmosphere, which would also turn the Moon red. In Chapter 6: Prophecies of the Maya and Egyptians, Maya elder Don Alejandro speaks of a dark cloud of contamination that will darken the sun for a period of 60 to 70 hours on March 31, 2013. The phrase "and the heavens split apart as a scroll when it is rolled together," possibly tells us what causes the pole shift. An asteroid (Wormwood?) will split apart and penetrate the atmosphere, and the impact and resulting expanding blast wave will resemble the unrolling of a scroll. When the verse says split apart, it means the asteroid *and* the atmosphere! According to the following verses, after this first "fragment" impact, we can expect silence for a while, and then solar flares or more fragment impacts followed by another impact from the main mass of Wormwood!

When the seventh seal is opened, there will be silence in the heavens. John saw seven angels that stood before God, who were given seven trumpets. The Bible reads:

Another angel came and stood at the altar, having a golden censer; and the angel took the censer and filled it with fire of the altar, and cast it into the Earth; and there were voices, and thundering, and lightning, and an earthquake. And the seven angels that had the seven trumpets prepared themselves to sound.

The first angel sounded, and there followed a hail and fire mingled with blood, and they were cast upon the Earth; and the third part of the Earth was burnt up and all green grass was burnt up. And the second angel sounded, and as it were a great mountain burning with fire was cast into the sea; and the third part of the sea became blood; and the third part of the creatures which were in the sea, and had life; died; and the third part of the ships were destroyed. And the third angel sounded, and there fell a great star from the heavens, burning as if it were a lamp, and it fell upon the third part of the rivers, and upon the fountains of waters; and the name of the star is called Wormwood; and the third part of the waters became Wormwood; and many men died of the waters, because they were made bitter. And the fourth angel sounded, and the third part of the Sun was smitten, and the third part of the Moon, and the third part of the stars; so as the third part of them was darkened, and the day shown not for a third part of it, and the night likewise. And the fifth angel sounded, and I saw a star fall from Heaven unto the Earth; and to him was given the key of the bottomless pit. And when the sixth angel sounded, he heard a voice telling the angel to loosen the four angels which are bound in the great river Euphrates. The four angels were loosened, which were prepared for the hour, and the day, and the month, and the year, for to slay the third part of men. And the seventh angel sounded, and there were great voices in the heavens, saying the kingdoms of this world have become the kingdoms of our Lord, and of his Christ; and he shall reign forever and ever.

And the first angel went, and poured out his vial upon the Earth; and there fell a noisome and grievous sore upon the men which had the mark of the beast and upon them which worshiped his image. And the second angel poured out his vial upon the sea; and it became as the blood of a dead man; and every living soul died in the sea. And the third angel poured out his vial upon the rivers and the fountains of waters; and they became blood. And the fourth angel poured out his vial upon the Sun; and the power was given unto him to scorch men with fire. And the men were scorched with great heat, and blasphemed the name of God, which hath power over these plagues; and they repented not to give him glory. And the fifth angel poured out his vial upon the seat of the beast; and his kingdom was full of darkness; and they gnawed their tongues for pain. Then the sixth angel poured out his vial upon the great river Euphrates; and the water thereof was dried up, that the way of the kings of the East might be prepared. And the seventh angel poured out his vial into the air; and there came a great voice out of the temple of heaven, from the throne, saying, it is done.

It sounds to me like the world is in big trouble after the sixth and seventh seals are opened! We can expect to see a pole shift of Earth, asteroid or comet impacts, and large bursts of solar flares that will hit Earth! Some of the verses suggest nuclear war and poisonous radiation that will cause sores that can't be cured. Our rivers and oceans turning to blood could be caused by asteroids, nuclear devastation, or "red tide," which is caused by single cell algae that destroy our oceans and turn them red. To see every ocean creature die would make me absolutely sick.

Wormwood definitely sounds like an asteroid or comet that hits Earth and causes Earth's pole shift. There are over 700,000 asteroids between Mars and Jupiter. An asteroid collision with Earth would cause a blast wave that would incinerate everything at its epicenter in seconds and would destroy everything within a radius of at least 70 miles. Sixty-five million years ago, a six mile wide asteroid hit the Yucatán Peninsula in the Gulf of Mexico. It released 100 million megatons of energy, or the equivalent of 100 million hydrogen bombs. Fires would have raged across every continent and would have been followed by global winter, where the Sun's rays couldn't penetrate through the debris in the atmosphere.

When reading the verse above that states "the second angel sounded and a great mountain burning with fire was cast into the sea," images may flash into your mind of an asteroid, comet, or the eruption of a super volcano. Scientists know of eight super volcanoes around the world, of which Yellowstone National Park is the biggest and measures 35 X 45 miles. Scientists know that Yellowstone has erupted many times, the most recent eruption being 640,000 years ago. These eruptions occur on a regular basis, about every 600,000 years, which means we're overdue. If Yellowstone erupted, the eruption would be 150 times bigger than the eruption of Mt. St. Helens and everything within a 100 mile radius would be cooked. These eruptions are caused by giant pools of magma that accumulate under the surface of Yellowstone. This magma builds up until it explodes and ejects over 100 cubic kilometers or more of ash into the atmosphere. Other chapters contain information on an eruption of Yellowstone, including Chapter 4: The Bible Codes.

The Bible codes and the Book of Revelation also speak of "the beast," whose mark will be 666. Many believe the beast to be the third Antichrist, who will start the wars that lead to the end of days. The third Antichrist was Mabus, or Saddam, as I explained in Part 1: The 2012 Phenomenon. The "beast" is communism, or communist dictators imposing their own will upon their people. As soon as communist rule came into play in 1917, God and the Blessed Virgin Mary went into action to start communism's downfall, as I revealed in Chapter 5: The Lady and Children of Fatima. Vague and ambiguous verses speak of the beast, but the only thing that leads me to believe that this would actually be a person is information found in several Bible codes that read "the microchip mark, of Satan, on his right hand for Satan," and "666 microchip, mark for the soul," and "a subcutaneous chip, 666 is its name." The word "subcutaneous" means under the skin. Do these Bible codes imply that a communist dictator will attempt to force their citizens to have microchips surgically implanted under their skin for identification and other purposes (possibly under the skin of their right hands)? According to the Bible codes, this subcutaneous IC chip is a bad idea and will only lead to terrible repercussions. Be leery of anyone trying to impose "big brother" ideals, communism, and forcing people to do anything against their will; these are evils that must not and will not be tolerated!

The final sign of Armageddon will be the final battle between good and evil. It's said that 200 million led by Christ (or at least His teachings) will prevail in the final battle. All will then be at peace for 1,000 years. Also at this time, all the dead from all times will be re-born and will rise from their graves. The faithful will receive their reward, which is everlasting paradise. The verse reads:

And God shall wipe away all tears from their eyes; and there shall be no more death, neither sorrow, nor crying, neither shall there be any more pain; for the former things are passed away.   *Rev. 21:4.*

John Nelson Darby, an English minister, developed his own end of days' theory.[2] He believes there will be a divine moment when God will call his faithful to Heaven to witness the end of times. He calls this event, "The Rapture." This theory has been the basis for the *Left Behind* book series. Darby and his followers believe that just before the Apocalypse, the righteous true believers of the Lord will vanish from Earth and be taken to Heaven where they will witness the destruction of Earth. This theory seems comforting for the righteous followers of Jesus, though this event is never actually mentioned in the Bible. Though the notion seems feasible and possibly logical, it also gives "the righteous" an easy way out. They may believe that as long as they're righteous, they will be saved. They may also believe that they don't need to worry about most of the problems of today's world and don't need to jump in and help solve these problems. They need only to take care of their own lives and not sin. These people must realize that the Rapture possibly does not and will never exist, and they are stuck with the same fate that awaits the rest of us and the planet. If they don't want this fate, they should rise up and help change the world's current path to destruction, instead of just saying that they will be saved, and they don't need to worry about these possible future events.

Once before Earth was destroyed by the flood of Noah's day, and the Bible says the world will be destroyed again, this time by fire. Many prophecies can be found throughout the scriptures of the Bible concerning the coming of an apocalypse. The following verses are but a few examples.

But the day of the Lord will come as a thief in the night; in which the heavens shall pass away with a great noise, and the elements shall melt with fervent heat, the Earth also in the works that are therein shall be burned up. (2 Peter 3: 10)

Behold, the Lord maketh the Earth empty, and maketh it waste, and turneth it upside down, and scattereth abroad the inhabitants thereof. The Earth also is defiled under the inhabitants thereof, because they have transgressed the laws, changed the ordinance, broken the everlasting covenant. Therefore hath the curse devoured the Earth, and they that dwell therein are desolate, therefore the inhabitants of the Earth are burned, and few men are left. (Isaiah 24: 1, 5 and 6)

The Earth is utterly broken down, the Earth is split through, the Earth is moved exceedingly. The Earth shall reel to and fro like a drunkard, and it totters like a shack, and the transgression thereof shall be heavy upon it, and they shall fall, and not rise again. (Isaiah 24: 19 - 20)

The mountains quake at him, and the hills melt, and the Earth is burned at his presence, yea, the world, and all that dwell therein. (Nahum 1:5)

Immediately after the tribulation of those days shall the Sun be darkened, and the Moon shall not give her light, and the stars shall fall from Heaven, and the powers of the heavens shall be shaken. (Matthew 24: 29)

According to Geoff Stray, in his book *Beyond 2012; Catastrophe or Awakening?*, the last verses of the book of Daniel actually give us the date of the end of days.[3] In the verses, it's written that Daniel overhears the conversation of an angel, where the question is asked, "How long shall it be to the end of these wonders?" The answer is given, "And from the time that the daily sacrifice shall be taken away, and the abomination that maketh desolate set up, there shall be a thousand two hundred and ninety days. Blessed is he that waiteth, and cometh to the thousand three hundred and five and thirty days. But go thou thy way till the end be; for thou shall rest, and stand in thy lot at the end of the days." The "abomination that maketh desolate set up" was Israel taking control of Jerusalem in 1967. In Bible terms, one day represents one year. So, if we waited 1,290 years after the construction of the mosques that were built on the Temple Mount, we would arrive at the year 1967. If we take the two figures of 1,290 and 1,335 mentioned in the verses, we find a difference of 45 years (that the "blessed" are to wait). If we wait 45 years after 1967, we arrive at the year 2012, the end of days!

Another figure is given in the book of Daniel, Chapter 8, verses 13 and 14, where it was asked, "How long shall be the vision concerning the daily sacrifice, and the transgression of desolation, to give both the sanctuary and the host to be trodden under foot?" The answer was given, "Unto two thousand and three hundred days; *then shall the sanctuary be cleansed.*" If we take the date that the Greeks invaded and took control of Israel, which was around 333 B.C., and add 2,300 years, we again come up with the year 1967, when the "sanctuary" (Jerusalem) shall be cleansed! After adding the last 45 years that are to be waited after the year 1967, we again arrive at the year 2012![4]

The Book of Revelation is filled with symbolism and colorful imagery, but when we examine these descriptions with a scientific lens, they don't seem to be so far-fetched. It should also be noted that the prophecies that span from the Old Testament to the New Testament all describe the same future, but were both written by many different authors.

Speaking of the authors of the Old Testament, this chapter would not be complete without information on the Essenes, Jewish mystics who compiled the Hebrew Bible and the Old Testament. Remnants of their work were found in 1947 by a nomadic shepherd named Muhammed edh-Dhib in a cave in the Judean Desert high above the Dead Sea. Archaeologists then found ten more caves with over 900 more documents written on animal skin and papyrus, which were all sealed in jars. These hand-written biblical texts took over 200 years to write and contain parts of almost all of the Hebrew Bible and the Old Testament. These documents soon became known as the Dead Sea Scrolls.

The scrolls were written by the Essenes, who lived by the Dead Sea in the city of Qumran from about 150 B.C. to 70 A.D. Among the scrolls is a document now being called "The War Scroll." This cryptic scroll tells the story of a fight between good and evil.[5] The apocalyptic scroll speaks of the "Sons of Darkness," who are the violators of the covenant, and the "Sons of Light," who are the defenders of the covenant. The Essenes called the evil leader of the Sons of Darkness "Belial," and they hid prophecies written about him in the caves before they were exterminated by the Romans.

According to the War Scroll, seven great battles will take place in the end of days. Many people say six have already occurred. The Bible and the War Scroll both clearly state that in the end of days, the tribes of Israel will gather and reunite, and the enemy will gather against them. The War Scroll also states that angels will fight along with the Sons of Light in the last wars. "They shall fight against Mesopotamia (Iraq and parts of Turkey, Iran, and Syria) and they shall fight against all the sons of Assyria and Persia (Iraq and Iran)."[5]

In 1917, Britain took control of Palestine and invited Jews from all over the world to come back to Israel (Isn't it strange that so many different major world changes began in 1917, including the events of Fatima and Russia?). On May 14, 1948, the state of Israel was established, but was not recognized by its Arab neighbors. Jordan, Lebanon, Syria, Egypt, and Iraq all attacked the next day. This began the first of the six prophesied battles. The scrolls say three times the Sons of Light will prevail, but will not win. Three times the Sons of Darkness will do the same. The seventh and final battle will supposedly be caused by Israel's actions on land rights issues concerning the Temple Mount.

The Temple Mount is held sacred by the Islamic faith and is the third holiest site in Islam. According to the Qur'an, the Prophet Mohammed ascended to Heaven from the Temple Mount. Al Aqsa Mosque now sits on the Temple Mount, as well as the Dome of the Rock, and has since 691 A.D. The Muslim world would be up in arms if the time-honored Dome of the Rock was destroyed and a third temple built. The Temple Mount is very sacred to the Jewish people. This is the ancient site of the Temple of Solomon, where Abraham was to sacrifice his son, and where David built the first temple that housed the Ark of the Covenant. Israel now has physical possession of the Mount. Some believe rebuilding Solomon's Temple will hasten Jesus' return. If the Dome of the Rock was destroyed and a Jewish temple built in its place, Armageddon would occur, triggering the final battle between the Sons of Light and the Sons of Darkness. Several verses give us information on the battle, stating the Middle East will be the battlefields of Armageddon. According to the War Scroll, the heavens open, the sword of God descends, and God intervenes with a "non-human sword" and defeats the Sons of Darkness. One verse reads, "The great hand of God shall overcome Belial and all the angels of his dominion, that wickedness be overcome without a remnant. There shall be no survivors of all the Sons of Darkness." Another reads, "For the God of Israel has called out a sword against all the nations, and by the holy ones of his people he will do mightily." As in verses of the Bible codes, Israel shall prevail, and Iran will be completely destroyed.

Are the prophecies that are revealed in the War Scroll and the Dead Sea Scrolls fated to occur, or will the warnings be heeded? Either way, we will finally have peace in the Middle East. The region's fate will depend on their actions in the next few years.

Again, all the prophecies of this chapter seem to warn us of the same fate that awaits us as is described in previous chapters. Many more details appear here, such as one third of Earth being destroyed by fire from solar flares, a comet, asteroids, or nuclear war. How many ancient prophecies that describe the same upcoming apocalypse do we need to absorb before we can finally admit there is a good possibility that these events will occur in or before December 2012 (March 31, 2013 according to the Maya)?

In closing this chapter, I would ask to take a few minutes of your time and reveal some of my beliefs about the powers of good and evil, Heaven and Hell. If you are simply not interested in my theories, please skip the next pages, but I believe that the information will enlighten many people, and that most people don't question or delve into religious beliefs and their origins as much as they should.

I'm a very scientific minded person. I believe in God, the Supreme Being, but I don't believe in the devil, or evil spirits (I explain why in a moment). An afterlife definitely exists, but there is no Hell. I believe in spirits and guardian angels, and that God has a soul mate as knowledgeable and powerful as God. I also hope there are other gods. Many religions believe that each of us has the capability to become a god after obtaining all of the knowledge possible here on Earth and in the afterlife.

I don't see God as the Romans did, or as many religious people do today; I see God in a scientific light. God isn't conceited and doesn't demand to be "worshiped." God doesn't get angry. Anger is much too primitive an emotion for an all-knowing spiritual being. God isn't magic. He's just much smarter than we can comprehend.

Before God created the Universe, He had existed forever, amassing all the knowledge that ever existed in His previous "dimension." To evolve and to grow, to experience more things, to learn more beyond everything that presently existed, God and others (possibly including you and I) created a new dimension, a physical world. They thought and planned for an eternity to create this new idea, the Universe.

Creating matter that had physical properties and natural laws where nothing had previously existed is beyond human comprehension. The amount of knowledge mankind has accumulated in discovering the origins of the Universe is absolutely nothing compared to the wisdom necessary to create physical matter and the natural laws that govern the Universe. Taking nothing and splitting this nothing into matter and antimatter, creating a physical plane of existence where nothing previously existed, seems absolutely impossible, but here we are!

Something or someone must have influenced the Big Bang to create our Universe. If there was nothing, including no God, the Big Bang could never have happened, because nothing can influence or create something from nothing! Some people would then ask, "How did God come to exist and how did He create something from nothing?" Obviously, this is an unanswerable question. Scientists have theories on how and when the Universe was created, but they have absolutely no idea who or what triggered its beginning. There are no scientific theories on how God came into existence. Scientists need to see that something ripped matter and antimatter apart, creating something from nothing. Obviously higher powers or God does exist, or we wouldn't. Scientists need to start seeing God in a scientific light!

Physicist Stephen Hawking argues in his new book *The Grand Design* that God did not create the Universe, and the "Big Bang" was an inevitable consequence of the laws of physics. He states that the Universe created itself from nothing. Hawking writes, "Because there is a law such as *gravity*, the Universe can and will create itself from nothing. Spontaneous creation is the reason there is something rather than nothing, why the Universe exists, why we exist."[6] This statement has one flaw. If nothing existed before the Big Bang, then *gravity* and its laws didn't exist! Gravity is the force of attraction between all masses in the Universe. If there wasn't any mass before the Universe was created, gravity wouldn't yet exist, which Hawking says was the *cause* of the Universe creating itself! If gravity *did* exist before the Big Bang, then my question to Mr. Hawking is "How did gravity come to exist?" In the beginning, God created *everything*, as well as gravity.

Long ago while growing up, I believed in the devil and his evil spirit followers, who would get into our minds and attempt to influence our decisions negatively; the devil on one shoulder, an angel on the other, with the devil trying to talk us into doing something we knew we shouldn't. I haven't believed in the devil or evil spirits for many years. Since then, no evil thoughts have entered my mind. If evil spirits and the devil were real, they would still be tormenting me with evil thoughts, constantly, regardless of my opinion on the matter. I now understand that these "evil" thoughts were just my conscience and normal brain thought patterns.

The following are flaws in the logic of believing in Hell, and are reasons why I don't believe that it exists. Every person's mental state is a product of society and their individual circumstances, environment, past experiences, physical brain pattern's development, and their brain's capabilities. If I would have been born in Adolf Hitler's body, I would have led Hitler's life and would have been influenced by the same things that he was, had his exact same biological and chemical makeup of his brain patterns, gone through all the same experiences he did, had all the same influences from others, and had all the same knowledge he used to make his decisions. I would have been Hitler. Hitler didn't go to Hell after he died, he went to an afterlife, where he was shown all his mistakes and what it was like to be one of the people he wronged, where his spirit was not limited to the thought patterns of his previous biologically faulty brain. He, like everyone else, has the chance to learn from their Earthly mistakes, which were based on decisions made purely from his circumstances, environment, and mental capabilities. Hell is reliving your earthly mistakes after you die, seeing and understanding what caused your mistakes, and witnessing the ramifications of your actions.

If a person is born in Africa and dies of starvation before they can speak, their spirit or soul goes to Heaven. Wouldn't you agree? If that same spirit or soul would have been born in Hitler's body, there would be at least a chance of that spirit going to "Hell." This isn't right, and God wouldn't believe that it's right either. All souls are savable when taught correctly and enlightened. I believe more in the idea that there might be separate levels of Heaven. The better life you lead and the more spiritual knowledge you possess, the higher of a level you would obtain when reaching Heaven, with the ultimate goal being to learn everything possible and to reach the highest level.

Some people will say that if their spirit was born in Hitler's body, they wouldn't have become the monster that Hitler did, and everyone has individual choice of decision. What are these decisions based upon? The person's knowledge, circumstances, environment, previous experiences, and their brains mental capabilities! All of these circumstances would be *exactly* the same for you, as it would have been for Hitler! Another way to look at it, is what if Hitler's soul was born into a starving African's body and died at one year old? Hitler's soul would have gone to Heaven! This would say that his soul was *condemned* when it was appointed to Hitler's body! Our all-powerful God is righteous and wouldn't let an injustice like this happen. He wouldn't have picked anyone's soul to be condemned to Hell as a result of which body it was placed in. When we're born, all memories of any pre-existence are erased. We all start with a clean slate. This would indicate that all our future decisions from the moment of our conception forward are based on the limitations listed above.

God (or higher powers that we call God), the pre-existence, and an afterlife definitely exist, but the only evils that exist in the world are the evils that mankind has created. The Bible tells us that if we conquer these evils in the end of days, evil will no longer exist, and mankind will live in peace for a thousand years. We must immediately eradicate all "evils" that humans have brought into the world, such as greed, envy, hubristic pride, poverty, hunger, despair, and the trashing of our planet. These are the evils that God wants us to eradicate, not imaginary evil spirits who attempt to control the minds of the innocent inhabitants of Earth!

PART 2
Solving The World's Problems

Introduction

When we think of the state of the world today, we can't help but picture all of the corruption that is transpiring around us. Most of the daily news we hear makes us sigh in disbelief. Contemplating the condition of the world forces us to wonder how mankind could have possibly evolved to its current state. Why do we feel so powerless to right the wrongs of this troubled world? Sure, there are elements of our lives that make it all worthwhile such as our loved ones, cherished moments, the pleasures of life, and experiencing the miracles of nature, but why should we accept the bad with the good, when we have the capability to eliminate the bad?

The world is full of hidden riches. Our existence is a marvel beyond human comprehension. We live to learn and grow spiritually in the hope of making life better for everyone. This is the purpose of our existence; to strive for a better today and tomorrow for us and future generations, to gain as much knowledge as possible, and to evolve to the highest level achievable.

With the troubles of everyday life consuming all our time, such as attempting to earn enough to pay the bills, worries of health and dental problems, unemployment, the declining state of the economy, the deteriorating environment, transportation issues, and the stress of just making ends meet, it's no wonder we don't have any spare time to get involved in solving the problems of today's world.

We push all the bad news aside, count all our blessings, and try to concentrate on the tasks that we need to accomplish to survive through the next days. Why continue like this? How can we go forward with our lives, knowing we could make a much better life for everyone?

"It's too hard to change things," we tell ourselves. "I'm only one person. What can I do amid the mountains of grief, despair, and worries of the world?" We can do a lot. I've reached a point in my life where I can no longer just sit idly by and watch the planet and civilization deteriorate! I'm an optimist. I don't dwell on the negatives of life and work constantly on building a better future for my family.

My children, spouse, and family are everything to me; all I do is for them. When their lives are disrupted or negatively affected by the wrongs we see happening today and no one seems to be doing anything to change it, it's time to assume the lead. One person *can* make a difference, and the time has come for me to be that person. If I can make the world a better place in which to live, it's my responsibility and duty to do so. I hope that you feel the same way.

I believe with every fiber of my being that we can change the face of the world and create a paradise where everybody would be happy. I envision a world where everyone could wake up in the morning and look forward to the day's challenges with none of today's major worries or fears. I imagine a world with no greed or poverty. If everyone could begin the day knowing these securities were in place, the world would be a wonderful place!

Most importantly, the people of this advanced world would be secure in the knowledge that they owned their own homes free and clear. Property taxes wouldn't exist. Health and dental care would be free. Education, including a four-year college or trade school, would be free to any American who has the desire to excel. Actually, free isn't the correct word. "No charge" or "funded" would be better words. The *Commonwealth* would pay for these essentials with the people's money, under direction of the American people. I say that the *Commonwealth* will pay for these essentials, because it must be clear that it's the American people that pay our country's debts. The government has lost sight of the fact that they work for us. We are their bosses and not their sheep. From this point forward, when I refer to the Commonwealth, I'm speaking of the new "People's government," where the *common* people of the country control the government, not the greedy corporations and the wealthy.

The time has come to *combine* capitalism with a *voluntary* socialist type outlook. We don't need or desire a *communist* society, we just require some of the morals and ideals that a *socialist* society is based upon. The last thing the United States needs is more government control. It's time for the American people to retake control of the government, not give it more power! I'm not sure a "voluntary socialist" society combined with capitalism is the correct wording. We just need many changes in our country's morals and views that would benefit the common people of the United States.

Please don't misunderstand me. There is a huge difference between socialism and communism. Previous communist governments have made a mess of the world. Forcing people to do *anything* against their will and limiting freedoms are definitely evils that we have expelled in the United States. The main "socialist" changes that are needed in the country's systems are how they're funded and who pays the bills.

These changes must be *voluntary* and supported by all Americans. The changes I envision wouldn't include the government running everything or everyone working for the government for their equal share of society's benefits. The changes would be limited to certain financial burdens of everyday life being paid by the Commonwealth. I recently discovered that Edgar Cayce foresaw that these visions of the future will become realities. He stated:

"... for changes are coming, this may be sure—an evolution or revolution in the ideas of religious thought. The basis of it for the world will eventually come out of Russia. Not communism, no! But rather that which is the basis of the same as the Christ taught—his kind of communism."

Christ's "kind of communism" is obviously socialism, where we start caring more about others and less about ourselves.

In a world where jet set millionaires gallivant from one place to another, adorned with million-dollar jewels, blowing thousands of dollars on extravagances, while many people, including children, are homeless and starving in the same cities, greed must be eliminated so that we might restore the balance between excess and deficiency. Our materialistic world, now glamorized, must be shamed. Greed, materialism, and selfishness have no place in an advanced society. I have no quarrel with people who possess expensive luxuries. We will always retain the freedom to live the American dream of becoming independently wealthy, and people who desire to hoard large sums of money should be able to do so, *as long as all other people have the basic necessities of a comfortable lifestyle!*

I strongly desire to stir up enough energy from Americans to get their circumstances changed for the better. If enough people envision the changes needed to solve our country's and the world's problems and gain enough ambition to see these changes through, I know we could transform this world into a better place, not only in which to live, but to embrace with delightful enthusiasm!

We must all see that we are running short on time to repair the world's problems. Realize it or not, we're at the dawn of a new age. Our actions in the next few years will determine the future of the entire world. The time has come to force our government's representatives to completely overhaul our capitalistic society. Capitalism isn't working as it should. The basic foundations that capitalism was built on are greed, pride, and envy, three of the seven deadly sins!

Every government needs an overhaul every few hundred years. As our society progresses, moral issues arise that we've never faced. It's no longer acceptable to care about only ourselves; we must help those who have less than we do. We must solve our country's problems immediately, so that we can concentrate on fixing the world's problems. It's time we combine all the good assets that capitalism has to offer with all the humane attitudes that socialism has to present. We must keep our free enterprise system, where everyone is encouraged to become the best that he or she can be and to strive for the American dream, but at the same time we must help people who aren't as lucky as we are to obtain an acceptable and happy standard of living. This means no homeless, no hungry, no unemployed, and no poverty!

Chapters in Part 2 concern solving the country's and the world's problems and changing mankind's current path to impending doom. This includes changing the nation's perspectives on many issues, becoming more spiritually enlightened, and creating a world where God and we would be proud of our achievements, thus saving the planet from the cleansing it presently requires!

10

PRESIDENT BARACK OBAMA

Americans don't just want change, they want major changes. This is apparent in the fact that we have elected our first African American president, President Barack Obama. We were looking for a leader who would represent the common people. *Someone who wasn't afraid of implementing changes!* We were looking for a person with morals and visions beyond capitalism. We desired new ideas and a better way of life. Since the early 1970s, I've dreamed of the day when our generation would finally assume control of the government and the nation's morality. Hopefully, that time is finally upon us!

We've all heard a lot about President Barack Obama's beliefs and opinions. Unlike some previous presidents, who didn't accomplish much while in office, Obama headlines the news every day! This man is involved with his job and isn't wasting any time or opportunities! His role in the events leading to the outcome of 2012 is revealed in many of this book's chapters. Most people admire his general outlook and desire to change our world for the better. Many people say that he's a socialist and his ideas refer to socialism. Others say he is sitting very far out on a limb. There's a big difference between socialism and communism. Many aspects of socialism can be praised, such as humanitarianism, and can be practiced voluntarily. Communism involves forcing people to do something against their will, or people forcing their will upon others. We should back the President's goals, but if we see any indications in the future that our American rights are being limited by the government, our views will change quickly. Change is drastically needed, but as American citizens, we must not allow the elimination of any rights we have become accustomed to.

My family lives near the Grand Tetons and Yellowstone National

Park, where people have compassion and feelings for the plight of African Americans and the American Indians. We have very few prejudicial people here, and what few we do have are looked down upon as ignorant, blinded, and narrow-minded people. President Obama didn't get our state's vote, but he sure got mine! The main reason Obama didn't get the majority vote from the people of our state is that they don't like his policy on gun control. They admire most of the President's goals, but his idea of eradicating all firearms from the United States must change!

Our country was built on freedom. It was protected and won by our people defending themselves with firearms. The right to bear arms is one of our constitutional rights, and this will never change. In 2004, 38% of American households and 26% of individual Americans reported owning at least one firearm.[1] These figures equate to 42 million households with 57 million gun owners! Long guns and rifles represent 60% of the privately held gunstock.

Forty-eight percent of individual gun owners reported owning more than four firearms, which equals one firearm per every adult in the United States! This is counting only the guns that the government knows about! Wouldn't you think that more than twice as many guns actually exist and are not reported? Attempting to remove this number of firearms from so many people would cause a civil war in our country. Guns would have to be pried out of our dead citizen's hands to enforce this policy! If we take everyone's guns away, only the criminals will have guns! Trying to confiscate everyone's guns is not the answer. The answer is eliminating crime, which is caused mostly by poverty and our country's drug problem. *Two Paths'* chapters on these subjects describe the solutions to these problems. When we finally eliminate poverty and our country's drug problems, there will be no need for gun control. When there are no criminals, there will be no criminal activity. Guns aren't the problem. People are the problem. When we repair society, we fix our gun problem!

Everyone should be very pleased to find that President Barack Obama is a sun sign of Leo, and his wife Michelle is a Capricorn. Knowing their sun signs tells us a lot. Oh, you don't believe in astrology, or don't know much about it? I didn't believe in astrology and didn't believe in horoscopes (and still don't believe in day to day horoscopes), until I made a bet that if I read the description of any one of the twelve zodiacal signs, that I could make myself that sign. I read each of the sign's chapters, their descriptions of personality traits, good and bad, and came to the conclusion that it was all a bunch of garbage! None of the sign's traits seemed to describe me, until finally I read my sign's chapter! I was speechless, in awe. The chapter described me *perfectly*, revealing everything from my outlook on life and personal goals, to my good and bad traits!

Reading my bad traits hit a nerve. I had a hard time admitting that a few of them were mine, but after realizing they existed, I've been able to work on eliminating them. I was reading from a large reference book called *Parker's Astrology*, written by Julia and Derek Parker, which I would highly recommend to anyone who desires to learn more about astrology. I cherish the book and have introduced its vast knowledge of astrology to many of my friends, who like me, didn't previously believe in it. Realizing and understanding your son's, your daughter's, your spouse's, or any acquaintance's personal traits, perspectives on life, and state of mind will help immensely in any relationship!

Many people believe that as a person grows in the womb after conception, the growth and development of his or her electrical brain patterns is influenced by the magnetic fields of our planet and the position and strength of magnetic fields of the Sun, the Moon, and other planets in our solar system. Ancient civilizations noticed that people born about the same time of the year exhibited similar traits and mannerisms. Knowledge they accumulated became structured into the twelve signs of the Zodiac.

You may ask, "What has astrology got to do with President Obama?" Knowing Barack Obama's sign tells us many things about him. President Obama is a Leo. According to Julia and Derek Parker (authors of *Parker's Astrology*) organization is essential for Leos, who must control their lives. Their organizational abilities *will spill over into the disordered lives of others.* Leos may be dogmatic and so must cultivate flexible minds and respect for other's opinions. Only then can their characteristic warmth, generosity, and desire to understand others be fully indulged. A powerful creative urge is present in every Leo and must be expressed. Otherwise, a very great deal of potential will be wasted. The Sun, ruling this sign, gives Leos infectious vitality. They must live life to the fullest *and like to see others doing so as well*. They have an inner sun that not only illuminates their lives and activities, but also lights up the lives of others or perhaps gives them energy. Leo days should be full with not a moment wasted, since lack of fulfillment, professionally or personally, will totally destroy them and cloud their personalities.

The traditional Leo traits are generous, warmhearted, creative, enthusiastic, broad minded, expansive, faithful, and loving. Leo's keywords are creatively, impressively, powerfully, and moodily. Leos are emotionally idealistic and surprisingly sensitive, making them wonderfully supportive *and often real powers of the throne*. Leos can take criticism to heart, and their enthusiasm lasts a lifetime.

Emotional involvement in a career is central if Leos are to feel fulfilled. They're at their best when able to use their creative potential and organizational abilities. Taking center stage comes naturally to the Leo, one of their biggest desires being *to improve the lives of others*. These Leo traits are exactly what the country is looking for in a president!

I've made several significant discoveries regarding President Obama being a Leo, whose astrological symbol is the lion. Obama has major roles to play in the next few years, as the Hopi and Nostradamus predicted long ago. Nostradamus knew of President Obama's presidency hundreds of years ago and depicted him in drawings of the "Lost Book of Nostradamus" as the "Lion King" and the "One Male" who will determine the fate of the world, which I revealed in great detail in Chapter 8: Lost Book of Nostradamus. Obama is also a part of Hopi prophecies, which I disclose in Chapter 3: Prophecies of the Hopi.

The Hopi are waiting for a white man they call Pahana, the True White Brother, who will not be greedy like the other white men and will bring a new unselfish plan of life to the world. Hopi prophecies state that the True White Brother will have two great and intelligent helpers, and that one of the two great helpers will have the sign of a

Celtic cross with red lines between the arms of the cross (representing *female* life blood). I show evidence in Chapter 3: Prophecies of the Hopi that this powerful woman is more than likely Oprah Winfrey or Hillary Clinton. The other great intelligent helper is a man who will have a *masculine* symbol of purity and the sign of the Sun. President Barack Obama is the astrological Sun sign of Leo, whose astrological "ruling planet" is the Sun. The "sign of the Sun" is Leo and refers to our Leo president. I believe President Barack Obama is Nostradamus' Lion King and One Male, *and* that he is one of the True White Brother's intelligent helpers who will help carry out a great new plan of living for the world!

We should be comforted by the fact that First Lady, Michelle Obama, is an energetic Capricorn. Capricorns are conventional, sometimes even slaves to convention. They always need to be seen as "doing the right thing." Cappies have strict consciences and force themselves to make morally correct decisions. Capricorns have a splendidly offbeat sense of humor, vividly contrasting with their strong tendency to grumble. They are practical, prudent, ambitious, disciplined, patient, humorous, and reserved. Capricorns can be so involved in their careers for the benefit of their families that they have no time to enjoy their home lives.

Cappies welcome a chance to sit in their own offices with many responsibilities. They set goals, climbing the ladder one rung at a time, the top rung of the ladder being their minimum goal. Their bad traits include being pessimistic, fatalistic, overly conventional, and rigid.

We should all be impressed with Michelle's track record. She attended Princeton University and graduated in 1985 with a BA in Sociology and a minor in African American Studies. In 1998, she received her law degree from Harvard Law School. She began her law career at Sidley and Austin, a Chicago firm, where she met Barack. In 1991 she began serving as Assistant to the Mayor of Chicago and later served as Assistant Commissioner of Planning and Development for the city. She became the Founding Director of Public Allies, a leadership training program that works with youth aspiring to careers in the public sector.

Beginning in 1996, she served as the Associate Dean of Students at the University of Chicago. During her tenure, she started the university's first community service program. She is presently Vice President of Community and External Affairs at the University of Chicago Medical Center. She also directs the hospital's Business Diversity Program.

Michelle was born on January 17, 1964, which puts her birth date towards the "cusp" (the beginning or the end of a sign), which gives her some of the traits of the next sign Aquarius. Aquarians are friendly, humanitarian, honest, loyal, original, inventive, independent, and intellectual.

All these traits that the Obamas possess will hopefully bring to the table what we need to change this world. I've been working on this book for years, while thinking that someday someone would be elected into office that would have enough courage to make the major changes needed to solve our society's problems. Years ago, I thought that this person may have to be me. I saw no other candidate who desired the massive changes the country required. Then along came Barack Obama!

Most Americans have great expectations for President Obama and wish him well. I hope that my plans catch his attention. One point that troubles me about his presidency is the fact that it could end prematurely. Many people in the world would love to see his presidency end, such as white supremacists and greedy capitalist robber barons, just to name a few. Many assassination threats have been made, including several that have been thwarted by the FBI. One of these assassination attempts was predicted in a Bible code found in Genesis 9:11.[2] The code reads "Barak Obama (spelled without the letter "c"), assassinated, blood, September, gunfire, crowd, Aryan Nations, guilty, Harry, prevented."

In mid-October, 2008, the FBI announced that they (or Harry, is Harry an FBI agent?) had prevented the assassination of presidential candidate Barack Obama. The assassination plot was planned by two neo-Nazis (Aryan Nations), who planned to assassinate him at the Democratic National Convention in Denver. Cousins Tharin Gartell and Shawn Adolf, along with their friend Nathan Johnson, went to

Denver with plans to assassinate Obama. On August 24, 2008, the three were arrested. The FBI found their truck filled with weapons and narcotics. Another code that possibly describes the same event reads "shooting of Obama, 2009 President, Island from Hawaii, not dead, from Kenya solved."

A second 2008 assassination attempt on Obama was stopped in Tennessee, when white supremacists Paul Schlesselman and Daniel Cowart were arrested on October 22nd. The two planned a murdering spree of 88 African Americans, most of which were young students of a predominantly African American school. Their plan was to end the killing spree by driving their vehicle toward President Obama and shooting at him through the windows. They told authorities that they intended to rob a gun dealer to obtain more guns before starting the killing spree.[3]

Several Bible codes contain information on the President's election. One from Genesis 3:6 reads "Joe Biden, vice president, Obama's choice, selection." The other from Genesis 17:5, reads "John McCain, not President," and "B. Obama will be selected."

Other Bible codes found indicate that one assassination will be completed. One reads, "from the back, B. Obama was killed, Obama and his assassination, in the head, in the shadow, a lion for the wound," and another reads "suspicion of an Obama assassination is in him as in them, it is a pity, what a pity for your wickedness, this is the cult." This would indicate that the President could be shot from behind, in the head, by a cult member hiding in the shadows. It's very interesting to note that President Obama is referred to as a lion, knowing that he could be Nostradamus' lion and Lion King. Another code, found in Genesis 29:15 reads "Barak Obama, assassination, gunmen, conspiracy, Tishri (September - October), he will die, panic, substitute, replacement." This code speaks of someone replacing President Obama after he is assassinated. Another code suggests who replaces him, which reads "Hillary Rodham, president, welcomes, accepts, honors, praises." Hillary has let everyone know that if she did become president, she would use the last name Rodham, not Clinton.

These prophecies could reveal two possible paths of the future.

The first possibility of the future results from the failed assassination attempt of Barack Obama, where he then becomes president, which is today's timeline. The second possible outcome of the future would have been if Obama had been assassinated and didn't become president, or if he's assassinated after becoming president and somehow Hillary Rodham succeeds the President and unknowingly ushers in the "times of the beast." The beast could be a symbol for communistic ideals forced upon the people. Could President Obama's assassination lead to the world's destruction? Could this be the turning point that determines which path the world follows? Another possible turning point of the future could be whether or not President Obama is reelected in 2012. Only time will tell. Many people blame him for the prevailing economic problems the country is facing. Obama didn't get us into this mess, but he *is* one of the people trying to get us out of it. The President's foremost role in solving the country's economic problems is revealed in Chapter 12: Housing.

This is the Obama's time, and with help from the people, they *will* change humanity! The time has come for *all* Americans, Republicans and Democrats alike, to stand up and back President Barack Obama!

11

THE ECONOMY

The economy—what a mess! Where do we start? So many different aspects of the economy have gone completely wrong, and others haven't been correct for hundreds of years! Today's situation stems from changes in our country's views on moral and ethical standards that occurred about 230 years ago, when suddenly greed, pride, and envy became accepted as good qualities to achieve on our way to the top rung of our capitalistic ladder!

Capitalism as we know it today was born in 1776. When we think of the year 1776, thoughts jump to the Declaration of Independence, but capitalism wouldn't have been born from the Declaration of Independence. In 1776, Adam Smith wrote a book called *The Wealth of Nations*, where he claimed that capitalism, self-interest of individuals, and greed might be good traits! What an innovative concept. Justifying selfishness and greed in the name of progress! Wow, and what a ride we've been on since, with everyone looking out for number one!

Today's capitalism is a big monster fed by greed, selfishness, envy, and pride. The American people must realize that there is no place for these primitive emotions in an advanced society such as ours. In 375 A.D., a monk named Avagrius Ponticus wrote about what he called, "The Eight Terrible Temptations to Mankind's Soul." In 590 A.D., Pope Gregory the Great revised the list and combined two of the terrible temptations into one.[8] Pope Gregory called his new list, "The Seven Deadly Sins." These sins included greed, pride, envy, sloth, anger, lust, and gluttony. Of the seven, the ones that pertain to my topics are the first three: greed, pride, and envy, which built today's capitalistic ideals.

Webster's dictionary states the definition of envy as "a feeling of discontent or resentment for another person's possessions or advantages." Envy, known as the evil eye and the green eyed monster, is resenting others for having something that you don't, which you desire.

In our present capitalistic society, possessions show who you are, how much you make, what you've achieved, and your position in society. Envy has been a major driving force for the country's progress in the last few hundred years.

Envy has proven itself to be an asset in that it makes us strive to do better when we see others doing better than us, which is one of the main foundations for capitalism. In the past, socialism's main concern was keeping everyone at the same level and sharing the prosperities of society. Past socialist societies have stopped the most skilled and talented citizens from aspiring and pursuing their talents, causing their country's development to stagnate.

Seventy percent of our economy is made up of spending.[9] Envy is all about relative status, having a nice house, driving a nice car, traveling, and showing off your success. This boasting is a form of aggression. Some hostilities and conflicts are caused by one nation being envious of others that have more resources, wealth, and a higher standard of living. Envy is one of the main driving forces of terrorism. With envy, we don't have peace. Without envy, we don't have progress. Some middle ground must be found.

Envy is a primitive instinct we have at birth. Studies of capuchin monkeys at the Yerkes Institute of Atlanta found that monkeys trained to exchange tokens for food became envious when they saw others getting exchanges of more highly valued fruit.[7] In fact some monkeys became so envious that they actually rejected the lesser food.

Is envy a primitive instinct that we can't avoid, or is it an instinct we should overcome? We need to be weary of its power, but used wisely it can result in better progress for our nation. A combination of capitalism and voluntary socialism would assist in keeping our envy under control.

Pride is a sense of personal dignity; a feeling of pleasure because of something achieved, done, or owned. Pride is considered to be one of the most dangerous of the seven deadly sins, a form of arrogance and vanity, which leads to an overpowering sense of self-importance. Pride always concerns a comparison and has always been a part of our capitalistic society. It's the reward for "doing well," which usually ends up with one person exploiting others.

In the 1850s, the Industrial Revolution came to the United States. The sin of pride became a virtue instead of a vice. A new type of "robber baron" came about as we switched from agriculture to industry. Their extravagant lifestyles met with much criticism, forcing the wealthy to find a way to justify their extravagant spending and consumption habits. These wealthy barons of the industrial age didn't want people to think that they thought they were better than everyone else, so they started giving to charities, transforming their image from robber barons to philanthropists. They found that in order to continue their lavish lifestyles, they had to give back to society to keep the public's approval.

Almost a century before Adam Smith wrote about the apparent advantages of greed, the Amish began a new tradition banning pride in all its forms. Humility replaced it as the most valued character trait. This culture shuns worldliness, believing that technology can only lead to the envious behavior of wanting more, ultimately leading to more pride.

In the middle of the 20th century, pride itself became something that made people proud. In our country's capitalistic society, we're encouraged to rise above the crowd, to live the American dream of becoming independently wealthy and to go from rags to riches, which creates pride. This says that pride is an accomplishment, a force that makes people want to do better, and is thus not a sin.

Psychologist Jessica Tracy's new research indicates there are two types of pride.[7] One leads to success, the other to "Hell." The first type is called "authentic pride," which depicts righteousness and includes confidence that comes from being productive and reaching goals. The second type of pride, which represents deceit, is called "hubristic pride," and consists of arrogance, egotism, and conceitedness. Pride of ownership, a hubristic pride, drives us to prosper and grow, which is one of the more destructive types of pride.

Scientists say pride comes from our genetic makeup and our ancestors. The History Channel aired a special where they talked to Laurie Santos at Yale University. She found that monkeys exhibit behavior a lot like human pride.[7] Pride causes a person to overvalue an item simply because they own it, which psychologists call "the endowment effect." Santos found that the capuchin monkeys she studied valued the cereal they already owned much more than an equivalent amount of apple. In fact, the monkeys would only relinquish the cereal they had after they were offered several apples. The capuchins, like humans, seem to take pride in the things they own.

Once the two types of pride are understood, it should become evident that hubristic pride would be associated with capitalism, while authentic pride would be more in line with socialism. The main driving forces that fuel capitalism's engines are greed, envy, and hubristic pride. Socialism is based on authentic pride and has nothing to do with greed, envy, or hubristic pride. After combining capitalism with voluntary socialism, hubristic pride would still exist, but would be looked down upon. Authentic pride would flourish in a system that combines capitalism and voluntary socialism. The hubristic pride that a person feels after purchasing an expensive item can't be matched by the feeling of authentic pride that would be felt by giving that item to another person.

Greed is a selfish desire to acquire more than a person needs (or perhaps deserves). It is the excessive desire for wealth or possessions that can lead people to cheating, hoarding, corruption, and crime. The problem comes when our possessions control us instead of us taking control of our possessions.

In 1776, Adam Smith's book changed the way the world thought about commerce. Capitalism was born. Smith, often called "the father of modern economics," originally wrote of greed in his 1759 book, *The Theory of Moral Standards*. He wrote then of the apparent benefits to society of people operating in their own interests. He called greed "the invisible hand."

Thanks to the influence of Adam Smith and a small group of self-interested individuals, the 19th and 20th centuries became centuries of greed, resulting in the stock market crash of October 29, 1929, which brought in the Great Depression. One of the main causes of the crash was the barely-regulated banking system, which allowed the greedy to gain extensive wealth at the expense of the majority of the population.

In the 1980s and 1990s and even today, the wealthy have become further glamorized as greed has become more accepted. This stands in stark contrast of thousands of years of human intuition.

Jesus denounced greed. Jesus said that the poor were the lucky ones, not the rich. Greed led to the betrayal and death of Jesus as Judas was paid in gold for his betrayal. To this day, religious people have frowned upon greed, for greed is "the root of all evil."

Islamic beliefs also condemn greed. The Qur'an, written by the prophet Muhammad in the seventh century, is the fundamental text of the Muslim faith. This book tells believers that in order to attain spiritual purity, one must avoid greed.

The Tao Te Ching, which is the central Taoist book, clearly condemns greed. This book, attributed to the great Chinese philosopher Lao Tzu, said that "greed is the source of all man's evil."[10]

Aristotle believed that one must find a balance between excess and deficiency. He encouraged the idea of what he called "liberality."[11] He believed that everyone should be able to receive everything they deserve.

Greed is the basis of the legend of King Midas. King Midas was so greedy that upon being granted a wish, everything he touched turned to gold. The king soon realized his greediness, when he could neither eat nor drink. His food and water turned into gold as soon as he touched them.

For centuries the Roman Empire embraced the seven deadly sins, trying to defy the consequences. By 500 A.D. the Roman Empire collapsed. Greed had helped destroy the most powerful state in the history of the world. Europe soon fell into the dark ages.

Greed may be a trait that all people share as a part of our fundamental nature, but that doesn't mean we don't have any power over it. Jesus, Lao Tzu, Muhammad, and Pope Gregory say that greed is evil. Robber barons, most politicians, and many Hollywood icons say that greed is good for society. Who do you believe is correct?

Hopefully, the evidence has shown that in 1776 the country's better judgment was clouded by the desire to achieve success and that greed, envy, and hubristic pride are not acceptable traits for a morally correct world and have no place in an advanced intelligent society. Once these negative traits are realized and no longer desired, where will this leave capitalism?

Our banking systems and the stock market are representations of our misguided desires to become financially successful and have always played a major role in determining the state of the economy. Since 2007, the stock markets have dropped 30%[12] and hundreds of thousands have lost their jobs and homes. Home foreclosures have doubled,[13] financial institutions are closing and going bankrupt, and automakers are on the verge of bankruptcy. Retirement plans are falling apart. Are we headed toward another recession? Didn't we learn anything from the stock market crash of 1929?[1]

Our recent economic troubles started to cascade in March 2008, when Behr Sterns nearly folded only to be saved by JP Morgan Chase. At this time, President Bush and Treasurer Paulsen insisted that the fundamentals of the economy were still strong, and they stated the situation had been contained.

By August, super giant mortgage companies Fannie Mae and Freddie Mac were the next to fail. On September 7, 2008, the federal government took them over at a cost of 5 trillion taxpayer dollars. What happened next was completely unexpected. Wall Street, as we've known it for many decades, collapsed within days. There were five big investment banks on Wall Street. All five are now gone! Morgan Stanley and Goldman Sachs have become depository banks, Lehman Brothers collapsed into bankruptcy, and Merrill Lynch and Behr Sterns were sold to depository banks.

AIG, the world's largest insurer, looked like it would be the next to collapse. The government stepped in supplying an $85 million dollar bailout, but the domino effect had started. Iceland declared bankruptcy, and it became obvious that the crisis had spread worldwide. The stock market again began to panic, and on October 10, 2008, the stock market had its worst week since the end of the Great Depression. In only one week, the Dow Jones had dropped nearly

25%, wiping out the gains of many years of prosperity. Many predicted we were headed for another Great Depression.

One of the biggest lessons learned from the crash of 1929 was that the government must act quickly. In 1929, Andrew Mellon, Herbert Hoover's Secretary of the Treasury, famously announced that the feds would stand by while the market worked itself out.[14] This turned out to be a devastating decision. All the major political figures of the time also assured people that their money was safe. The people didn't believe them, and they lined up at the banks to get their money. Of course, there wasn't enough money in the bank's vaults to pay everyone. The people's money was in investments. Banks soon ran out of money and panic followed. People had either lost their life savings, or had lost all their money in the stock markets. Soon, over 5,000 banks collapsed and everyone's money evaporated.

In the 1930s, foreclosures were so common that you could look around and see many people's furniture in the streets. Neighbors would band together to save each other's homes at auctions. They would bid low, keeping outsiders from bidding up the prices. By 1933, 1.5 million people were homeless. The American dream had become an American nightmare!

After the crash, President Hoover became the most unpopular man in the country. He attempted to fix the economy with a $2.5 billion bailout, but it was too late.

 In 2008, the Bush administration decided that they didn't want to make the same mistake. They couldn't allow major financial institutions to fail, because the effects of the failure would be too great on the country's economy (as we experienced in 1929).

If you compare what happened in the 1920s with today's economic problems, you'll see many similarities. In both instances, the rich were getting richer, while the poor became poorer, with easy credit being the cause in both situations. The following is a very important statement. *Credit has caused most of our country's financial problems since it was introduced!*

Easy credit was invented in the 1920s. Before then, people saved money until they had enough to pay for something. This new innovation called "credit" was unbelievable. You no longer were required to save money to purchase an item. In fact, having money was not a requirement for buying something on credit. A simple agreement of future payment was all that was necessary to acquire possessions. Many people realized that this new credit system was a snake in the grass, and others saw only its benefits. As the '20s progressed, easy credit steadily became more available. Before long, Wall Street was playing the credit game and soon became the way to make easy money. Even women were involved. Beauty parlors had tickertape machines installed for women to do their trading while they did their hair. The stock market boomed in the '20s, mostly due to the expansion of credit. Many people were buying stock on credit, which made the stock market "bubble."[15]

Just like in the 1920s, easy credit helped today's housing market bubble. When the feds dropped the overnight rate to 1%, mortgages became so cheap that almost anybody could afford to buy a home. With rates so low, people started borrowing money on their homes though they couldn't afford the payments. The large increase of lending and excessive borrowing continued with home equity lines of credit and 0% APR interest credit card loans. Everyone seemed to be getting in on the lower rates, until one day it crashed!

Sooner or later, overvalued markets run out of gullible buyers. In the 1920s we had a stock bubble; in 2008 we were in a housing bubble. At the time, excessive speculation had driven stock prices far above any resemblance of the actual value of the commodity. The same thing happened in our housing market. By October 2008, 70% of all homes purchased after 2006 were not worth their mortgage balances. Many homes across America have lost over 30% of their previous value.[16] Since real estate was overvalued, all the securities that had been based on the higher prices of these homes became worthless. Our new financial structure tumbled down!

Federal Reserve chief Ben Bernanke, having studied the great depression extensively, urged Congress to pass the $700 billion bailout plan. Had President Bush and Ben Bernanke not been able to persuade Congress to follow through with the bailout plan, our country would have been plunged into another Great Depression! The question is, "Did the government bail out *the right people?*"

Now that all the financial institutions have been bailed out, we find that it will cost American taxpayers twice the amount originally anticipated for these bailouts. It's time for the government to stop bailing out financial institutions and start bailing out the people of the United States!

I researched how much it would cost to put every American adult into his or her own home with a clear title. This figure is substantially less than we just paid for these financial institution's bailouts, stimulus projects, and future stimulus packages combined, which are expected to double the national deficit![3] (Chapter 12: Housing contains statistical information.) The country would be in much better shape right now had we paid off everyone's home mortgages and purchased homes for all of our renters. We could have accomplished this feat and *still* spent less than our current spending plans! If everyone owned their own home and didn't have any rent or mortgage payments, our economy would blossom! Our economy is built on spending. We wouldn't know what to do with all our extra money! We could even work on paying off our national debt!

Here is where we now stand with the economy: *We are doomed! We're cooked! We're finished, washed-up, ruined, done-in, kaput!* Our federal government has dug us such a deep hole that unless we completely change our ways of thinking, we will never again see the light of day! Most people believe that our existing national deficit is about $13 trillion, which equates to each working American owing over $119,650.[4] It would be nice if these figures were correct! Actually, we're in the hole *much* deeper than this.

According to most sources, including the national debt clock website,[4] our present national debt, which is about ten percent of our country's total unfunded debt, equals roughly $13 trillion. That is $13,000,000,000,000! In 2009, we spent $320,650,178,293 in interest payments alone! Can you imagine what could be done every year with this much money? Lately, about 5% of the budget is allocated to service debt interest payments. It's estimated that in 5 years the national debt will double and is expected to triple before 2020.[24] If the national debt doubles and then triples, so will our interest payments. Our estimated yearly interest payments in 2020 will be $960 billion!

Where is all this money going to come from? Supposedly it will come from the greedy corporations and the wealthy. Well, they don't have that much money. Since 2005, average after-tax U.S. corporation profits have steadily dropped from $1.45 trillion to $650 billion in 2008. Wal-Mart only showed a profit of $13.3 billion last year (in 2010).[17] If we took 50% of the after-tax profits from all U.S. corporations in 2008, we would have enough money to pay the *interest* on the national debt for the year. Of course, this doesn't account for paying anything on the national debt itself!

Our nation's total debt per family household is $688,000![4] The average family income is only $50,300.[22] If we took all the personal income from every American taxpayer for the next 13 years, we would still not have enough money to pay off the national debt, even if you *exclude* interest over the next 13 years! This would also leave *zero* dollars to fund the government over those 13 years! Our present spending trends are absolutely unsustainable!

In fact, our national deficit is a *small problem* compared to everything else our economic recovery is up against. The projected upcoming tidal waves of Social Security, Medicaid, and Medicare costs are expected to expand the federal public debt to nearly 300% of the gross domestic product by 2050 and over 850% of the GDP by 2080.[18] The governments General Accounting Office projects payouts for these programs will significantly exceed tax revenues for the next 75 years![19]

In addition to the burden of our national deficit is the fact that our Social Security system is in disastrous condition, and its future looks particularly bleak. The government takes a percentage of our paychecks to "invest" in the Social Security Trust Fund, where it supposedly collects interest until we retire and are able to start receiving payments from the fund. Actually, our money is *not* saved for us until we retire. The money is presently being spent by the government! According to the NCPA, our verified shortfall in this fund is over $17.5 trillion,[2] this being a conservative figure. Other sources show this figure to be much higher.

Medicare *funding* is also a joke! Combining the costs of Medicare Part A (which pays for hospital admissions and visits), Part B (which covers doctor's visits), and part D (for prescription drugs) results in a total Medicare debt of $89.3 trillion,[2] this figure also being very conservative.

This brings our total unfunded obligations (including our national debt) to a grand total of $119.8 trillion![3] A national debt of $13 trillion is starting to sound pretty good right about now, isn't it? This figure is a very conservative estimate, and in all likelihood we have much more debt ahead of us to repay. At this minimum figure of $120 trillion, this puts each American's share of this debt at over $353,000! Our family of four's debt would be over $1.4 million!

If our national deficit doubles by 2015 as predicted, our national deficit would be $26 trillion. If the deficit triples by 2020, we would be in debt $39 trillion. Medicare is presently a minimum $89 trillion in the hole. Most of this has been incurred since the start of the programs in 2006. The amount this unfunded obligation will incur in the next 10 years could be three times bigger than today's loss, for a total loss by 2020 of $268 trillion! Adding this to 2020's projected national deficit of $36 trillion totals $304 trillion, and on top of this will be added the losses for unfunded obligations to the Social Security Fund for the next 10 years! This figure will be outrageous! With well over $355 trillion of debt 10 years from now, which is $4.2 million per family of four, *we're doomed!* The following statement is very important! *The only way we'll ever recover from this mess is to completely restructure our system of economics!* We can avert this impending financial disaster by implementing reforms you will read about in this book's upcoming chapters, such as eliminating housing costs for the average American family, *forever!*

It should now become apparent that the combined totals of our national deficit and other unfunded obligations are far beyond our ability to even begin to pay. That is why I say, *"We are doomed!"* Something must be done to *"change our current path to impending doom!"* We must reverse our climbing government deficit, *NOW*! Our gross national debt has risen from 52.4% of our gross domestic product in 1940 to 90.4% of our GDP in 2009![25]

Congress has passed many irresponsible mandates lately, including pay raises for themselves and increasing our "debt ceiling" every two years or so. Our country's debt ceiling is supposedly the maximum amount our country can be in debt. On February 12, 2010, the U.S. Congress passed new laws raising our debt ceiling to its present $14.3 trillion limit.[5]

With our economics going down the tubes, it's no wonder that people are losing faith in capitalism. Polls taken recently show that 53% of Americans were for capitalism, 20% for socialism, and 27% were not sure.[21] Among the younger generation, 37% were for capitalism, 33% for socialism, and 30% were undecided. None of these people polled were asked if they would favor a new type of government that combines *both* capitalism with a responsible voluntary socialist outlook. Maybe the polls will be different when such a society is proposed!

Now that our economic situation has been revealed, it's time to discuss solutions. The main economic remedy this book prescribes deals with housing and is discussed in detail in this book's housing chapter. We should press Congress to grant every American of age $100,000 (*in the form of a housing credit*) to pay off or purchase their home ($200,000 per couple). Homes *must* appraise at a minimum acceptable amount of $100,000 ($200,000 for married couples, since they may separate). This home could never be taken from the individual(s) who owned it. The next chapter shows that we could accomplish this, in retrospect, *for free!*

Anyone who desires a home worth more than this figure can pay cash or borrow the amount needed from *the Commonwealth,* not a bank, at *very* low interest rates. If a more expensive home ever became unaffordable or undesirable, the minimum equity of $100,000 per adult would always be available to purchase a lower–cost home. Home equity loans would only be given on appraised amounts over $100,000 per adult, so that *all* homeowners would retain a minimum equity of $100,000 in their homes. Creditors would not be allowed to touch this minimum equity or payments for home purchases from the Commonwealth.

The time has come to overhaul our economic systems. One of the first things we must understand is that we can no longer let the stock market and financial institutions dictate the condition of our economy! Interest payments made on home mortgage loans and most types of credit are unnecessary evils. Banks and mortgage companies have become tyrants, getting away with charging as much as they possibly can for their fees. It's not uncommon for CEOs of these institutions to make $10 million yearly. These outrageous profits come from you and me.

These institutions and their immoral practices aren't needed anymore! The government collects our money and lends it to the banks, and the banks in turn lend it back to us and demand interest. It's our money! (Saying this reminds me of the J.G. Wentworth commercials, "It's our money, and we want it now!)

I propose the "People's Bank" for everyone's personal banking, an institution to be owned and run by the people! We need to change our economic ideologies by eliminating home mortgage and rent payments and limiting all existing interest rates of credit to very low percentage rates. Most people's credit card interest rates are so high (19% to 29% are common interest rates) that they may never be able to fully pay off their balances!

Physical money must also be eliminated. It costs 1.67 cents to make a penny, 7.7 cents to produce a nickel, and 10 cents to make a quarter![26] When it costs more to make a coin than it's worth, the time has come to rethink physical money! Most illegal activities revolve around cash, and many of them couldn't operate without it. Eliminating cash would save us billions of dollars in its production and would also shut down many black markets.

We must all agree that when it comes to money, many Americans *are* greedy and selfish. Capitalism isn't working correctly when we have 37 million American workers below the poverty level.[6] This is one out of six of our working men and women! Upon studying our country's income levels, I'm stunned. I truly believed that the average American earned more money. I discovered that in recent years 26% of our working population made less than $7,500 annually, and 52% made less than $31,000 per year.[22] After computing figures from the U.S. Census Bureau, I found that 8% of the working population made

36% of the total U.S. income in 2008![6]

This is the United States, the land where you can become rich beyond your wildest dreams. Capitalism, our way of life, rewards you for your hard work and strife. Isn't this correct? Sometimes it does, other times not. Most Americans work their tails off only to *almost* make ends meet. Many of us have worked at a job for years, putting everything we had into the company or privately owned business, only to be laid off, or have the business go under due to circumstances beyond our control. One out of a thousand of us reaches our dreams fully and becomes independently wealthy. Today, more people become wealthy through inheritance than hard work. Capitalism is failing the expectations for the country. More and more, the rich become richer and the poor become poorer. Now days the saying goes, "It takes money to make money." This has become even more accurate as availability of money has plummeted with the recession. With the economy in today's condition, loans are accessible only when you don't really need the money. Newly passed laws that impose stricter loan guide lines now make it even harder to obtain home loans.

In a perfect world, everyone of age would have an average-sized home, completely paid off. All utility companies would be purchased by the American public and their operating costs paid by the Commonwealth. Use of electricity, heating, and phone services would be given to all households at cost. Individuals who over-use the services might be charged more than the base fee. People would still work for their food, clothes, vacations, and the luxuries of life, but we would have plenty of money to do so if our homes were paid off and utility costs were reasonable! Everyone would still work for their hard-earned money, just as they do now.

I'm not proposing a communist government, where everyone is controlled by and works for the government, where freedoms are limited and personal growth stagnates. I'm envisioning a society where people will start to care more for others and less for themselves by implementing ideas designed to benefit all of society. I envision a society run with today's capitalistic ideals of freedom and choice, while still taking care of the common person's needs. Please hold off judgments on visions of this new society until the end of the book. I recommend implementing only a few changes now that could be labeled as "socialist," but the majority of Americans will agree that they are much needed changes.

This perfect world of the future many of us envision is exactly that, a future world. It will be years from now before our society becomes enlightened, civilized, and intelligent enough to bring about all these changes. For the moment, we must concentrate on altering the country's views and implementing the most needed changes on prevailing issues and today's problems. The American people must focus on correcting issues on housing, health care, the country's drug problem, over-population, and environmental destruction. Other aspects, like Commonwealth-owned utilities will follow as society becomes more enlightened and less selfish.

The future world envisioned is so much different than our own that converting to such a world would need to be done in steps. The first step must be housing reform, because it is the simplest way to increase everyone's expendable income (please see Chapter 8: Housing for further details). Advancements from there could only be made with nationwide support. It may be a while before the greedy people of the country would consider other changes.

Let's pause for a moment and look at ramifications that would be caused by implementing these systems. Many thousands of jobs would initially be lost with the collapse of unnecessary businesses like *some* banks and mortgage companies, but hundreds of thousands of jobs would be created. The American people need to take control of the morality of the nation's banks. The Peoples Bank's should open, transferring their new customer's loans from banks that have adopted policies that take advantage of people. Many of the failing banks would be taken over by the government and converted to the People's Bank with no employee losses. The only job losses which would occur here would be limited to the "top brass," the CEOs, presidents, and others who pocket the big profits of these unnecessary banks. These people should be presently living comfortably anyway. If job losses occur to the common American worker because of national system changes, the Commonwealth could offer these people new and better careers and could pay for their schooling and training as well.

Implementing these systems, along with other economic system changes such as health care reform, would create more career openings than job losses caused by switching to the new systems. Thousand of new doctors and dentists would be needed after medical and dental care become part of every U.S. citizen's rights. Seventy percent of our citizens need some type of medical treatment, but don't have any health insurance, or can't afford the deductibles. Ninety percent of Americans need some type of dental work, and most have no dental insurance. Preventative maintenance in both medical and dental fields is almost nonexistent for most Americans! Chapter 13: Health Care Reform goes more in-depth on the reasons for and benefits of change, but the main change that would occur in our medical fields (besides everyone having health insurance) is the Commonwealth would pays the bills, not the insurance companies who presently pocket a large percentage of the scheduled payments we make to them. Insurance companies can make their profits in other areas, but profits made from our health insurance system should be eliminated. Every American could be covered for less than we pay now!

We would require hundreds of thousands of new workers in the home construction industry. Many people deserve a new home or a home makeover. Many cities have complete neighborhoods and large housing areas that would be deemed unlivable and surely condemned. All of these housing units would need to be replaced immediately.

Hundreds of thousands of people would receive new jobs setting up new educational facilities, which would include colleges and trade schools built specifically to handle the overflow of new students desiring to better their lives. In our new system all education would be free, which would easily pay for itself in the long run in increased productivity. The last years of medical and dental graduate schools could be funded by government institutions, the graduates in turn possibly working for the Commonwealth or their alma mater after completion of their schooling.

The automotive industry, now going bankrupt, would need thousands of new employees. We must replace all of our nation's gas guzzling vehicles with environmentally friendly vehicles that don't use fossil fuels as their energy source. The economics and expenses of these newer clean-running vehicles would no longer be a factor in their production and distribution. Older vehicles, which put out more pollution than newer models, would be replaced first, their owners finally getting a new car they greatly deserve. Eventually (the sooner the better), all gasoline-burning vehicles would be re-placed by vehicles which produce no pollution.

People on welfare should be required to work, if they are able to do so. If people want benefits, they should work and do their part to assist society. If a person needs and desires a job and can't find one, society could help find one for them. If a person has disabilities, jobs could be found for them that use their talents. There would be no more freebies, government, or state handouts. Everyone would con-tribute to society for their benefits.

Upon implementing all the ideas contained in this book, we could put every person to work rebuilding the country. After American businesses stop giving away jobs to China, Korea, and other foreign countries, we'll need hundreds of thousands of new workers to make our own products in the USA. We all have high hopes of turning over goods in the supermarket and again finding the proud label, "Made in the USA"! Churches and other organizations could awaken, stepping up to build new homes for their congregations and lifting up all their members to a comfortable standard of living.

No one should be jobless. Unemployed people could work for the Commonwealth. They could contract their labor for the mutual bene-fit of all Americans. All Commonwealth industries would be non-profit organizations, their sole purpose being to supply jobs and save the common people money. Everyone working for the Common-wealth would be paid well for their share of their contribution to so-ciety. Hard and tedious jobs could be made easier with everyone's help.

If every American worker had the knowledge that most of their income would be "frill" money, life would be great! Everyone's atti-tude would be soaring, while their *debt load* plummeted! Income now spent on scraping to get by could be used for the pleasures of life, like remodeling, new furniture, and vacations. Hundreds of thousands of people who can't afford to take any time off work would be able to take much needed vacations. New types of vacation sites would spring up everywhere. People would gladly put in their ten hour work day, four days a week (this is our new 40 hour national workweek, with three-day weekends!) knowing that more of their income would be going to the pleasures of life.

Take just a moment to consider the proposed four-day work week. Think about the positive aspects gained by converting to such a system. American workers who now put in an 8-hour work day (often extended by an unpaid lunch) find that by the time they get home from work, not much time is left to do anything worthwhile or rewarding. One extra day off a week could be used to accomplish a lot! Our country would instantly reduce transportation costs by 20%. Fuel consumption, air pollution, and vehicle wear would all instantly be decreased by 20%. When you're talking about most of the country, that's a lot of savings and less wear on Mother Earth! More quality time with the family would be a major plus. Everyone would still put in their 40 hours, but in four days rather than five.

In the future, the "keeping up with the Jones" attitude (where people are envious of their neighbor's possessions and attempt to acquire the same material wealth for themselves) will fade and disappear. Everyone will have all of the basic needs of life, and the idea of trying to live better than others will slowly fade. Jet set lifestyles will be frowned upon instead of glamorized. All people of the world will do their part to conserve resources.

No, this book doesn't have all the answers, but the basics are laid down. Americans need to take these ideas, modify and expand them, and run with them! Once we repair our economy, we could then set our sights on saving the environment. Cost efficiency of environmentally-friendly methods wouldn't be so critical anymore. We could support American businesses offering higher quality, eco-friendly goods, and we would feel good about supporting their production as well as respecting the planet.

Some people would suggest that bailing out the citizens instead of the institutions would give benefits to some undeserving individuals. As an example, let me propose a hypothetical situation: A homeless and unemployed 40-year-old man needs help. Circumstances for this person have plunged his life over a cliff, and he has hit rock bottom. He has recently resorted to stealing food and begging for money to survive. Does this person deserve help? Or better yet, do you think this person can help *us?* Let's say we give this man a job working for the Commonwealth as farm help. We also set him up with his own home. We teach him what he needs to know to perform his job and offer him free schooling in the evenings to better his career opportunities. This man would be very thankful! He would be crying, as he humbly accepted our help! Soon, he would be able to wake up in the morning in *his* bed, in his home, knowing that no one could ever take it from him. He would look forward to the day's challenges, feeling secure about his future. He would proceed with a bright outlook throughout the day, making plans of what he might do with the extra money that he's earned. Who's to judge this man and say that he doesn't deserve this help?

Almost everyone more than deserves the benefits that a Commonwealth perspective could provide. Thousands of people across the country have worked too much of their life at a job, slowly paying off their home mortgage, only to have their employer close for various reasons, causing the loss of their retirement plan, income, and eventually their home.

This "caring" Commonwealth society seems like a dream, but think of the possibilities. All problems could be worked out and solved. With the right leadership, this "paradise" could be implemented. Without the burden of today's normal worries, we could set our sights on visions not yet realized or dreamed. If you don't agree with the ideas in this book, don't just put them down, revise them! With everyone across the country inserting their own ideas, we can become Americans again!

Our country's main obstacle in converting to such a system is today's capitalistic views that are based on greed and selfishness. It is morally wrong for many of the wealthy to ornate their bodies with million-dollar rings and necklaces, while others in the same cities have no housing, food, or basic necessities! To them, social responsibility means to appear in public wearing their best custom designer clothing. Hoarding large sums of money accumulated from the masses is not only selfish, but damages our moral sense of responsibility. People who desire more material wealth than others need to take a good look at their ideals. Some of the wealthy need to realize that their money comes from the common people and that their outlandish spending is unconscionable. We must renounce lifestyles that glamorize high-dollar sports cars, multimillion-dollar mansions, and outrageous spending habits. This mentality must go! Everyone should be happy with a nice home and a stylish environmentally friendly car.

We Americans need to realize that we're seen by most of the world as being a selfish, materialistic, greedy, capitalistic society, whose wealthy residents live among the homeless and hungry. Terrorist countries, along with other countries who believe wealth, materialism, and capitalism are evil, would marvel at our new system and the changes it brought about. They would praise our newly-founded utopian society and after seeing it work would implement the systems themselves. This revolutionary ideal of mutual generosity could eventually wipe out world poverty, hunger, terrorism, and all wars. The United States could be at the center of organizing the New World structure. Until we change, we can't expect the world to change.

Implementing new policies that strive for a morally correct world (one Earth under God, that exists without poverty, homelessness, or hunger), would change the lives of every person on the planet. The United States must now lead the way for the world, but first we must solve our own problems.

Changing America's greedy and selfish ways, along with enacting other changes presented in this book, will repair our economy and determine the outcome of the future as well. Our economic habits coupled with our disregard for the planet and its resources make our present standard of living absolutely unsustainable. Changes are not only needed, but are essential in order to stop mankind from destroying itself and all other life on Earth! Changes envisioned in upcoming chapters that will transform our economy include:

1) - Eliminating our country's biggest financial burden, housing costs, for every American adult (We could put every American adult into their own home, paid off with a clear title, and in retrospect, five years from now, we would find that it would have been accomplished for free!)

2) - Implementing dental and health care reform that will cut America's health care costs in half (We can supply coverage for *every* American for the same cost that we're now paying for less than half of us!)

3) - Changing direction in fighting America's drug wars (Upon placing this book's ideas into effect on the country's drug problems, we will *instantly* shut down all drug trafficking, drug lords, and gang activity, unclog our court systems and jails, and eventually eliminate 95% of the nation's crime. All previous attempts to accomplish these goals have failed. Why would my plan succeed? Please read this book's chapter about our country's drug problem!)

4) - Implementing a "buy American campaign," where we quit giving away our jobs to foreign countries (It will save us billions of dollars every year and create hundreds of thousands of American jobs!)

5) - Demanding world peace, now (Defense costs have become major financial burdens world-wide. We must set time limits. No more war mongering after a certain date, or your atrocities will be swiftly dealt with *by the world!*)

6) - Offering trade school or college educations to our children, free (Educating our citizens must be one of our upmost priorities, especially regarding our younger generations. Poverty and lack of education are synonymous. Educating everyone with a desire to learn could turn our economy around!)

7) - Changing the world's outlook on the inevitability of population growth and reducing the world's population to a sustainable level (The planet no longer has the available resources to sustain its existing population, let alone supporting the world's *growing* population! We must decrease the world's population by one-half!)

The economy seems to be the main concern of most Americans,

but we must not lose sight of the fact that we can't sacrifice our planet and its resources to better our economy. What good is a stable economy with a trashed planet? Getting the economy back on track is a must. The only way that this will be accomplished is by making major changes, *immediately!* If anyone has any better ideas or visions to modify mine, then let's hear them! Otherwise, let's get rolling! We've almost run out of time to save our world!

12

HOUSING

After reading this book's chapter on the economy, it becomes obvious that the country is in serious financial trouble. Not even by combining the annual income of the poor, middle class, rich, and greedy corporations can we presently acquire enough money to pay our national deficit and unfunded obligations. Where will this money come from?

Unfortunately, it will eventually come from you and me. At this point in time, my family doesn't have our share of the country's unfunded obligations and national deficit, which is about $1.4 million per family of four.[8] The only way that the country will be able to recover from the federal government's spending sprees is by *dramatically reducing everyone's personal debts!* Only then can Americans hope to move the mountain of debt now resting on the nation.

The most burdening expense for most Americans today is housing. According to the U.S. Census Bureau, more than one third of households in the United States are spending at least 30% of their annual incomes on housing expenses.[2] Most Californians, Nevadans, and Floridians spend over 40% of their income just to put a roof over their head.

When early settlers first established the American colonies, they found suitable places to build a home, claimed available land and built homes at reasonable costs, if not for free. Even when it was necessary to purchase land and building materials for their homes, early Americans' costs weren't proportionally anywhere near what we pay today. If you had told Thomas Jefferson that someday people would make payments on their land and home for 30 years or more and in the process spending up to hundreds of thousands of dollars for principal and interest on an average-size home, he would have been in disbelief.

Today, housing costs are ridiculous! The average American home owner can plan on paying up to four times the original price of the home once the mortgage and interest are paid. Today's housing costs are driving the average American into an early grave! This doesn't have to be the case! We can eliminate this burden from everyone's shoulders, *forever!*

In today's system, the government collects our money in taxes and then lends it to banks at very low interest rates. Banks then lend the money back to us at higher rates, so that we can buy our land and homes. This sounds like the type of government we revolted against hundreds of years ago! The government has become a separate entity from the people. We must retake control of the government and our money! Lately, the government has attempted to prevent economic collapse by funding banks directly, but since 2008, 59 banks have collapsed.[5] *The time has truly come to bail out the people, not the banks!*

Our society has progressed immensely in the last few hundred years, but our expectations have not yet caught up with what we could deliver to each citizen in this nation. Land and home ownership should be an American right! Every American should be able to own a home and at least a small parcel of land, and no one should *ever* be able to take this from them. There is plenty of land to go around; many states still have vast open areas.

The time has come to make major changes in how we view real estate and housing. Our society is evolving to a higher level of consciousness. As our technology and the morality of our society grow, material items will dwindle in importance. Acquiring new views and compassion for our fellow Americans will lead us to become less primitive and more spiritual, and we will realize that sharing good fortune with any who are less fortunate is the only way to raise the bar of what is possible for all of humanity.

All American citizens who have been very fortunate must now help the people that haven't been so lucky. I say that some Americans have been fortunate because they have their homes paid off. The U.S. Census Bureau reports that approximately one third of Americans own their homes outright.[9] These are the lucky ones who have not lost their homes like many Americans have. They didn't get sick and cave under insurmountable medical bills because they couldn't afford health insurance, or their health coverage was inadequate. They didn't lose their job of 30 years through no fault of their own, their retirement fund disappearing with the occupation. They didn't get laid off from businesses downsizing because of the bad economy or lose their job to industry outsourcing to China. These Americans remained safe from natural disasters like hurricanes, tornadoes, or floods. Yes, this 33% of the country's households should count their *many* blessings and be very thankful that circumstances allowed them to live their dreams of becoming the sole owner of their homes. But what about the rest of the American households that weren't so lucky?

All Americans need to reach out to each other in order to make the American dream of home ownership a reality for everyone! If every American could get up in the morning and have the security of knowing that they own their home with a free and clear title, life would be so much better for everyone! We have enough housing to accomplish this task. As a matter of fact, according to the U.S. Census Bureau, fourteen percent of the country's housing units are vacant![2] Can you imagine the majority of Americans having 40% more of their income going to other necessities and desires? The economy would skyrocket! Without a home mortgage payment, our household would pocket an extra $22,000 a year. How much would *you* save?

My concept for a better country would start with everyone of age owning their home, free and clear, with no property taxes. When I say everyone of age, I mean *everyone!* There is no reason that we should still have citizens of this country who are homeless. A beneficent United States would see no more foreclosures, no more families living out of their cars, and no more people with nowhere to turn!

This plan can provide a home that is paid off for 100% of Americans! So far, the lucky 33% who have their homes paid off completely have been mentioned. We should allocate a standard amount of $100,000 to the 34% of American adults who currently have home mortgages. Renters, who are 33% of the population, would also receive a one-time payout of $100,000 per adult from the Commonwealth in order to purchase a home. These funds could come in the form of a "home credit." The "People's bailout" funds would be better used if the funds were used for nothing but purchasing housing, but people's circumstances always vary. If *all* American adults received a bailout check for $100,000, regardless of whether their homes are paid-off or not, then many could use part or all of the money for other purposes (home improvements?), if they can show that they already have $100,000 of equity in their home ($200,000 per married couple) or require less than this amount to gain the minimum required equity.

After setting up all Americans with their own paid off homes, we would then need to do the same for our children. Upon reaching the age of 21 (to 22) *and graduating trade school or college*, the Commonwealth should *reward* each graduate with $100,000 or enough money to purchase a home, condo, or apartment (wouldn't we all like to see *every* student continuing their education into college or trade school and living at home longer in order to mature a bit more before finally moving into the real world?). We now pay for at least 12 years of our children's education, why don't we finish the job correctly and send them to trade school or college?

If a person ever sold his or her home, the first $100,000 of equity ($200,000 per couple) would be given back in a "home credit," which would be required to be used on the purchase of the next home. Exceptions could apply, such as emigrating from the country permanently.

This standard amount of $100,000, or $200,000 per couple, would be enough to purchase a nice home, considering the average American family home is valued at $167,500.[4] This home could never be taken from the individual(s) who owned it, and immunity from property taxes would put even more money back in the pockets of citizens. We should press Congress to grant every American of age $100,000 to pay off their home, which *must* appraise at a minimum acceptable amount of $100,000 ($200,000 for married couples, since they may separate; trust funds could be set up for couples who require $200,000 of equity and own homes that appraise for less than $200,000).

I would like to clarify my statements regarding "putting every American into their own paid home." With the understanding that the median home in the United States is valued at $167,500, and that the Commonwealth would be giving $100,000 to each American adult, $200,000 per couple, in order to pay off their mortgages and purchase homes, from this point on when I speak of the People's bailout paying off everyone's homes, I'm assuming that most homes could be paid off (and/or remodeled?) for this amount.

Anyone who desires a home worth more than this figure can pay cash or borrow the amount needed from *the Commonwealth,* not a bank, at *very* low interest rates. If a more expensive home ever became unaffordable or undesirable, the minimum equity of $100,000 per adult would always be available to purchase a lower–cost home. Home equity loans would only be given on appraised amounts over $100,000 per adult, so that *all* homeowners would retain a minimum of $100,000 equity in their homes. Creditors would not be allowed to touch these payments from the Commonwealth.*

Using figures from the U.S. Census Bureau, I calculated that paying $100,000 both to every adult in the country who has a mortgage and to every citizen who rents in order to purchase a home would initially double our national debt. Our country's deficit is getting outrageous. But, if you knew that every American could have a home, paid off, free and clear of any debt, wouldn't you *gladly* see the national deficit *initially* double?

Though the national deficit would initially double, the United States Treasury would ultimately save money by taking this step. Most mortgages are taken out through banks that borrow from the

---

Just a quick note on credit and creditors, if I had my way, all unsecured credit would be limited to a 5% interest rate, and suing people for nonpayment wouldn't be allowed; bad credit scores are punishment enough in today's economics! I despise people and companies that make outrageous profits from extremely high interest rates on people's credit accounts. Many credit cards and second mortgages have rates as high as 30%. People who get caught in this type of scam see very little progress in paying off the debt over many years. This raping of the people's dignity must stop! If we put a 5% cap on all interest rates, then most interest in making greedy profits would disappear!

government. If mortgages were paid off, it's likely that the bank would soon pay back their own loans from the Treasury. This would not be true if the bank borrowed funds internationally or loaned from its own revenue; however, these must represent a minority of banks' loans considering the obvious monetary support our government offered big banks during our most recent economic crisis. A good majority of the money paid out would return to the federal government. The people of our country would also save hundreds of trillions in future mortgage, interest, and rent payments.

Our present government deficit is about $13 trillion. We would spend about $12.9 trillion upon giving $100,000 to every adult who currently rents or has a mortgage payment. This figure could be reduced by trillions after the government received all the banks payoffs, or even cut in half depending on how we set up our renters in new housing.

For example, the Commonwealth could build new homes at one third of the cost of purchasing an existing home. It's a fact that contractors who build a home usually mark up its price by an average of 67%.[10] The government could also build multi-unit homes for less than the cost of individual homes, and these homes could be built on government or state-owned land to save money.

Depending on how we went about purchasing or building homes, where the new homes would be built, and exactly how we went about paying off everyone's mortgages, my first (and most recommended plan) would increase the total amount of the nation's debt and unfunded obligations by only 5 to 10%! Projections of existing spending proposals show our country's national debt and total unfunded obligations of $119.8 trillion will increase to over $355 trillion in the next 10 years. This would be three times our country's total unfunded obligations! Taking care of the problem now for 5 to 10% of our nation's total unfunded debt, sounds much better than 300% later, with no end in sight!

If we continue on our current path the remaining balances on people's mortgages will not have changed much five years from now, and people who rent will probably still be renting, but the national debt will have doubled! This means that the amount each American taxpayer owes to the national debt will have doubled, indebting each working American over $236,000!

Luckily, this prospect of cascading debt doesn't have to be the case. If my plan to virtually end housing costs for every American is implemented, the national deficit would at most be doubled. At this point, we would be in the *same* situation as five years from now (when the national debt is projected to double), *except* that our homes would be paid off! If paying off everyone's home now puts us in the same financial situation as we would be five years from now, comparatively speaking, putting everyone into a paid home now would be *free!*

This would also force us to deal with the problem today, rather than five years from now. Facing the problem of inflation and mounting governmental expenses would be infinitely easier if everyone's homes were paid off first! With our homes paid off, we would have more available money to deal with the national deficit! There's no way that our economy could be in worse condition five years from now, if we implement my plan now!

If anyone can think of a better idea, rather than putting every American into their own home today, with a clear title, which is a $13 trillion accomplishment, plus saving the country from the agony of scraping up $550 billion to pay for their homes in the next five years, plus saving each American adult hundreds of thousands of dollars over their lifetimes in housing payments, and set up our future generations *forever*, we would all like to hear it. Otherwise, let's get moving!

Let's just implement this plan now, pretend that five years have passed, and now the national deficit has doubled. Either way, we would have the same results; we've just reached the conclusion sooner, with a better outcome! The only negative factor would be that our interest payments on the national debt would double now rather than five years from now, but it must also be noted that by jumping five years ahead, we will have saved *the exact same amount* by not paying five years of interest on the national debt! As people say, "In the long run, it all comes out in the wash." Had we waited the five years and not paid off homes for everyone, the deficit will have doubled anyway, and we will have paid five years of interest payments on the national debt in the meantime! If we pay off a home for everyone now, the deficit doubles now, and our interest payments double now, but we save paying this same exact amount by jumping ahead five years and not paying five years of interest on the national debt!

The obvious difference is that if we put everyone into their own paid home now, we could more easily solve the debt issue, now, saving trillions of dollars in interest payments on the national debt over the long run. Can you imagine the relief you would feel knowing that your home was paid off and guaranteed to never again be a drain on finances for you or your children and grandchildren? Everyone's attitudes and the economy would soar! Implementing this plan would not only fix and expand our economy beyond our wildest dreams, but it would permanently set up our children and grandchildren!

Speaking of our descendants, Chapter 21: Population Growth states that it is absolutely necessary we decrease our country's and the world's population by one half before the year 2100. If the rest of the world decides to emulate America's middle class rather than to collectively protect our planet from future damage, we'll need five more planet Earths to trash.[7] Earth can't go on like this, and curbing our population growth would also reduce the number of homes that will need to be built as our offspring reach maturity. If houses are built more solidly and designed to withstand the elements of time, children will be able to inherit their parent's homes. If we're lucky, in a few decades we may have many more homes available than people to live in them!

When considering my proposals, it should be noted that a fair way to evenly split the $13 trillion in People's bailout money among American adults who don't have their homes paid off wouldn't exist, if we used figures that are based upon numbers of households. My original quest was to pay off most, if not all, of the country's existing mortgage amounts and purchase homes for our renters. Many American adults live with their parents, and some are homeless. These adults also deserve a home of their own.

Using figures of the total adult population, rather than figures based on household numbers, would result in each American adult receiving $88,000 rather than $100,000 (based on a $13 trillion bailout), or $176,000 per couple rather than $200,000 per couple (calculations are shown at the end of this chapter). With this reduced amount, a couple receiving $176,000 would still have enough to purchase a home (with the average American home being valued at $167,500). We could also increase the bailout amount to $17 trillion and still give each adult $100,000.

Many people would state that most Americans would want their fair share of a People's bailout regardless of their housing situation. Wouldn't you imagine that the top 10% of wage earners (who make 40% of the nation's income[11]) would not need or ask for bailout funds? If the other 90% of the adult population asked for help, $13 trillion would be split between 201,344,000 adults. Even at $64,566 per adult or $129,000 per couple, a People's bailout would still improve our country's situation a thousand fold more than bailing out any institution! We could also increase the amount of the People's bailout from $13 trillion to $20 trillion, giving 90% of American citizens $100,000. This $7 trillion increase would only be a 6% increase in our nation's total unfunded debt. Most people would recommend this route, since the 6% increase would result in an additional bailout amount of over 50% per adult. A check for the People's bailout in the amount of $100,000 should be paid to every American adult who requires or deserves it.

We could also view the funding of this plan from another angle. The People's bailout could be added to our country's total unfunded debt rather than the national deficit. The People's bailout plan would be a national stimulus plan and wouldn't need to be funded by borrowing from China and Japan. We presently don't pay interest to ourselves on most of the country's total unfunded obligations such as the Social Security and Medicare deficits. If funds were allocated in this manner, our national debt would remain the same, and our country's total unfunded obligations would only increase a maximum of 12% (0 to 12% depending on whether you view it in retrospect or not and whether each adult receives $88,000 or $100,000)! Wouldn't you gladly pay your share of a *zero percent* increase in taxes to fund the program in return for a check written to you in the amount of $100,000 ($200,000 per couple)? Even a 12% increase in taxes wouldn't be bad when comparing the rewards.

I made two graphs that compare implementing my plan; Graph A shows the People's bailout funds added to the national debt (See Fig.15), and Graph B shows the funds being added to the nation's total unfunded obligations (See Fig.16). The People's bailout would be added to one of the two, depending on how we propose to fund the plan. Both graphs also show what will happen if we do nothing to prevent our national debts from doubling in five years and tripling in ten (as financial analysts have projected).

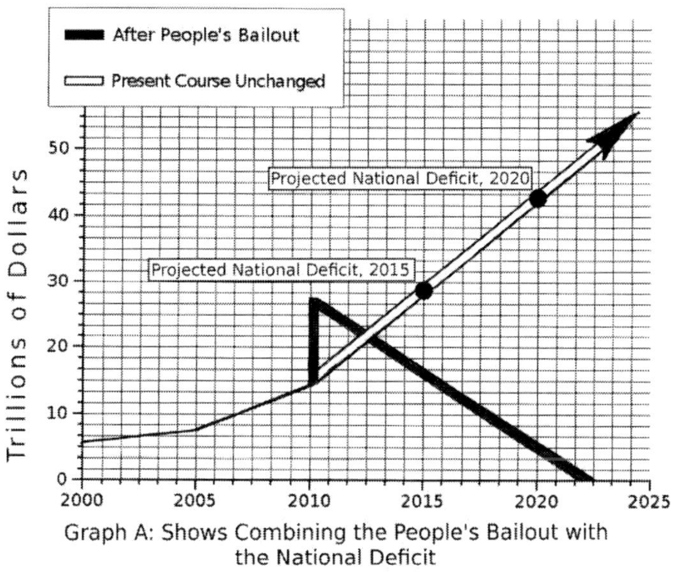

Fig. 15. Graph A.

The two graphs are very basic; the projected statistical lines don't contain any ups *and* downs, because it's a *future* projection graph. Unless you have information that the rest of us don't, all anyone can say is that the two graphs show exactly what is projected for the country's finances and what is occurring now; our deficits are doubling every five years! Graphs usually don't contain arrow tips on their statistical lines, but the "point" that needs to be stressed here is that these lines will continue upward as we persist in beat our heads on walls, or downward after we free everyone from their daily burdens of debt. The choice is ours. Fix the problem *now and forever*, or let it cascade until the country goes bankrupt!

Graph A (Fig.17) shows the projected rise in our national debt required to put my plan into effect, and that in 2015 the national debt will be much lower if we implement the People's Housing bailout now! In retrospect, we will have paid off a home for everyone, for free (and reversed our upward course)! In Graph B (Fig. 18), which shows the People's bailout added to the nation's total unfunded obligations, the projected increase to enact this housing plan is *barely*

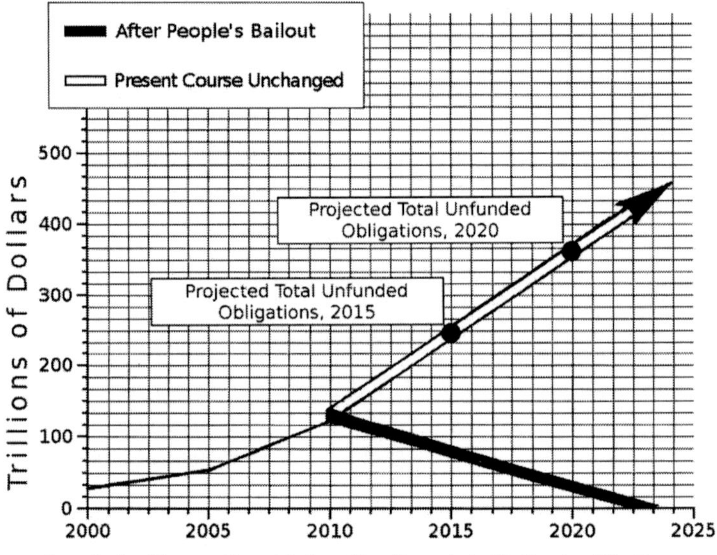

Graph B: Shows Combining the People's Bailout with the Nation's Total Unfunded Obligations

Fig. 16. Graph B.

perceivable! The increase is *over-exaggerated* just to make it noticeable (the increase in debt is the width of the statistic line)! The decreases in debt shown "after the People's bailout" on both graphs may be exaggerated, but doubtful. Americans are very enterprising, especially after receiving a check for $100,000 each.

Paying off a home for the average American would free us from most of our daily financial worries, and the economy (which is built on spending) would blossom! Right now, few people have extra spending money, and stimulus packages here and there aren't helping much, they're just tiny temporary patches, when we actually require major overhauls!

By now many of those who have already paid off their homes are thinking this proposal is absurd! Most of these people have worked long and hard to get their mortgages finally paid off. Some people may have inherited a home or purchased one with windfalls, but most people have labored for many years to pay off their homes. These are the fortunate people. They were born without major disabilities and had the right circumstances to allow them to accomplish this feat. Many of our country's adults are not as fortunate.

Others, who have a long way to go in paying off their mortgages, might comment that this plan seems unrealistic. Why would the people of the United States who have worked hard for their dreams and now have their homes paid off, help other Americans who aren't so fortunate? As we become more civilized and intelligent, greed and envy drive our decisions less often.

When the government implemented the "cash for clunkers" program, qualifying citizens received a $3,500 to $4,500 credit to be applied towards purchasing a newer more environmentally-friendly vehicle. Americans didn't complain that some were receiving benefits that others weren't. In fact, most Americans who owned newer vehicles were happy to see these less fortunate people get into new models. They realized that the country and environment would be in better shape, so they weren't jealous in the least! They didn't say, "These people don't deserve the money and will just trash their new vehicles because they didn't earn the money and won't have respect for its value." This sentiment wasn't heard because the general public believed these people *deserved* a new vehicle! Now that they have their new vehicle, they're overjoyed and thankful! They'll take care of this new vehicle just as any other American with a new vehicle would. Many of these new car owners will take even better care of their vehicle than others might after appreciating its normally unobtainable value.

If there were any greedy, selfish, or jealous views from fellow Americans, I didn't hear of any. If there are any who object to the People's bailout for selfish reasons, I urge them to see that now is the time for them to gain spiritual enlightenment, to accept that their circumstances and good fortune allowed them to gain what they have and to help others who haven't been so fortunate. The time has come for an end to greed, selfishness, and envy in our society! I honestly don't think there are many people in the country with this attitude of hostility toward mutual benefit. Maybe the people of today's society aren't as greedy as they're thought to be.

This same attitude should prevail when we help people pay off and purchase their own homes. Americans who have their homes paid off shouldn't be envious of others receiving help who haven't been as fortunate as they. Most financially stable Americans would be happy to see everyone enjoy at least the minimum comforts of living as they do and would help others to obtain this dream.

Some people would argue that these "handouts" would be going too far; that some people don't deserve to live in a home that is paid off by the Commonwealth and that lazy people would take advantage of the system. Who is to judge which people do or don't deserve help? Most people's circumstances have earned them a "home makeover." There will always be lazy people. Society now takes care of many of them. As we repair society, and as we become more enlightened, the number of these people will become fewer.

If Americans across the country were given all the information presented in this book on the subject and polled on whether or not they would support the idea, the majority would vote in favor of the proposal, because two-thirds of the country's adults don't have their homes paid off. Furthermore, most of the Americans who do own a home free of debt would support the People's bailout, because most of them have religious beliefs.[6] These spiritual people will know deep in their hearts that this plan conforms to religious teachings and would be supported and blessed by God.

Some people will say that this plan is virtuous, but unrealistic. Sticking with our current economic situation is unrealistic, unsustainable, and detrimental to most American families! We can't even begin to pay off the national deficit itself, let alone all of our total unfunded obligations, if average Americans have as little extra income as they do! We must take these small steps to make a hugely positive impact on all citizens!

Hopefully, most of you are now thinking that the People's bailout proposal might actually work and that I'm correct after all. How could it make things any worse if everyone's homes were paid off? So many benefits would arise from the plan's implementation. Many spouses could possibly afford to stay home and teach proper living skills to their children, resulting in better lives for their children and many job openings for others. If everyone had their home paid off and the economy boomed, small businesses would spring up everywhere.

Another option to alleviate the burden of housing costs, which wouldn't help near as much as my recommended plan, would be to compel the government to give home loans at 0% interest. After all, why should we have to pay interest on our own money? Only loans for the first mortgage on a home would be given at 0% interest (up to $100,000 per adult). This plan contrasts sharply with today's loans, where most of the amount paid on mortgages in the first years goes to interest. When we first started paying for our previous house, $950 of our $1140 monthly payment went to pay interest! Imagine how much quicker people could pay off their home with a 0% interest loan! If you purchased a home for $100,000 and paid $1,000 a month with a 0% interest loan, your home would be paid off in 100 months (about 8 years), compared to well over 30 years at today's interest rates. Now imagine what you could do with an extra $1,000 a month for the remaining 22 years! With all that extra money, you probably wouldn't mind paying higher taxes to compensate for the People's bailout. Why should the government finance banks with our money and not us?

In summary, the United States could pay off the average mortgage for all mortgage holders and purchase homes for all of our country's renters for less than our current spending plans on bailouts and stimulus packages.[1] Which would help our country more, continuing to pay bailouts and stimulus packages that we make payments on *forever*, or paying off the homes of every adult in the country (in retrospect for free)? According to CNN's Bailout Tracker (cnnmoney.com), we have already invested 3 trillion in bailouts and have committed to another 11 trillion. This $11 trillion would set up most of us for life!

The time has truly come for a change in views, now, before we spend the remainder of this money *needlessly*. The people of the United States must encourage President Barack Obama to change paths and implement the People's bailout, immediately! He will find that the country's people will be easier to work with rather than our elected officials (who probably have their homes paid off). If our elected officials object to this plan, they can be *replaced* with others who see the light. Obama must now help the common people of the United States, not the rich; he must bailout the people, not the corporations! This would result in less money spent *for a thousand times the outcome gained!* If President Obama made this plan a reality, he could change the world and would become a hero for 90% of the country's people, if not more!

This plan should be very acceptable to the majority of Americans. Most people would gladly pay for a 0 to 12% increase in our nation's total unfunded debt payments (which currently aren't being paid anyway) and an increase in taxes, if they could eliminate their house payment and up to 30 years of compounded interest payments!

Hopefully, the evidence presented has shown everyone that the People's bailout is not only a good idea, but its implementation is *absolutely necessary* to repair the country's financial problems! The only question at this point should be, which of the two ways should we use to fund the program, and who will receive the funds? Greed will play a major factor in making the latter of the two decisions; how greedy and selfish have Americans become? If a large cake was given to the people of our country (as payment for the People's bailout), who would desire a piece of it? Thirty-three percent of the country's households have already received their cake; will they want more? Many people haven't eaten yet, others are starving. Nationwide polls could be taken to determine everyone's views. Applications could be submitted in order to receive a share of the

People's bailout funds. If anyone deserves a piece of the cake, he or she should receive it!

Solving the problems of the world and the destruction of Earth begin with fixing our economy, our view on economics, and our housing issues. We can't concentrate on the real problems of the world until our daily problems are solved. Implementing these ideas on housing will get us a head start on repairing our economy and the rest of the world's problems! Any way you look at it, the country would be in much better shape if we bail out the people of the United States rather than continuing to see our economy flounder. If this plan doesn't fix our country's economic problems, *then nothing will!*

It now becomes obvious that if we don't bail out *the people*, the country will soon go bankrupt. What have we got to lose by enacting the plan? Not much if we're going bankrupt anyway. What have we got to gain? *A new beginning for everyone across the country!*

In closing this chapter, I have added the following information that I obtained from the U.S. Census Bureau, so that anyone can calculate and verify my findings.[2] All of the following information has been previously disclosed, but is shown here in more detail.

The following housing unit figures, which are for the third quarter of 2008, show breakdowns of the country's 111,730,000 occupied homes.

All housing units:	130,357,000	100%
-Occupied	111,730,000	86%
-Renter	35,834,000	28%
-Owner	75,896,000	58%
-Vacancies	18,627,000	14%
-Year-round	13,841,000	11%
-For rent	4,012,000	3%
-For sale only	2,227,000	2%
-Other	7,602,000	6%
-Seasonal	4,785,000	4%

Home owners with mortgages:	50,091,360
Total renters:	35,834,000

Total households with homes not paid off: 85,925,360
Total married couples with unpaid homes: 43,704,112
Total singles with unpaid homes: 42,221,248

We have 43.7 million married couples who now rent or have home mortgages. After multiplying this figure by two, we come up with the total number of married people in the United States, who rent or pay home mortgage payments, equaling 87.4 million. Upon adding the 42.2 million single people who rent or pay mortgage payments, we come up with a total of 129.6 million people who do not own their own homes outright. If we multiply this figure (129.6 mill.) by $100,000, we come up with $12.9 trillion, the *maximum* total necessary to put every American into their own paid-off home!

Using figures of the total adult population to calculate each American adult's share of the People's bailout (money to be split between people who don't have their homes paid off) rather than figures based on household numbers would result in the following figures. According to the U.S. Census Bureau the adult population of the United States is equal to 72.4% of the population.[3] Our total population is about 309 million, which equals 223,716,000 American adults. If one third of these adults have their homes paid off, then 147,652,560 adults who don't own their homes outright would split $13 trillion, which equates to about $88,000 per adult, or $176,000 per couple, this amount being higher than the median family home value in the United States of $167,500.

Calculations for paying the People's bailout to 90% of the country's adults are given in the chapter above and equal $64,500 per adult or $129,000 per couple based on a $13 trillion People's bailout. Increasing the bailout figure to $20 trillion would net each adult $100,000, or $200,000 per couple. Increasing each adults share from $64,500 to $100,000 would raise our total unfunded debt by 6% and would be well worth the more than 50% increase per adult. I recommend a People's bailout of $20 trillion, $100,000 per adult, which would setup the average American and *instantly* reverse our economic trends!

13

HEALTH CARE REFORM

I began writing this chapter four years ago with the hopes of revealing the true situation of the country's health care system and to suggest ways of reforming it. It now looks as if the United States will finally establish a new health care plan, since a resemblance of one was passed into law. After reading this chapter, people will better understand why we desperately need health care reform and will agree that politicians have messed up its implementation. President Obama has been forced into settling for a "capitalist" health care system, where American corporations, insurance companies, and Republicans can still do business as usual, rather than a universal health care system funded by taxes only, where unnecessary profits aren't made from the system.

The solution to the problem of 46 million people in the United States being without health insurance is *not* enacting laws that force Americans to purchase health care insurance! People that can't afford the insurance today won't be able to afford it tomorrow just because somebody passed a law making it mandatory! What's next, solving the ailing Social Security system by forcing everyone to purchase retirement plans with money that they don't have? After that, we may as well pass laws that force drivers of gas guzzling cars to purchase new fuel-efficient models. If you don't have money to purchase health insurance, pay for your retirement plan, and buy a new car, you'll be fined or jailed! Give me a break! These are not fixes! They just compound the problems!

In Canada and other industrialized countries, you can walk into any hospital and be treated, free, with proof of citizenship. Can our citizens do this here in the United States, now that health care reform has been passed? No! We must now find an insurance company to be a middleman and pay them money that we don't have! This is ridiculous. The following is my original chapter.

An estimated 46.6 million people in the United States don't have health insurance. They simply can't afford it! It's hard for me to believe the United States is the *only* major industrialized nation without a universal health care plan! All other industrialized countries have universal health care plans that work great, but our capitalistic ideals seem to be getting in the way. Here in the United States the government leaves it up to the employers to supply health care insurance. Another 40 million in the United States are underinsured, with more and more employers cutting back on health insurance every year. Many Americans who have coverage are finding that their policies are completely inadequate. All types of limitation clauses and pay out maximums are extinguishing the expectations of policyholders. Many who have health insurance have still gone bankrupt from overwhelming medical expenses!

Half of bankruptcies in the United States are due to health care costs. Our country spent $2.24 trillion on health care in 2007, an average of $7,421 per person! The average cost of health care for other countries that have universal health care systems is less than half our costs.

It's morally unacceptable that we can ration health care by our ability to pay for it. Health care should be available for all Americans. Here in the USA, with the loss of a job, all insurance premiums paid go up in smoke! Unemployed usually means uninsured.

Over 82 million people under the age of 65 were without health insurance during some portion of the last few years. Harvard/Harris polls show that 66% of Americans recently needed some type of health care, but didn't get it, 58% of which either didn't have an insurance policy or not enough money to pay for the services needed.[1] Some that had insurance didn't have money to pay the required deductibles.

Of Americans polled, 82% support changes in our present system and 79% think health care should be a right. Every year, health care costs soar in the United States with no end in sight. What is the answer? We must look at other countries' successes. Many Americans are looking at Canada's health care system, called Medicare. The United States needs to start a comparable system. After extensive research, I learned a lot about Canada's system, mostly from doctors such as Karen S. Palmer MPH MS of the California Physicians Alliance. Here's how Canada's system works, along with information on misconceptions of the system.[1]

Canada began their Medicare system in 1947, and by 1971 all Canadians were covered by this universal health care system, which combines capitalism with social responsibility (as you know, I believe that all our country's systems should combine capitalism with social responsibility). There is no limit to what the system will pay to an individual over their lifetime. Every Canadian who is a legal resident is entitled to the same health care. Nobody may be discriminated upon based on income, age, health status, race, gender, or any other reason. When you are sick and need health care, you're treated equally. You don't have to be a Canadian citizen to receive health care in Canada; you need only to be a resident, which means living in Canada at least 183 days out of the year. Canadians are never denied health care or forced to wait for care for lack of funds or because of pre-existing conditions. In Canada, a major health problem doesn't result in financial ruin. Canadian doctors seldom know whether they are treating the rich or the poor. They're responsive to your needs rather than your pocketbook. Canadians receive quality health care for their tax dollars. In the United States, we pay slightly lower taxes with soaring health insurance premiums!

According to Harvard Medical School, Canadians are healthier than Americans, and their survival rates for most types of cancer are higher than ours.

In Canada, if a person loses their job, they still have all their health and medical needs met. In the United States, unemployed usually means uninsured.

The Canadian government, unlike popularly believed in the U.S., does not decide who receives care; the doctors do. You and your doctor decide what you need. The government's responsibility is to collect the money and distribute it to the provinces. The provinces, which are comparable to our states, are locally run.

Though considered a nationally funded program, Medicare is actually ten different health insurance plans that are partially funded by insurance premiums as well as general taxes from the residents. In seven of the ten provinces, health care is paid by taxes alone. The other three provinces charge insurance premiums as well as general taxes and will subsidize up to 100% of the premiums if you can't afford it. They also have federal cost-sharing, so poorer provinces have the same standards of health care as wealthier provinces.

General hospitals in Canada are typically structured as nonprofit corporations and their practitioners are self-employed and not accountable to the government in any way.

Canadians who travel to other provinces can also receive medical treatment there. Bills for these services are sent to their province of residence.

The Canadian Health Act is very simple, having only 14 pages, compared to President Clinton's plan, which was over 1,000 pages. Of course, no plan is perfect, and as times change, the Canadians work hard to update their health care plan for the greater benefit of all their residents.

The main problems we have now with our country's system of health care are limited access to health care because of no insurance or high deductibles, the rising uncontrolled costs of health insurance premiums, and the rising cost of health care itself.

When Canada first switched to a national universal health care plan, many doctors went on strike. The Canadian government brought in doctors from Britain to replace them. Many initial problems were overcome in the implementation of the plan, but now Canadians are very proud of their success. When the Canadians talk about their health care system, it's like Americans discussing the Constitution. Canadians consider their universal health care system to be the greatest thing that their government, or maybe any government, has ever successfully implemented.

Many Americans have untrue beliefs and myths concerning a universal health care plan and either have a financial gain in not converting to one, or are simply afraid or not informed on the subject to make a change. The main myths and misconceptions are as follows:

The first misconception is that the government decides which people receive care and when they receive it. This sounds like our country's HMOs! Wrong! There isn't an HMO-like preauthorization by a clerk who is practicing medicine without a license! You and your doctor decide what care you need with no outside interference. Doctors are self-employed and only answer to their patients.

The second misconception is that Canadians have long waits to get medical treatment. Waits here in the United States may be shorter because less of us are being treated! In Canada, there are no waits for urgent care or primary care and very reasonable waits for specialist care. Elective surgery is the only wait, and if you want your facelift or such done quickly, you can always pay for it yourself. To address this issue, Health Canada has now funded "The Western Canada Waiting List Project," which systematically studies the waiting process.

A new rating system implemented in 2000 is based on objective clinical assessment of each patient's medical needs and expected benefits rather than the order in which the needs were listed or requested. In very rare instances, if waits are too long, patients are sent across the border to United States doctors, with all expenses paid by Canada. Eighty-six percent of Canadians said that their wait was very acceptable for medical testing, and 83% said their wait for specialist care was fine. Longer waits to see a specialist are very common in the United States even with good health care coverage!

The biggest misconception U.S. citizens have is that Canadians are taxed to death to pay for their universal health care system. This is not true. Americans say this only to impede implementing a single payer universal health care system, or from lack of information on the subject. When comparing tax bracket rates from the United States to Canada, tax percentages are very compatible. Canada also levies 5% surtax on wealthier residents who pay in excess of $12,500 in yearly taxes, effectively raising their top income bracket tax rate from 29% to about 31%.[1]

At the end of the day, Canadian workers enjoy about the same share of their gross earnings as the citizens of the United States. After all figures are considered, such as tax credits and social benefits, United States taxpayers pay 1% less than Canadians.[1] Most Americans would gladly pay 1% more in taxes for their health care costs!

Another myth is that the Canadian Medicare system is going broke. This is not true either. The system has had its ups and downs as health care changes, and the Canadians adapt with those changes. In 2005, the Canadian government delivered a $41.3 billion, 10 year plan to strengthen Canada's universal health care system.

Other misconceptions are that since medical charges and costs are controlled by the government, there aren't enough existing or new doctors, and that Canadian doctors aren't being paid enough. Most Canadian doctors are self-employed practitioners who work independently or in group practices and enjoy a high degree of self governing. Some work with community health care centers, hospital-based practices, or outpatient hospital offices, all of which are not accountable to the government in any way. With less malpractice costs and less billing and office expenses, the average Canadian doctor pays far less in expenses than a doctor here in the United States. Canadian physicians can also "opt-out" of the system and bill their own patients. Many Canadian doctors bring in over $1 million yearly. That's over $80,000 a month!

The Canadian health care system definitely works. Ninety-two percent of the Canadians who have medical treatment are satisfied with their system. Many other countries, including Japan, Germany, Norway, Sweden, Great Britain, France, and Switzerland, have made universal health care work for their people. Isn't it time we did the same for Americans? Most Americans believe so.

The Bush administration endorsed and funded a universal health insurance plan. The problem with his plan is that it was designed for the people of Iraq, not our country's people.

Besides Republicans, one of the main barriers impeding our progress in implementing a universal health care system is the selfish view of the snobs in our country who *presently* have health insurance and don't want to share their benefits with anyone else. Citizens who don't have health coverage and others who aren't selfish would love to see the system implemented. Many of the selfish Americans who do have coverage are upset because they believe that they'll have longer waits for their personal care. This was evident in an advertisement that was aired on cable television.

In the commercial, a women's group (I won't name them specifically) had a representative from their organization griping about the possibility of changing to a universal health care system. This representative stated that thousands of American women could possibly die in the next few years, because their life saving treatment would be delayed by the treatment of other Americans who don't have any insurance now! What do these people think about the thousands of lives that could be saved by treating people who can't even afford a checkup? And are they concerned about all the American women who will die in the next few years who have treatable illnesses? What kind of selfish garbage is this talk? We may die because others are treated and saved before us! What an unbelievable outlook. I wonder how many people phoned this women's organization to ask why they thought that their lives were more valuable than other American women's lives!

Obviously all industrialized countries that have universal health care systems rank their scheduled appointments according to the critical nature of the illness. The only people that would be treated before these selfish people would be others with worse conditions! Not wanting others to have coverage because it might detract from their coverage is about the most selfish thing I've ever heard! Absolutely unbelievable!

The time has come for Americans who are lucky enough to have health insurance to stop being selfish and to help all Americans who aren't as lucky to receive the same benefits. In a perfect society, everyone would have health care, whether they could afford it or not! If we change the way that we pay for our health care, everyone can have health care for less than we're presently paying for those who do have it!

Health care reform will not change how health care is delivered, just how its bills are paid. Health care providers will do business as usual, competing with each other and trying to do their best, and in return will have guaranteed paid procedures with coverage for all. Costs would not constantly increase to cover lost revenue from unpaid services. Health care providers would pocket more money than they presently do!

Medical institutions are so worried about their costs and who will pay for them that people are routinely turned away who need urgent medical treatment. Many urgent-care centers want full payment before treatment is rendered. If people don't have health insurance or enough money on hand, they're turned away. This mentality must change!

Another aspect of health care that must be addressed is dental care. Ninety-percent of the country's people currently need some type of dental work. More people now need some type of dental work rather than medical treatment. Many people who are lucky enough to have health insurance don't have dental included in their policies. Dental care should be a part of every universal health care plan. If everyone who needs dental treatment received care, we would need thousands more dentists and dental assistants, creating countless new jobs and enterprises.

More hospitals and medical practitioners would also be needed and in turn would create many jobs and careers in the medical fields. Our colleges would need to be ready for increased class sizes, possibly funded by the government or states. Any costs paid now would result in later paybacks far beyond our expenditures. Eager students who might become practitioners, but don't have any way to pay for medical college, could be funded by the states or the government. After graduating, they could run nonprofit hospitals set up by the states in order to handle overflow from private practices.

Our country was founded on the premise of working together and striving for equality for all. Many things have changed since then, mostly because of declining morals and ethics. Today there are urgent calls from voices across the country that desire health care coverage. All we need now is the collective will to implement the plan.

If the federal government can't get their act together, each state should take the initiative and implement its own health care plan. Soon, other states would follow suit until all Americans enjoyed full medical coverage as other industrialized countries do. When the United States finally converts to a universal system and all Americans who need health care receive it, our standards of living will rise.

Previous administrations have impeded our conversion to a universal health care system, and until we alter "business as usual" in our government, needed changes will be hindered, but they will occur. Politicians preach change, only to become part of the self-serving system, voting themselves pay raises when people in our country have no homes, food, or health care. The time has arrived for outsiders, common people like you and me, to penetrate the thick walls of our government. *All politicians doing business as usual must be replaced!*

President Barack Obama is an advocate for universal health care reform. I give him all my blessings. The President has his work cut out for him. Many greedy capitalistic Republicans who don't have all the facts or have a financial gain in not converting to such a system are against health care reform. These greedy Republicans already have free health care, why should they worry about the rest of us? As our politicians battle on the outcome of health care reform, Republicans may try to force Obama to compromise goals, possibly by attempting to break the package into different components that are paid by different sources. We must not settle for "going halfway." The system needs to be implemented completely, and we must not settle for anything besides a single-payer system, where all costs are paid directly by the Commonwealth, not by insurance companies that presently pocket most of our premiums paid!

This is the chapter as it was written four years ago (the previous paragraph was added in 2009). Our country must not settle for anything but a single payer system, where as in other industrialized nations with legitimate universal health care systems, the government pays the health care costs using taxes collected from the Commonwealth, not percentages of income from insurance companies!

The average annual income *per employee* of an insurance agency in the United States is close to $200,000![2] And this doesn't include top brass salaries! Insurance companies need to be eliminated from the picture. Insurance companies can still make plenty of profits from home, car, and life insurance. Everything we pay into our health care system should be applied to health care costs, not to greedy insurance conglomerates!

Forcing everyone to purchase health insurance is un-American. Enacting laws that force people who can't afford health care insurance to purchase coverage from these insurers reeks of capitalistic robber barons! Some people say mandating health insurance is like mandating liability insurance for vehicle drivers. This isn't true. A person may decide not to carry liability insurance and not drive at all. The government shouldn't be able to force anyone to do anything against their will! What will be next, gun control, racial profiling, and forcing us to have microchips surgically implanted under our skin for cataloging purposes? When it comes to cooperating with the government while they're doing anything that infringes upon my rights as American, you can count me out.

Most people's expectations were that after the universal health care reform bill was passed, all Americans would have access to medical treatment and the world would be a better place. Nothing has changed for the majority of us. Most of the previously uninsured are still uninsured, still don't have access to medical treatment, and are not enthused about or looking forward to purchasing insurance for which they don't have the money!

Sooner or later, health care reform will become a reality for the United States. What we do with the system after its enactment is our choice. It can be changed, shaped, and molded to fit our society, but we must eliminate capitalism and all insurance companies from the funding aspect of our new universal health care system and make health care a benefit, funded with taxes collected from the Commonwealth, not a burden, funded by *portions* of our money that we pay to insurance companies!

14

OUR COUNTRY'S DRUG PROBLEM

One of the biggest problems that the country faces today is drug abuse. It is deteriorating our society, and the problem only worsens every day. Drug related crimes account for 90% of the nation's criminal activity.[3] Our daily news recounts stories of people being shot or stabbed in order for drug addicts to obtain money for drugs, dealers being killed for drugs, robberies being committed to supply money for drug habits, burglaries perpetrated to gain sellable goods to purchase drugs, and goods being stolen that the drug addict needs, but can't afford.

The main tragedy of drug addiction is that the children of our addicts are forced to endure the consequences of their addicted parent(s) actions. They are constantly neglected and often forgotten. Money that should be spent on food, utilities, housing, clothing, and special needs is absorbed by the addicted parent(s) drug purchases. Often, drug users are forced into dealing drugs in order to support their habit, which also puts their children at risk. Children that grow up in this environment may become drug addicts themselves.

Present and past government administrations have failed to stop drug trafficking and black marketing of drugs. Gangs continue to flourish and are centered on drug sales and usage. Drug lords continue to supply the United States with trillions of dollars of drugs that are transported over our borders yearly. Our justice system is overwhelmed by drug cases. Our prisons and jails are overcrowded with inmates serving time for drug related crimes. The cost of maintaining our existing system has become outrageous! What can we do to eradicate this infestation? We hear about the consequences of drug usage in the news, the police see first-hand results of drug addiction, and our courts and judicial systems witness the cascading effects of the drug world, but to truly understand the situation in-depth, you must have either been an addict yourself, or really listen to someone who has.

I have seen many friends trapped in this nightmare. Most didn't wake-up and escape until after they hit rock bottom, which was usually about two years into their calamity. Some have never awakened and are still addicted today. I've watched the wasted livelihoods and downfalls of many friends. I've seen the neglect of children and stagnant lives going nowhere except downhill. I have observed relationships being torn apart by the altered and disillusioned mental states caused by drugs. I've seen finances tumble downward and witnessed goals and ethics being thrown aside for lust and drugs.

For the addicted person not much matters except maintaining their high, having a good time, and being around other people in the same state of mind. Faithful partners succumb to lust, responsible people become irresponsible, work habits falter, jobs become meaningless, and good parents lose sight of their parenting responsibilities. The existing moment in time is the only thing that matters to the drug user. Future plans and goals slip away, and until the addict becomes aware of the drugs consequences, and decides that he or she doesn't want this way of life anymore, no one can help them. What can be done to hasten this process?

Education is a major part of the solution. We must educate the people who haven't yet become addicts and show the addict what the drugs are doing to their lives. They're caught up in their own little world and concerned with limited problems, none of which is the extended welfare of their families, children, and spouses. We must show the addict the real world beyond their currently limited vision. How can we do this?

Police departments have their DARE programs. These very successful drug deterrent programs are designed to educate our kids about drug addiction and usage and are greatly needed, but there is one item these programs are missing. Police officers tell stories of drug addiction and its consequences, but the students know that these officers have probably never experienced drug addiction and the circumstances of the drug addict themselves. Sure, the police see the results of drug addiction, but to really convey the knowledge in the manner needed, we need ex-drug addicts to teach along with the officers! Kids need to hear stories of true-life experiences that are told first-hand from real addicts who have been through the trenches. Then, and only then, will the hard-hitting truth sink into the minds of the students. As kids fall off track and find themselves in circumstances that may lead to drug use, they become apprehensive towards police and the law. Having true ex-drug addicts to relate their bad experiences and downfalls with drug addiction would immensely reinforce the officer's teachings.

One main truth must be instilled into our children's minds. This next sentence may be the most important message taught. *"There is no such thing as trying drugs!"* I've repeated this statement to my kids many times. Drugs are addicting by nature. Once you try drugs, most assuredly you will be *instantly* hooked! This is especially true of methamphetamines. Of all the people I know who have tried methamphetamines (more commonly known as crystal meth), every one was instantly hooked!

I watched friends and others use meth and saw it destroying their lives. Goals that were previously important to them slipped away, as their ethics and morals fell apart. The only cares they possessed were of their drug habit and friends that were into the same trap. I saw some become so involved with meth that they began shooting it up with hypodermic syringes to receive a better high, while using less of the drug. I hate meth. I hated meth addicts who were turning others into addicts. I hate needles. I preached anti-meth to all my friends, especially to the ones who became meth addicts themselves.

The mentality of the meth addiction is as follows: Once a person is addicted, he or she wants others to know how it feels to be on the drug and desires others to be in the same state of mind. Addicts have no way of knowing what lies before them, which is a road to self-destruction. They only care about the here and now and have no idea of the misery that awaits them. People need to understand that listening to an addict about "the awesome feeling and experience" of the meth or "crank," is like talking to a person on a cell phone who's riding on a new roller coaster ride. "Oh, this is awesome! I've never had such fun in my life! You've got to try this ride!" Then just around the corner and at the peak of the ride, the addict suddenly sees a two hundred foot drop with jagged rocks piled at the bottom of the drop! Before entering the ride, a smart person would talk to someone who has finished the ride and discovered the plunge to the rocky bottom and then make a wise decision to never take the ride.

Unfortunately, most addicts who recommend the ride haven't yet reached the summit and haven't experienced the plunge downward to their destruction. Kids and adults must speak to someone who has finished the ride before they make the decision to try it themselves.

Again, I emphasize teach your kids, your family, and friends as I have. "There is no such thing as trying drugs." Our citizens must either say no, *or expect to waste many years as drug addicts!* They must expect to lose their ethics, morals, family, friends, and loved ones, and to have their lives turned upside down. They must also anticipate putting their hopes and dreams on hold and waiting for the worst to happen, because it will.

I repeat "the sentence" at least a few times a year until my kids say, "I know dad, there's no such thing as trying drugs!" They not only state this, but they also believe it.

Drug addiction is a result of a person's circumstances and fate. Anyone can become a drug addict. Most addicts were convinced to try drugs by people who haven't yet finished the roller coaster ride. Had the addict on the ride not been in the new user's life, the new user wouldn't have become an addict. Some people don't stop to think how others become addicted. We've all heard "Lock them up and throw away the key, or shoot them all" and such, until it's their son, daughter, or spouse who becomes the addict. People must realize drug addiction is a social problem, not a criminal problem. Addicts are usually not criminals, just misled victims of circumstance! Addicted people must be educated and shown that their misguided ways are hurtful to everyone, especially themselves.

Everyone must agree that in our society it's okay for a person to have previously been a drug addict, realized the problem, and somehow escaped its lifestyle and corruptions. Once the person is away from the drugs and he or she is "normal" again, society, the courts, and police commend the ex-addict. Many celebrities and prominent figures have been addicted to drugs such as heroin, meth, and cocaine, and have finally escaped the drugs grip. Later, after getting off the drugs, were they jailed, prosecuted, or charged with drug use? No! They were forgiven, because they had been addicted to drugs "against their will." They were not in full control of their faculties. They were applauded because they had the courage to tell others of their plight and were no longer addicted.

This is not so if a person comes forward and says, "I robbed a bank last year" or "I murdered a person a few years ago." These crimes were committed against humanity and something is done about them, regardless if they were committed yesterday or five years ago. Drug addiction is the only crime where people are instantly forgiven for their past transgressions and understood. This shows drug addiction is not a criminal offense, but a social problem such as alcoholism and should be addressed as such!

Our government's attempts to shut down the black market, gangs, drug lords, and the drug trade have failed. Jailing traffickers only results in other dealers taking their places. When most addicts are released from jail, they resume their habits. People don't quit drugs until they're ready to do so, until they've "seen the light." What can we do? We can't continue to let the drug problem in this country devour more and more victims! What is the answer?

Continuing to educate the public is the first step in stopping people from becoming addicts in the first place. We must continue our DARE programs and include ex-drug addicts to teach along with the officers.

The next step includes one major step that many Americans might be against, mostly because of lack of knowledge, fears of worsening our problems, or lack of experiences in such matters. We must learn from other countries' successes in eliminating their hard-drug problems. Advanced European countries such as Norway, Sweden, and many others have found a working solution to the drug problem. They've succeeded in eradicating their country's drug problem, where here in the United States we've failed drastically for many decades. Our educational programs have helped, but the time has come to completely eliminate our country's hard-drug problem, not just reduce it. What's the first major step we here in the United States are so afraid of? We must legalize marijuana.

Please don't criticize this statement until we look at all the facts! First off, I don't condone the use of marijuana. I wouldn't suggest smoking pot (or drinking) to anyone, but I don't denounce it either. Every American citizen should be able to make their own decision without any public interference. It's a free country until you violate another's rights.

Many pot smokers are "go-getters" and marijuana helps them relax after a hard day's work. It has little negative effect on their overall performance and helps them have a good attitude on doing whatever they may be doing. Pot smokers are definitely less stressed than non-smokers. Most lazy, pot-smoking bums would actually be lazy bums anyway if they didn't smoke pot!

The main stigma with marijuana is that it's directly linked to harder drugs. In the minds of people who have never smoked pot, marijuana is clumped into the same category as cocaine, heroin, or meth. This is true because it's been proven that smoking pot leads to harder drug usage. Why? Because they're all illegal and people who try pot and like it, surmise the populace was wrong about pot, and therefore must be wrong about cocaine and other harder drugs. As long as marijuana is linked to harder drugs, people will most likely try harder drugs after trying pot! *We must disassociate marijuana from harder drugs by making it legal!*

Other highly developed countries in Europe have done so, thus eliminating the link from marijuana to hard drugs. In Holland, politicians decided over 25 years ago to separate marijuana from the illicit drug market by permitting coffee shops all over the country to sell small amounts of marijuana to responsible adults. These countries' marijuana use is *less than half* that of the United States! This shows legalizing marijuana didn't lead to more pot smokers, *but less!*

Denmark, Sweden, Holland, and others have eliminated their hard-drug problems. They regulate, tax, and profit from selling legal marijuana. When asked of a pot smoker in these countries, "Have you tried or would you ever try cocaine, heroin, or meth now that you are a pot smoker?" The answer was invariably something to the effect of "Are you crazy? Of course not, I don't want to be a drug addict, you know!" This is because they've disassociated marijuana from hard drugs! Smoking marijuana rather than drinking alcoholic beverages is a normal occurrence in these countries.

In their countries, hard-drug addicts are a very small percentage of the population, the "bums" of the society and are looked down upon greatly. Their governments give drugs to these addicts free, teach and regulate them, trying to get them to become productive citizens. Supplying them with their drugs keeps them from criminal behavior and allows the government to monitor their activities. These addicts are known to be the scum of their society. They are tolerated and citizens feel sorry for them, but they definitely aren't leading desired lifestyles. Most Europeans despise their existence, and being one of them is the last thing on their minds. In the United States we've glamorized the drug world to such an extent that we've made it desirable and profitable for millions. We must learn from these countries' successes and legalize marijuana in our country!

People who smoke pot will continue to smoke pot, whether it's illegal or not. If drug education works, people wouldn't start smoking pot just because we legalize it. My kids wouldn't start smoking marijuana just because it was legalized; they've been educated properly. We need to make it illegal to be a neglectful, uncaring parent! If all parents did their jobs, numbers of new pot smokers would be at a minimum. As in the case of prohibition, making alcohol illegal didn't stop people from producing and consuming it. Prohibition didn't work. It caused more criminal activity, which is the same effect that the illegalization of marijuana is causing on our society now! Many of today's criminal activities began when alcohol was illegalized. Today's consequences of the illegalization of marijuana are much more disastrous! We must legalize marijuana, tax it, and eliminate its link to hard drugs!

Most Americans have no idea how many people smoke pot in the United States, let alone the whole world. According to federal government statistics, *over 80 million Americans* admit to having smoked marijuana.[1] This is a huge percentage of our population! The United States has roughly 309 million citizens, including children. Statistics show over 40 million people regularly smoke marijuana. This estimate must be too low, since many pot smokers haven't yet come out of the closet. Most of these 40 million smoke to unwind after a busy day or to relieve stress. It's been proven that pot smokers are much less stressed than non-smokers. Some smoke for religious or spiritual reasons, for meditation, to be more self-conscious, or to enhance their awareness. Others smoke to relieve symptoms from cancer, stomach problems, glaucoma, and other body pains.

The vast majority of marijuana smokers are otherwise law abiding productive citizens, despite the federal government's decision to make possession of marijuana a criminal offense. More than 800,000 American citizens were arrested *last year* on marijuana charges, more than 5 million in the past decade.[1] With such staggering numbers of people who have smoked marijuana, are now smoking, or were previously arrested for marijuana charges, how can the government not see that it should be legal? No other crime is practiced by such a large percentage of our population! This shows that the elected officials that we put into office are afraid of fixing the mistake of illegalizing marijuana. Many people are firmly against legalization of pot, such as Daryl Gates, outgoing Los Angeles Chief of Police, who testified before the Senate Judiciary Committee, stating he favored the death penalty for even casual users of marijuana![4] Imagine that, executing 80 million Americans (more than one out of four) for having smoked marijuana! This is the 21st century, not the 15th! Oh, never mind that statement, marijuana was legally used back then!

In fact, cannabis has been growing and used by humans on Earth for thousands of years and grew long before humans even occupied the planet. In Asia, cannabis grows naturally everywhere, covering entire hillsides and valleys. Our ancestors grew cannabis and used hemp to make clothing, paper, and rope. A pair of pants made from hemp will far outlast a pair made of cotton.

In 1937, President Franklin D. Roosevelt and the U.S. Congress outlawed the cultivation and use of marijuana for any purpose. In fact, few if any of the congressmen who voted in favor of the illegalization of marijuana had never heard of the word "marijuana," and didn't know that hemp and marijuana came from the same cannabis plant. These congressmen were never told that they were actually outlawing the hemp crops that were familiar to them, because most of them grew up with marijuana growing on their farms! In early colonial days, it was the law to grow your share of cannabis. Thomas Jefferson and many other well-known columnists grew marijuana!

The illegalization of cannabis is strongly believed to be a monumental mistake, even worse than Alcohol Prohibition by hundreds of millions of people around the world. People familiar with the benefits of this "weed's" industrial uses, state the problem isn't that we've made mistakes; it's that we have failed to learn from these mistakes. We have failed to realize the country's war on drugs needs to change direction. It's very probable that Alcohol Prohibition contributed to the 1929 stock market crash and the Great Depression of the 1930s. If we don't address the economic and judicial issue of hemp, more problems will escalate, including an increasing number of hard-drug addicts.

Fourteen states have now legalized marijuana to some degree, despite the recent Supreme Court ruling that the U.S. Justice Department, including the DEA, may prosecute state authorized medical marijuana patients for violating the Federal Controlled Substances Act.

Marijuana is the third most popular recreational drug in the United States today, despite harsh laws against its use. Millions smoke it responsibly. Our public policies and laws should reflect this. Marijuana is far less dangerous than alcohol or tobacco, which are the top two drugs used in the United States today. *It fails to inflict serious health problems that these other two legal drugs cause!* Almost 50,000 people die each year from alcohol poisoning, and more than 400,000 die from tobacco related illnesses. Marijuana is non-toxic and can't cause death by overdose. According to the prestigious European medical journal *The Lancelot*, "The smoking of cannabis, even long term, is not harmful to our health."[1] Cannabis is obviously a lesser threat than alcohol or tobacco. Many Americans smoke marijuana rather than drinking alcoholic beverages.

Wouldn't you much rather be on the roadways with someone who has been smoking marijuana than someone who has been drinking alcohol (not that either should be tolerated)? Marijuana stimulates and heightens awareness, while alcohol diminishes your senses. Marijuana is the only natural drug of choice, alcohol is man-made, thus the saying, "God made marijuana, humans made alcohol. Who do you trust?"

Speaking of God and marijuana, cannabis is mentioned in the Bible codes. Codes found by Iciple can be viewed at the website in this book's notes.[2] The codes include the words and phrases "cannabis, measure in her not and the need to purchase (which means it should be given freely), the medicine with beautiful characteristics, my gift to explore, to sense, to feel, to cure gloomy origin, heal, rejoice, glaucoma to prophecy, sickness help, calmness, meditation to spend time, to analyze disparity, medicinal heap abundance, prescription, handpicked vineyard, to produce forbidden, inhale, marijuana, grass, hashish, wonder in it, there to explore, Jesus behold, heal to rejoice and to sing."[2] After reading the phrases of these tableaux, God's position on marijuana is very clear. It is interesting that the code states producing it is forbidden and that you must have a prescription to receive your marijuana that is handpicked from the vineyards. God may have "given it freely" to mankind, but it's far from free for most smokers!

Medical marijuana that is now available through the black market, to anyone, sells for up to $400 an ounce! In many areas of the world this ounce of "weed" can sell for as much as an ounce of gold, or more! This is ridiculous! How can a weed be more expensive than gold? It's more expensive, because it's illegal! Many Americans can't afford to buy their marijuana and resort to growing it despite the fact that growing pot is usually a felony. Others grow it strictly for profit. Farmers of a certain county in one of our central states were all over the news a few years ago for growing crops of marijuana (I won't be specific on which county or state because they don't like the publicity, and I respect this attitude).

Most of the county's residents were farmers that had experienced several years of crop failures and many were losing their farms to foreclosure. Some of the county's farmers had been growing marijuana to subsidize their incomes, and soon 98% of the residents were growing pot on their farms!

The farmers were frustrated after not being able to pay their bills and decided that growing small crops of marijuana paid outrageously more than growing large crops of corn and grain! They decided that if everyone in the county grew pot, no one would be arrested, because the sheriff wouldn't jail and charge the entire county with felonies! They were right!

When reporters interviewed residents, they discovered that even the elderly and retired were growing pot! Most residents stated they didn't smoke marijuana, but saw nothing wrong with joining the bandwagon and growing it. Upon interviewing the county's sheriff, he was asked why he wasn't arresting the growers that were committing felonies. He said that he couldn't arrest the whole county, and if he did, he would be out of a job after the next election! If 98% of a community is breaking the law, the law is completely unjust! It makes me wonder how many people are presently serving time in prisons for growing pot! It seems outrageously ridiculous to me that in one state you can legally grow your own marijuana and in the next state be charged with a felony and put away for years! What other crime is this way?

I'm also aware of other instances where government agencies arrest American citizens for possessing and smoking marijuana, while looking the other way when others commit the same crimes several hundred feet away. In 1978 while in the Navy, I was stationed in the Great Lakes area around Chicago. I attended electronics school there and lived in one of the large dormitories that housed the students who attended the Navy's technical schools on the base. Our dormitories were searched by drug dogs while clouds of hashish smoke poured from windows in the Iranian's dormitory only a few hundred feet away. The Iranian students were allowed to smoke their hashish in their dorms due to their "religious" beliefs. This double standard upset many of the students of our dorm that were court marshalled and prosecuted for smoking pot, of which there were many.

Don't get me wrong. I don't condone, recommend, or encourage the smoking of marijuana. This is a free country. The choice should be up to each and every adult. We just need to stop harassing, arresting, and imprisoning responsible marijuana smokers! Most pot smokers are good citizens with good morals and standards. They are hard-working assets to society who are trying to raise their families responsibly. It's unfair and unjust to treat them as criminals! Think about it. We're arresting people for smoking a *weed* that has been smoked by hundreds of millions of people for thousands of years!

Hemp is a weed! Its nature is to survive better in the harshest environments. Since the weed is so easily grown, it makes the perfect crop. There are over 25,000 environmentally friendly products that can be made from hemp. More than 30 industrialized countries commercially grow hemp today, including England and Canada. The European Union subsidizes farmers to grow the crop, which is legally recognized as a commercial crop by the United Nations Single Convention on Narcotic Drugs, as well as the North American Free Trade Agreement, NAFTA. If these countries have realized its benefits, why can't we? Ask our politicians!

Who was behind the illegalization of marijuana? Our politicians were. Who is afraid to address the issue of legalization of marijuana now? Our politicians are. Who doesn't want pot legalized the most? Drug lords, pot dealers, the black market, gangs, Mexican Mafia, Colombian cartels, smugglers, and others who would lose their income that presently comes from this illicit market!

Politicians need to get involved and solve this problem! Legalize, regulate, and tax marijuana, *while making it affordable* for the general adult public who choose to smoke it, for whatever reason. Taxing legalized marijuana would bring in much needed revenue that would stimulate and add to the economy's recovery. Funds created could be used to replace and eliminate property taxes. There would be extra funds for schools and education. *Trillions* of dollars now flowing past our borders would stay here in the USA. Today, all profits from selling medical marijuana out of small shops across the country stay in the pockets of American growers and distributors. The government could profit on many aspects of the market, including taxing its sales.

Parents, teach your kids about alcohol, tobacco, marijuana, and hard drugs, and quit worrying about pot being legalized! If your kids are going to try marijuana, the decision will be made from circumstances, their education, and their knowledge, not whether it's legal or not. We must legalize marijuana, disassociate it from hard drugs, and teach our children about the consequences of drug usage, thus saving the futures of millions of our kids!

Now it's time to raise more eyebrows! Once we legalize marijuana and disassociate it from hard drugs, it's time to eliminate our country's hard-drug problem! How can we possibly accomplish this? We completely shut down all foreign imports of drugs. We shut down all drug lords, drug smugglers, the Mexican Mafia, the Colombian cartel, the black market, and gangs. Past administrations have attempted this and failed. With such an impossible task, how can it be done?

Again, we learn from other countries' successes. We get our politicians to grow a backbone and quit treating our country's drug problem as a criminal problem, and act on it for what it is, a social problem. We shouldn't legalize hard drugs, but we should quit prosecuting them as a criminal offense, which has done *absolutely nothing* but overwhelm our court system and fill our jails and prisons, forcing us to release true criminals early, or not jailing them at all for lack of space.

As other highly developed countries have done to eliminate their hard-drug abuse problems, *we give out drugs free!* Yes, you read that correctly. We give the addicts their drugs free. *Then, we take charge!* We take control of this currently uncontrollable problem. Instantly, we will be in the driver's seat! We will know exactly who the addicts are. We then open drug clinics at our health departments, register our drug addicts, and give them their drugs free until we can save them from themselves. We can then monitor them and their families. We can teach and show them what the drugs are doing to them, their families, and their lives. The glitzy allure of the drug scene would disappear. Addicts would be faced with the fact they're doing something wrong and unacceptable. When all addicts are in treatment, there would be no allure for newcomers. Society would see drug addiction for what it is, and nobody would desire becoming an addict, just to go into drug treatment. Once addicts begin treatment and are educated, they would no longer be recruiting new addicts. Sure, some addicts will never be saved. At least we could monitor and control this small percentage of addicts and keep them out of trouble.

When these addicts come to our clinics once a week to get their free drug, they must first watch a movie. They would learn about their addiction and be shown what the drugs are doing to their lives, families, and their futures, and would start noticing in their daily lives, the truth. Slowly, they would realize for themselves that these chemicals are destroying their lives and bodies.

We must go all out on this plan. If the addicts' behavior or drug problem is negatively affecting their children, we put a health care worker, a relative, or a friend in their home to become secondary parents, or remove their children from the environment.

Money now spent by the addicts for drugs would then be spent for housing, food, and bills. We could find jobs for our jobless addicts; they could be employed by their city or state if nothing else. Lives could be turned around, and children could have hope for their parents and their own futures.

When addicts get their drugs free, most crime associated with drugs would cease. There wouldn't be any more muggings, burglaries, robberies, and murders to obtain drug money. Law enforcement would be free to track down and deal with true criminals. Our courts and judicial systems would become unclogged and able to concentrate on real issues. Black market drug lords, mafias, cartels, smugglers, and gangs would cease to exist without drug sales at their core.

A television commercial aired years ago, where the President sat behind his desk (I believe it was President George Bush, Sr.), and on the desk in front of him sat a large bag of chemicals. The President said that someday the bag of powder in front of him would be seen as just a bag of chemical garbage. Why can't we make this day come sooner?

Implementing these systems will be a lot tougher than it sounds. Many obstacles would have to be overcome, but our country could make it happen. Wasted lives could be reclaimed! Future lives and dreams could be saved, and most importantly, hundreds of thousands of children could live better lives!

Volunteers to help these addicts would emerge from everywhere. Churches and organizations would come to the aid of our addicted American brothers and sisters. Each addict could have ten or more "saviors" to help guide them and their families. The United States could come alive!

We must press our politicians to put these plans into effect. We can't *afford* to wait any longer! Our country could be making a profit of billions of dollars per month, instead of shelling out billions on the drug war, jails, and prisons as we do today. The time has come to replace all politicians who are doing "business as usual."

Drug laws have become completely crazy. People need to realize drug addicts don't care about laws on drugs, and increasing penalties for drug abuse only furthers our problems. In some states that have legalized possession of small amounts of marijuana, it's still illegal to sell or purchase marijuana! What is this? You can have pot, but you can't buy it? You can have marijuana, but you can't grow it? What are you supposed to do, steal it? A person can legally grow marijuana in one state and in a bordering state be sentenced to 10 years in prison for committing the same act! Give me a break! Come on politicians, finish the legalization of marijuana, correctly, quit harassing good, hard-working Americans, and get all our hard-drug addicts into treatment by giving them their drugs free, thus eliminating the drug trade and all the crime associated with it!

15

FOREIGN-MADE PRODUCTS

One of the main causes of the economy's recent collapse, which makes most of us madder by the day, is that we are outsourcing our industry to China and other countries. Americans are sick and tired of going shopping for something we need and almost everything we attempt to purchase has a label with three degrading words printed on it, "Made in China." Degrading is a harsh word, but that's how it makes us feel! We have pride in American-made products and we're proud to purchase a product labeled "Made in the USA." When we buy something that was made in China, we feel like we're letting the country down, selling out to China and other foreign countries, and giving out jobs to other countries that our country needs! Everything from kids' toys to Craftsman tools are made in and imported from foreign countries. Have Americans forgotten how to manufacture products? No, we have just forgotten how to stand up for what we believe in.

The obvious reason why Americans are selling out to China is the economics involved. The "robber barons" have a much bigger profit margin selling cheaper products that are purchased from China and other countries rather than distributing American-made products. Americans are *forced* to overlook the fact that products from many foreign countries are made with slave labor and American jobs are lost when we purchase imported products, because either we can't afford the American–made product or it's no longer made in the USA. It really bothers me to think that most products we buy from China are no longer made in the United States, because American producers of the products were shut down *long ago* by people purchasing the cheaper Chinese products! This cycle must be stopped!

In some instances, it might not be so aggravating, but the main problem with products made in China and other foreign countries is that they are usually inferior quality products! In the past, Americans were more proud of the label "Made in the USA" than they seem to be today. I will always be very proud of this label. When I purchase a product that reads Made in the USA, I can usually be guaranteed it will work well and be durable for its intended purpose.

Products like Craftsman tools, once a sure bet that they were manufactured in the USA, have "Made in China" stamped all over them. Twenty-five years ago, my electronics repair shop purchased several small pairs of Craftsman brand wire cutters. They were made in the USA. After having cut thousands and thousands of leads and wires over many years, their cutting surfaces began to wear down. Upon replacing them last year, we were very upset after pulling the new cutters from their Craftsman packages and discovering the "Made in China" labels! The new wire cutters looked exactly like the "Made in the USA" versions, but guess what? Yes, you guessed it; they didn't perform in any way like the old ones. Within weeks, the cutting edges dented, because they had been made from inferior metal and couldn't cut leads and wires sharply. Then, to our complete disbelief, the entire cutting nose on every pair cracked and fell apart!

We took the cutters back to Sears and complained about Craftsman outsourcing to China and were given three new pairs of wire cutters, which of course were also made in China! These three pair lasted just as long as the previous Chinese-made cutters! We again returned them to Sears, informing them we were totally unsatisfied with their inferior garbage and were told, "Don't worry, they have a lifelong warranty!" What good is a lifelong warranty for a product that repeatedly only lasts two weeks? We refused to take the same type of cutters and were forced to trade them into another type, also made in China! Of the many varieties of smaller cutters Sears sold, they didn't carry any that were made in the USA. Since then, I've been forced to change brand names in small cutters.

What's the deal with China's quality control? Many products are manufactured and shipped to the U.S. without any product testing what so ever! I've purchased many products throughout the years and after unwrapping the product discovered that they were made in China and then found that the product didn't work correctly or didn't work at all! I'm sure you've had the same experience! We must admit that the quality of their products has increased in the last few years, but they still have a long road ahead of them.

A few years ago I purchased a pipe wrench. Upon trying to adjust the wrench to open wider, I found that the teeth weren't spaced evenly and the wrench wouldn't adjust past a certain tooth. I then found the "Made in China" label. I returned to the store and found that every wrench of the same type had the same defect! Our countrymen, or should I say our robber barons, had purchased these wrenches without any testing being done by the distributors or the Chinese manufacturers. As far as I'm concerned, the words "quality" or "quality control" don't belong in the same sentence as "Made in China."

Americans need to buckle up, pay the extra money for quality American-made products and quit selling our jobs and livelihoods to foreign countries! Products that were previously made in the USA and proudly bear that label are no longer made here, because we put our fellow Americans out of a job by purchasing the cheaper version made in China, Korea, Malaysia, Thailand, or Mexico. American manufacturers need to follow the lead of companies such as the Henry Repeating Arms Company, a manufacturer of rifles. Henry's slogan is "Henry rifles will only be made in the United States or they won't be made at all." Now that's my kind of company!

Today, people complain about our ailing economy, but continue to put up with robber baron distributors replacing American–made products with products made in foreign countries. The problem has cascaded so badly that most people can no longer afford the remaining USA-made products and are forced to purchase foreign-made products. Once we repair our economy, more people will be able to afford products made in the USA, but a good portion of fixing our economy relies on no longer purchasing foreign-made products!

The electronics industry is a good example of lost American industry and jobs. Televisions such as RCA (which stands for Radio Corporation of America), Zenith, and Magnavox were giants among the American electronics manufacturers. Our RCA TV was made in Canada. Our Zenith DVD player was made in Korea. Today it's almost impossible to truly know who made or designed an electronics item. Many popular brands are designed and built by another manufacturer, but still carry the name of the popular brand. Today's Magnavox brand electronics are built by Funai/Symphonic to be price competitive. The problem with this (in my professional opinion after repairing electronics for over 25 years) is that Funai/Symphonic units are the most poorly designed, made with the lowest quality parts available, and are the cheapest pieces of garbage on the market today. We call their VCRs "toys," because at first glance, you wouldn't think that there are enough parts in the units to make them operate.

Funai's cheap VCRs and DVD players have put almost all credible manufacturers of these items out of business. People purchase these cheap, poorly designed units and are mad that they don't work correctly or don't last long before they break down. The consumer must stand up and demand that *quality* electronics again be made in the USA! We must also stop buying cheap electronic equipment from China and other foreign countries (such as LCD TVs). Replacement parts aren't available, and the units are made with inferior parts that last for only a few years!

Toys are among the biggest imports from China. Action figures and such could easily be made in the United States. I always tell our kids that toys are now made in China because Americans forgot how to make toys. Actually, it's because *we've forgotten how to be Americans.* We've forgotten how to stand up for our beliefs. Or could I be wrong? Do Americans prefer that their toys be made in China rather than the United States?

Do you remember when Wal-Mart first opened in your hometown? They sell everything as cheap as possible, which means many of their products are made in China. Many stores around my city that sold American-made products (as often as humanly possible) were forced to close because they couldn't compete with Wal-Mart's prices. I would love to get a bunch of investors together and open a chain of department stores called, "Made in the USA," where *everything* that we sell would be produced or manufactured in the USA!

It becomes obvious that we're selling out to China and other countries when we look at the list of foreign holders of U.S. treasury securities. China and Japan are at the top, with 24% of our national debt owed to China and 21% to Japan!

Most of this information isn't new to the majority of Americans. We recognize all these problems. Clearly, many changes are needed, but we feel powerless to challenge the industries and the politics of change. It seems nobody is willing to stand up and demand the changes necessary to solve our problems. After all, the voice of one doesn't do much, right? Maybe, maybe not, but the collective will of many voiced by one can move mountains!

Please stand up with me, and let the robber barons know that we're not going to put up with this garbage anymore. A national campaign to buy American needs to be implemented now! Products no longer made in the USA, which are now imported, need to be produced in the USA again, creating hundreds of thousands of American jobs. Trillions of dollars now exported to other countries would stay in the USA. Quality would replace inferior products.

Americans need to start a New Year's resolution in 2012, to quit purchasing items made in China and other countries that can be produced and manufactured in the United States. Americans would then create and restart businesses across the country, which would spur economic growth beyond imagination. We shouldn't have any problem with distributors purchasing products from other countries, as long as the United States doesn't have the proper resources to produce the product, but when American manufacturers are shut down because foreign labor can manufacture the product cheaper, we should have a big problem with this.

According to many ancient prophecies of 2012, there are two possible paths of mankind's future. We are currently traveling on the Hopi's upper path of scientific development and devastation of the planet, which will lead us to disaster. We're running out of time to change to the lower path where we co-exist with nature, a path that leads to paradise and happiness. Unless we change our capitalistic views and idealisms and repair our economy, we're in no shape to help ourselves, let alone helping and changing the rest of the world.

Initiating actions from this chapter (and other chapters) will put the economy back on track and allow us to lead the rest of the world to peace and harmony rather than self-destruction!

There is one last item that should be addressed concerning China, another reason to boycott Chinese products; China's appalling record of animal abuse. PETA, People for the Ethical Treatment of Animals, talks for the animals, because they can't tell their own story. PETA tells us that intelligent cats and dogs that are as loyal as the dear ones we have in our homes urgently need our help! PETA Germany and PETA Asia Pacific have seen firsthand and recorded on videotape the *extreme* cruelty happening in China.

Nearly 2 million cats and hundreds of thousands of dogs in China are tortured and killed for their fur each year, and many are skinned alive! German shepherds, golden retrievers, and defenseless cats are slaughtered for their fur. PETA's investigators witnessed trucks transporting up to 800 animals in tiny cages to fur markets across China, some of the cats and dogs still wearing the collars their former owners had given them. Cages were so full the animals couldn't move and none of them had food or water. Dead or dying cats and dogs are crammed together along with the living, and the living ones are driven insane by these conditions. Some lash out, terrified, others are limp with exhaustion and fear. Cages were tossed from tops of trucks to the ground below, shattering the bones of the terrified animals inside.

Methods to kill these cats and dogs include anal electrocution, bludgeoning and kicking, strangling with wire nooses, drowning by forcibly hosing water down the animal's throats, and skinning alive. The fur from these animals ends up as collars on coats, as lining in gloves and boots, or even in rugs or trinkets. Even kittens and puppies aren't exempt. Gruesome evidence collected included a coat made from the fur of 42 German shepherd puppies. Frequently, items like these are purposely and misleadingly labeled as anything from "Asian jackal" to "rabbit."

Undercover footage that was taken shows scenes more disturbing than any horror film. If you have the stomach, you can view this undercover footage at PETA's website. I must warn you, it's very graphic and *absolutely horrific.* Living cats and dogs were filled with terror and pain as they were hung up by their legs and tails and had their fur peeled from their flesh. Stripped, bleeding bodies were tossed onto a pile of other bodies, where animals' hearts continued to beat. Meanwhile, the other helpless caged animals waited their turn in the cold and filth, covered with feces and urine, watching and listening as others around them were painfully killed.

We have two cats and a German shepherd. Can you imagine this happening to your animals? The thought of it turns my stomach and brings tears to my eyes. China has a major problem with human rights issues. What can we expect from them when it comes to animal rights?

Besides boycotting Chinese products, there are things you can do to help reduce the terrible suffering of these cats and dogs. Never buy or wear fur. Tell everyone you know the terrible price that animals have paid for it. You can also join PETA, the only true political power influencing the fashion industry. Call 757-622-PETA (7382) or go online at peta.org to join by sending a small membership donation of $16 or as much as you can afford, so that you can make a difference in these animals' lives.[1]

Again, I would like to emphasize the fact that Americans need to put a deadline (January 1, 2012) on purchasing any more foreign-made products that can be made in the USA. The next time we contemplate buying a Chinese product over an American product, we should remember what these animals are presently enduring.

16

TERRORISM AND WARS

President Bush did a great job with the war on terrorism, Saddam Hussein and Osama Bin Laden definitely needed to be unseated. Our country's other needs were greatly neglected, but his war mongering was completely necessary.

As the years pass and civilization advances, fewer wars occur. If wars do erupt, they're always incited by savage, uncivilized countries with terrorists or dictators who believe they have the right to invade and conquer other nations. All developed countries with intelligent leadership and citizens view war as barbaric, uncivilized behavior and only get involved to end another country's inhumane acts. War will be a concept of the past once people become more intelligent and civilized.

It's the 21st century, not the 14th. We have space travel and unbelievable technologies. We're prolonging life by finding cures for many diseases. We have vast amounts of knowledge in countless fields, but there's one thing we don't have. We don't have time for terrorists and dictators, or for people who terrorize and oppress the innocent. The time has come to completely eradicate all terrorists, wars, and inhumane atrocities that are occurring around the world!

Middle East people voluntarily segregate themselves, due to differences in religions and beliefs, which contributes to their wars and terrorist activities. The mentality of wanting to kill people that don't have the same outlook and beliefs as they do doesn't coincide with their main ideals. In the Middle East, they start wars and murder in the name of their god. This goes against all their religious teachings! Do they realize this? Surely God won't answer their prayers by helping them kill people, but they believe this to be true! How can they justify their reasoning? If someone's beliefs and principles are different than yours, then just kill them? Give me a break!

These people are raised in an environment where religious beliefs are not questioned and modern ways of thinking are oppressed. It's *our* responsibility to change their views on human rights issues and how they view the people of the United States. We're not all jet-set millionaires abusing our status.

In some ways, their society's morals surpass ours, but in other ways their beliefs and actions show immoral, primitive behavior. Many of the concepts that built the Middle East are based on religion. If everyone practiced the teachings of Jesus and Gandhi, wars and terrorism wouldn't exist. Most Middle Eastern cultures believe materialistic possessions hurt a person's soul and that selfishness and greed are morally wrong, which are also basic Christian beliefs. If all the people of the United States and the Middle East practiced the teachings of Jesus and Gandhi, we could finally bring peace to the world!

One of the biggest tools we have to eliminate terrorism is the terrorist's own countrymen. We need national campaigns to convince all countries to eradicate the infestations of terrorists living around them. Large rewards, such as a minimum of $50,000 per head should be offered to entice the common people to turn in these murderers. Bombing innocent by-standers, children, women, the elderly, and the working class people can't be tolerated any longer, and every means available should be taken to exterminate the responsible murderers. A reward of $50,000 per head would be well-spent money.

In order for a country to be freed of all terrorist activity, the country's people must first demand it. Until their people are ready to eliminate all terrorists from their countries, it will never happen. As the years pass, more people desire world peace. As these people's standards progress, we must empower them with the realization that with our assistance, they have the capability to eradicate all terrorists and dictators. We must show the oppressed people a vision of a better life with no wars, killing, or persecutions.

Time limits must be imposed on their governments. We must inform all oppressors that their behavior will no longer be tolerated and the time for their people's freedom and a unified world has arrived. Freedom must become a global realization, with all people of the world equal under God. All uncivilized countries must be given ultimatums, and we must stand behind the demands given to these dictators: Bring freedom to all the people now, and change your ruling ways. Accommodate the people's needs, or be eliminated by your own citizens with help from the United States and the world. When people of oppressed countries realize the rest of the world is behind them, massive change will occur. The time has come to eliminate all senseless conflicts, wars, and worldwide atrocities. *The world* must not tolerate these acts any longer!

There are more reasons why the time has come to end all wars and terrorism. Many prophecies from numerous sources speak of the worst type of war imaginable, nuclear war. Fabrice Bect of France and LOrd KyrOn of Spain, both accredited to having discovered many Bible codes that have later come true, recently found Bible codes revealing information on nuclear war, which verify our worries concerning countries that are about to join the nuclear club, such as Iran and North Korea. One matrice that doesn't require any explanation, reads "I will vow, the country, of Iran will be destroyed, fire by God, by the hand, of Israel." This is very ironic, because Iran's President Mahmoud Ahmadinejad has publicly announced that he will destroy Israel as soon as Iran gains a nuclear arsenal. Another matrice reads "atomic holocaust, dreadful, in one day they shall die, for the judgments, Lebanon, Israel, Lebanon, (Lebanon listed twice!) Egypt, quarrel, consumed, silenced, fulfilled a prophecy." Still another reads "he will strike, a heap is Iran, they will be destroyed, end of the tree." It could also be translated "he will strike, a heap! Iran will be destroyed, an end of the tree."

Two other codes found seem to echo North Korea's fate. The first reads "you will proceed to an atomic holocaust, repent! It will be destroyed, North, Korea," and the second reads "atomic holocaust, he gave them my treaty of peace, Seoul, North, Korea, Israel, Japanese, alliance, warned, abrupt, death, panic, desolation, shocking, terrible, thundering, vaporization, ablaze, burnt, consume, doom, the big one." If Iran's and North Korea's leaders don't get their heads on straight soon, they won't need to worry about the future!

One main thought must be realized when proposing terrorism's eradication: We may slowly eradicate terrorists, but to completely eliminate all terrorism, we must fix the root of the problem. Why do terrorists exist? What are their fundamental goals? *Terrorist's goals are to change the views of the "materialistic pigs" and eliminate the evil, capitalistic governments that support them!* Why do terrorists think of us as materialistic pigs, and why do they believe that our government is evil? Because they see many of our wealthy citizens as *extremely* selfish and greedy people that are living lifestyles well beyond the means of the average person on Earth, who don't care about the plights of the poor and disadvantaged. They also see our government officials who encourage this way of thinking and profit from it. These greedy people are trashing our ideals of freedom and equality and make very poor examples for the remainder of the world's population! If poverty-stricken countries didn't look down on capitalism as much as they do now, terrorism would have no basis or legitimate goal! After we show the world that the people of the United States can unite to become a country of thoughtful and unselfish people, who truly believe and practice human equality, only then will terrorism die and become a part of ancient history!

In the Main Introduction and Chapter 11: The Economy, I prescribe a new way of life that combines our capitalistic views with a voluntary commonwealth vision, where everyone tries to help each other rather than caring only about themselves. Once we change our country's views and other countries finally glamorize us for the right reasons, negative images caused by capitalism will change. *Only then, will we finally eliminate terrorism!*

We must solve our country's problems *immediately*, so that we can concentrate on helping less fortunate countries obtain a reasonable standard of living, showing the people of Middle East that we *are* a morally correct people and capitalism *can* work with voluntary socialism. We must prove that we can make the American dream come true, while at the same time taking care of our less fortunate citizens and helping other countries around the world to obtain acceptable standards of living!

17

OUR SCHOOL SYSTEMS

Education beyond high school should be free to anyone who has the desire to better their lives and should be a must for our future young adults. We pay for our children's education for 12 years. Why don't we finish the job correctly and send them to college or trade school? When a person reaches the age of 18, they're old enough for many responsibilities, but aren't really ready for the real world. After college, students have a few more years under their belts and they blossom!

When finishing high school, I didn't see college as an option, because I didn't think I could afford it. So, I joined the Navy to learn electronics and completed some of the best training available in this field. During high school, I developed my art skills and was headed toward a great career in art. If college would have been an option, I would have traveled that path and would now be working as an artist rather than an electronics technician.

Millions of teenagers coming out of high school don't have any plans for the future and become burdens on society. These teenagers deserve a chance to create a better future for themselves and the country. Finances shouldn't limit any person from achieving desired educational goals. It seems California is leading the country in this direction, but it's hard to get into a California college if you're not a resident, because they're taking care of their own students first. All other states need to follow their lead. Education, including college, should be a right of every American citizen and should be free!

Many of the country's problems stem from our citizen's lack of education. Once colleges become funded by the Commonwealth and the states as proposed, high school students who now can't afford college will have the capability to continue their education past high school, with goals of becoming professionals in technical fields. This added incentive may drive students to better use of their time and skills in pre-college schools. Today, most students who come from families that are financially strapped don't try their best in junior and senior high schools, because they know that they'll never have the chance to attend college, due to lack of finances.

Most of our public schools are failing. Compared to other countries and our own country's private and charter schools, our public schools are inadequate and require complete overhauls. Lucky children are able to attend private schools, where they surpass expectations. Consistently throughout the years, these children excel far above the country's educational standards and test several levels above their actual grade.

Private and charter schools have been proven to provide expected results from our students, and most graduates of these schools proceed with further schooling, because these students have realized and used their full potential. These schools are found to be costly, and most communities, cities, and parents can't budget them into their finances. We pay for public schools, just as private and charter schools are financed in some way. Why can't our tax dollars produce the same results in our public schools as our private schools? They can! Public schools must be converted to run and operate as private schools. The future depends on our children's education!

We need more teachers per student, more control in our public classrooms, and more parental participation, the latter being most important. As parents, it's our responsibility to ensure our kids are working at their full potential. With more communication between teachers and parents and with better teaching methods, we can change our children's futures.

Many states are implementing budget cuts in teacher salaries and educational programs. State's leaders must find alternatives to cutting resources and limiting personal growth. In the worst-case scenarios, states are forcing their best teachers to seek other employment and students to drop out because of lack of funding or programs. Funding our country's educational systems must become one of our top priorities!

After repairing our country's educational systems, the time will come to tackle the issue of education around the world. As a world leader, it's our responsibility to lead the rest of the developed world in helping poverty-stricken countries to build and set up schools. We must help these people to help themselves.

Education is a large part of the solution to most of the world's problems. We will eventually solve all of humanity's dilemmas as society becomes more intelligent and enlightened, but the problem with this is that we don't have much time remaining to make the needed changes! We desperately need to fix our economy immediately and make the funds available that are necessary to repair our educational systems. Knowledge should be free to anyone who has the desire to learn!

18

GLOBAL WARMING

We've all seen or heard evidence related to global warming. Years ago, the debate regarding global warming's validity raged onward. Many people believed that the warming trends we were experiencing at the time were natural and weren't much to worry about. In 2006, a special produced by NBC news for the Discovery Channel and narrated by Tom Brokaw[1] aired, which confirmed my beliefs that global warming is very real and is occurring on a larger scale than at any time in mankind's history. After recovering from the shock and realization that humans are the cause of most of the damage being inflicted to the planet and its ecosystems, I've been very worried about the world's future.

Every few months, we hear of another part of the world that's being affected by global warming. Scientists say that if we quit pumping tons of CO_2 into the atmosphere today and didn't put any additional CO_2 into the atmosphere, the existing CO_2 levels in the atmosphere would still require thousands of years to dissipate! We see efforts being made to reduce emissions and hear about new ideas being implemented, but we're not yet doing enough to solve the problem! We must immediately stop all polluting of the planet! God, Mother Nature, or higher powers won't tolerate the trashing of Earth, and if we don't change our ways, we will soon be exterminated as an infestation!

Evidence showing that global warming is definitely occurring is mounting all around us. Earth's climate has changed throughout its history, rising and falling through the different ages. The reason we're so concerned today is that changes, which normally occur over thousands of years, *are taking place in only a few decades!* It doesn't take much for an ice age to occur; a small drop in temperature could start our next one.

My family lives in the Rocky Mountains, where we see ice capped mountain peaks throughout the year. We live close to Montana and its Glacier National Park. The park's 8,000 year-old glaciers are melting rapidly and could disappear completely in the next 50 years. Montana's Glacier National Park once had more than 150 glaciers, which took thousands of years to form. Today, after only a few decades, less than a third remain. The same thing is happening in Alaska, Greenland, Patagonia, and the Andes.

In the last 10 years, 15% of the mass of the glaciers in Patagonia have disappeared. These glaciers, which lie between Chile and Argentina, are the largest fields of ice besides Antarctica and Greenland. Glaciologist Stephan Harrison[1] and his teammates have studied these ice fields for over two decades. Some of the hundreds of glaciers here are more than half a mile thick and have existed since the last ice age. These glaciers are melting at a historic rate, creating rivers through the ice, which are forming underground lakes and tunneling holes deep into the glaciers. The same catastrophe is occurring in the Arctic. As glaciers melt, more of the ground underneath them is exposed to the sun. Heat that is normally reflected by the ice is absorbed by the ground, which causes the ice to melt even faster, creating a cascading domino effect.

This warming cycle also happens with the atmosphere. As the ice melts and temperature rises, the atmosphere's water vapor content increases. The water vapor then absorbs more heat, causing temperatures to rise even further. These cycles of feedback that cause the temperature to increase could raise Earth's temperature 6° by the end of the century.

According to Stephen Pacala, director at Princeton Environmental Institute, ice ages were climate changes brought on by natural cycles.[1] He says every 100,000 years Earth's orbit becomes slightly elliptical, taking us further away from the Sun. Coupled with other cycles, such as times when the planet tilts away from the Sun, Earth's climate can be cooled down more quickly than usual.

Dr. Nick Lunn[1] and his colleagues at the Canadian Wildlife Service in Church Hill, Manitoba, Hudson Bay studied the polar bear population in the most in-depth study ever made on the subject. They tranquilized polar bears and recorded data on size and weight among other things. They've discovered that the polar bear population has declined 25% since 1980. This is a decrease from 1,200 to about 900. Lunn also found that the bears are starving, with the average weight of the polar bear decreasing 15% since 1980.

Thirty years ago, the Arctic sea ice covered 1.7 billion acres, which is about the size of the United States. Since then, it's lost an area about twice the size of Texas. Polar bears depend on this ice for their survival! If melting continues at this rate, by the middle of the century there will be no sea ice left during the Arctic summer.

Polar bears are now exhibiting activity that scientists have never witnessed, such as attacking huge walruses (these attacks are mostly unsuccessful)! Years ago, they hunted small seals on the frozen ice. Now, with all the frozen ice caps melting, the areas they used for hunting have decreased, and the bears are running out of smaller prey. It's estimated that we will lose 45% of the polar bear population by 2050.

About 10% of Earth's surface is covered by ice, most of which lies in the Polar Regions. As this ice melts, our sea levels rise. Antarctica and Greenland's ice contains 75% of our fresh water. In the last 18 years, the rate of outgoing icebergs from Greenland has doubled and then doubled again. If this persists, the Greenland ice sheet will collapse. As this warming trend continues, it could cause irreversible melting at both poles, causing unbelievable rising sea levels. If Greenland's ice caps melt completely, they would release enough water to raise global sea levels about 23 feet! If the West Antarctic ice sheet melted, it would cause a 20-foot rise in our sea levels. As we lose large amounts of either, coastal life as we now know it will disappear. Fifty years from now, New York, Boston, Philadelphia, Washington D.C., and Florida could all be underwater. Many people who live on low elevation islands are already seeing problems from the rising sea level.

The island of Tasmania, off the coast of Australia, has one of the oldest tidal gauges known to exist. Sea levels have been carved into the rocks, showing that the sea level has risen 6 inches since 1840.

Global warming has also caused ocean temperatures to rise. For every inch of sea level rise, 100 feet of beachfront along the Atlantic coast will be submerged. When ocean temperatures rise, the atmosphere reacts, causing dramatic global weather changes. A simple 1° rise in our oceans temperature can have devastating effects and cause more storms and hurricanes.

In 2005, temperatures in the Gulf of Mexico set new records with all-time highs. That year's hurricane season broke all previous records, with 28 documented storms ranking as the worst storms to hit us in over 75 years. With more moisture being drawn into the planet's atmosphere in recent years, the intensity of hurricanes has increased, and scientists predict it will only worsen until it becomes the norm.

Rural villages in northern China have seen less and less rainfall over the last three decades with hardly any rain falling in the last few years. Every year, 1,000 square miles of their farmland turns into desert. This is also happening in South Africa, India, and in other places around the world.

Mark Serreze of the National Snow and Ice Center in Boulder, Colorado, studies thousands of ice core samples that were recovered from drilling deep into the glaciers of Antarctica and Greenland. These ice cores contain over 600,000 years of Earth's climate history. By studying these cores, we can better understand today's climate change.

At the Ice Core Laboratory in Boulder, scientists can measure small samples of atmospheric gases that have been trapped and preserved in the ice. In layer after layer, going back hundreds of thousands of years, they found that one gas in particular matches the rise and fall of temperature almost exactly. This gas is CO_2. They found that when temperatures increased, there was more CO_2. When temperatures decreased, there was less. In test after test, scientists recently found that CO_2 concentration levels are now higher than we've seen in the past 600,000 years! CO_2 is essential for life, but when we have an overabundance, it traps and holds energy in the atmosphere and causes the greenhouse effect. Since human beings have been in existence, CO_2 levels have never been higher than they are now! The causes are obvious and include deforestation, the polluting of the planet's oceans, pumping thousands of tons of CO_2 into the atmosphere, and destroying ecosystems.

The Amazon forest, which is about the same size as the United States, contains billions of trees that absorb CO_2 and are the lungs of the planet. 2005 was the driest year on record for the Amazon, because climate changes are steering rainfall patterns away from it. Trees in the Amazon require up to 100 feet of vertical draw to get moisture to their tops. These trees' roots run 40 feet down into the earth, but when the ground runs out of water and there isn't enough rainfall, the trees die. Many of these trees have absorbed 20 years of global emissions of carbon into their tissues. After they die, the CO_2 stored inside them is released into the atmosphere, thus increasing the domino effect. If global warming continues, this domino effect will cause global repercussions.

In 1896, Swedish scientist Svante Arrhenius suspected that burning coal, oil, natural gas, and carbon-based substances could change the atmosphere.[1] Sixty years later, climatologist Charlie Keeling studied the rise and fall of CO_2 levels. He found that the normal ups and downs from the changing seasons were not following their usual patterns and that they were actually climbing! He found that more and more CO_2 was remaining in the atmosphere each year. His graph, known as "The Keeling Curve," showed a 15% increase in CO_2 levels from 1960 to 1995. This proved that fossil fuels, which took millions of years to form, were releasing massive amounts of CO_2 into our atmosphere.

Professor Peter Cox, at the Hadley Center for Climate Research in Exeter, England, heads one of the largest climate study efforts in the world.[1] His studies show that temperatures rise proportionally to the amount of CO_2 in the air and that increases in levels of CO_2 emissions are increasing.

Dr. Jim Hansen said that in the history of Earth there have been five or six massive extinction events that were caused by significant climate changes. This may reoccur soon. Scientists believe temperatures are rising so fast that we'll soon reach a tipping point—a point of no return—where there's nothing we will be able to do to change or undo what we've done. Once we pass this tipping point, the world will be condemned. Our lands will continue to turn into deserts, with less and less fresh water available.

If our warming trends continue, by the year 2100 the summers would become unbearable, no one would be able to go outside, and there would no longer be enough food or fresh water to sustain Earth's nine billion people. We could lose half of the species of the planet by then, but some species would flourish. Insects, which do well in hotter temperatures, would have rising populations resulting in more diseases such as West Nile virus, yellow fever, and malaria.

Marine biologist Ove Hoegh-Guldberg studies the Great Barrier Reef of Australia, which is the largest structure of living organisms on the planet.[1] Coral that is usually brown is now bleached white because of rising ocean temperatures, which has also driven away the normally abundant algae. Most of the algae that remain have been damaged by heat and light, and as time progresses it only worsens.

All over the planet, people depend on glaciers and mountain snow for their fresh water. The Amazon rainforests and their rivers are the largest source of fresh water in the world. If global warming continues as it has for the last 30 years, in 50 years there won't be enough fresh water to sustain the world's population. What kind of a world are we leaving to our kids and future generations? Is it already too late, and if not, can we change the prevailing ways of the United States, and then the world?

China has over one billion people alone and is now experiencing an unprecedented industrial revolution. China continues to build new coal-fired power plants, and the amount of their CO_2 emissions is rising rapidly. China is now the second leader in CO_2 emissions in the world. The leader is the USA. We are responsible for 25% of the CO_2 emissions globally. The United States is only 5% of the world population, which means we put five times our share of CO_2 into the atmosphere!

With China and India's growing industrial booms, there's never been a greater need to take control of the problem. We need aggressive measures now, let's hope it's not already too late! We can't tell the poor people of China, India, Iraq, and Mexico that they can't have what we have and can't cause all the pollution that we do. We must show them how to create a sustainable happy lifestyle, without trashing the planet. First, we must do it ourselves!

Over 160 nations have now ratified a plan known as "The Kyoto Protocol Treaty," where industrialized countries commit to reducing CO_2 emissions levels. Under the Kyoto Protocol, nations that don't meet their CO_2 emissions goals must buy carbon credits from countries that do. This creates incentives to comply with the Kyoto Protocol, and penalties are incurred for violating the terms of the agreement.

In 2001, the United States administration withdrew the United States from Kyoto, saying that their goals were unrealistic, that it would hurt the economy, and more studies were needed to prove human activity is causing the greenhouse effect. We didn't hear much about it here in the United States, but the international community criticized us greatly. Since then, our country's emissions have increased dramatically.

In December of 2009, representatives from two hundred countries met in Copenhagen, Denmark, with the mission to draw up new strategies and create a global agreement to slow down and stop global warming. The last such meeting failed miserably. The council couldn't agree with each other. People weren't impressed to hear that 1,200 limousines brought representatives of the 200 countries to the conference in 2009, and many of them came in private planes, of which there were 140!

There is one other major cause of global warming, and the general population knows nothing of it. Chapter 1: The Earth's Decreasing Magnetic Field tells how global warming is being affected by our planet's rapidly deteriorating magnetic field. We've trashed the planet's atmosphere for decades, and now the problem has been worsened in the last years by our deteriorating magnetic field, which has allowed more solar radiation to pass into our atmosphere, resulting in more global warming.

We must accept the fact that we're causing a good portion of global warming, and that if we don't stop polluting the atmosphere, we'll soon pass the point of no return. Many countries are beginning to take major steps in cutting CO_2 emissions. Big ideas are emerging. If we can repair our economy, most major steps needed to stop emissions could be accomplished without the worry of cost effectiveness.

The Sleipner Natural Gas Rig off the Coast of Norway uses "carbon sequestering" to capture all the CO_2 that it would normally emit into the atmosphere. This CO_2 is converted into a liquid form, where it's then put into a large underground reservoir more than 3,000 feet beneath the sea bed. Almost 3,000 tons of this liquid are pumped into this massive underground storage container every day! Scientists don't know if the CO_2 will leak out of the ground and into the sea and atmosphere. This sounds to me like a very temporary solution and reminds me of storing containers of nuclear waste at Yucca Mountain in Nevada. In doing both of these things, we're passing our problems down to future generations.

Brazil produces ethanol from sugarcane, which is their biggest crop. Ethanol is used as a gasoline additive. It burns cleaner than gasoline and reduces the amount of CO_2 released into the atmosphere. Brazil is the biggest producer of ethanol, which has completely eliminated its need for foreign oil. We must do the same!

Scientists believe that the way to save the Amazon is through "carbon trading," where money is paid by nations who don't meet their CO_2 emission reduction goals to the loggers and farmers of the Amazon in return for not destroying the rain forests. South American countries are proposing that they receive additional credits by proving that they're contributing to CO_2 reduction goals by preventing the deforestation of their forests.

After admitting that mankind is a major contributor to global warming, we must then admit that we're also responsible for the destruction of the world's forests that normally control CO_2 levels. Only 20% of the world's ancient forests remain. We need to redirect the tearing down of rain forests to acquire land for agriculture, by finding less precious land to use. We must find areas that will sustain certain crops over other crops, *but leave the forests alone!* Fifty percent of tropical wood sold in Europe is illegally logged. Avoid purchasing the following types of wood: abachi, afrormosia, azobe, bangkiria, hemlock, iroko, mahogany, merbau, okoume, ramin, red cedar, red meranti, sepeli and sipo (African mahogany), teak, and wenge'.

Even today, TV programs show forests being torn down by "extreme" logging operations. In my opinion, these shows reveal true to life and tragic scenes taken directly from the movies *Avatar* and *Fern Gulley.* Completely stripping forests of all their trees must stop! Selective harvesting, where only trees that have reached their prime are harvested, is the answer.

We should look at what ecologists call "sustainable development." It's about protecting Earth's natural resources, while at the same time meeting human needs. When we pollute our atmosphere, oceans, and waterways, and chemically pollute our lands, this is definitely unsustainable. We must face the facts of what we're doing to the planet and correct it all, now! We can also help eliminate global warming by making small changes in our own lifestyles.

Every year, fifty tons of CO_2 are generated from a normal family's emissions. Half of this comes from our vehicles, and the other half comes from our comforts of living such as electricity, which is usually generated from electric plants that burn fossil fuels. With more than 110 million households across the U.S., over 7 billion tons of CO_2 is pumped into the air annually! We now know that burning fossil fuels is a major cause of global warming. Each person must do as much as possible to reduce and stop CO_2 emissions.

Don't buy regular filament light bulbs anymore! If every household across the country changed one light bulb to a long lasting energy efficient fluorescent bulb, it would be like removing one million cars from our roads. Newer electronic items consume power whether they're turned on or not. Connecting them all to a power strip, which can be turned off would save 40% of the electricity used to power them. Turning down your thermostat by only a few degrees in the winter and up a few degrees in the summer would stop tons of CO_2 emissions every year.

We need to immediately eradicate our country of gas guzzling vehicles and replace them with energy-efficient electric cars. We must stop all imports from China until they stop pumping billions of tons of CO_2 into the air. We're contributing to their pollution by buying products from manufacturers in China.

Unless we reduce emissions and develop new energy alternatives around the globe, greenhouse gases will double in the next 50 years. Most people on the planet are eager to solve the problem of global warming. No one wants to leave a trashed world to their children and grandchildren. We need the collective will of all our industrialized countries to band together and eliminate all emissions of CO_2! We must share technology with all these countries. We must see things on a global level, instead of on a national level! We must implement all the technology we have today, whether it's cost effective or not! We can't put a price on Earth and its resources!

We can't just sit idly by any longer and watch the planet being trashed! We must face the fact that we must change our ways, now! The Bush administration pulled us from the Kyoto Protocol Treaty, stating it was bad for our economy, and the goals were unrealistic. It's unrealistic to think of economics, instead of saving the planet! All countries, including the United States, must join the efforts of the Kyoto Protocol.

Goals must be made and met. Unless more things are done now, we'll soon pass the point of no return. Which is more important, our children, grandchildren, and our planet, or the economy? With an uninhabitable Earth, what good is an economy?

New York City, once known for its pollution, is now known as "The Green Apple." Today, it is one of the most energy-efficient cities in the United States. New Yorkers are using hybrid and electric taxis and more mass public transit than anyone else in the country. New York has the largest hybrid electric bus fleet in the nation. Ellis Island and the Statue of Liberty are now run from electricity generated by wind power. Buildings are being constructed with recycled material from other buildings that were torn down such as the Hearst Tower, 80% of which was built from recycled materials. All cities around the world need to adapt plans such as these.

We must stop polluting the planet and eliminate all toxic chemicals. We have an obligation to recycle every product and container we produce. We need to backtrack, look at every aspect of civilization, and eliminate everything negative that we've brought to the world. If enough people across the country band together and make their voices heard, massive change would occur.

Tom Brokaw said, "In the 3 million years since humans have walked the Earth, we have been at the mercy of the climate. Now, the future of Earth's climate is in our hands. If enough people around the world do their part to change, we can become a collective force of change."[1]

Between 1930 and 1936, massive dust storms swept our prairie lands. The dirt and dust was inescapable. Many people and most animals died slow deaths after their lungs filled with dirt. The "Dust Bowl" was the result of *mankind* causing major ecological and agricultural damage to the land. People tried to farm land that didn't have enough rainfall to support their crops. High winds blew their dry topsoil across many states, hundreds of miles from its original location. Just as what happened in the 30's, mankind has caused Earth's weather problems that we are presently experiencing. Soon, if we don't reverse our ways, we will turn the entire planet into a giant dust bowl.

We have the technologies to stop Earth's destruction. As Tom Brokaw said, we need only to rally the collective will of the country to implement them. Our previous government administration wasn't willing to do so. Our present administration concurs with my views, or should I say our views? The time has come to inform all world leaders that we're ready to rally and eliminate all sources of global warming. Our futures depend on repairing the planet, and future generations are depending on us. Let's not disappoint everyone!

19

OUR OCEANS

Our oceans are presently being "trashed" and converted into giant landfills! The dumping of toxic chemicals, plastics, and trash is destroying marine ecosystems around the world! This became physically evident to my family and me about four years ago while we vacationed in Maui, Hawaii. We love Hawaii and try to vacation there as much as possible. We also love Hawaii's beaches. They are one of the main reasons why we love Hawaii so much.

During this particular visit, we hit the beaches the first day we arrived. We were shocked to find the water at our favorite beach had become oily, discolored, and foamy, and it emitted a foul odor reminiscent of garbage. We couldn't believe this was happening! People of the world had polluted our oceans to the extent that we were observing the effects in the middle of the Pacific Ocean!

We waded in the water along the shoreline, not wanting to swim in the now polluted water. Later that day, we noticed the skin on our legs had become red and irritated with small red and purple spots. We didn't go back into the ocean for the remainder of our vacation. Upon returning to the same beach two years later, we were absolutely overjoyed and relieved to find that the pollution had moved on and our beach was back to normal, but we all wondered where it had gone and what damage it was causing now.

Along with polluting the oceans, mankind has also recently caused other major problems with our oceans. Marine ecologists and Greenpeace say the biggest single threat to marine ecosystems today is overfishing.[1] Giant ships, using state of the art equipment, can quickly and accurately pinpoint schools of fish. These industrial fishing fleets have exceeded the oceans' ecological limits. As larger fish are wiped out, the next smaller fish species is targeted. Canadian fisheries expert Dr. Daniel Pauly warns that if this continues, our grandchildren will be eating jellyfish![1]

More and more people are competing for less and less fish. Scientists are warning that overfishing is resulting in profound changes in our oceans, perhaps changing them forever. The fishing industry is given access to fish stocks before assessing the impacts, and regulation of the fishing industry is terribly inadequate. Fishing vessels far outmatch nature's ability to replenish fish. These ships are fitted like giant floating factories, containing fish processing and packing plants, huge freezing systems, and huge engines that drag enormous fishing gear through the ocean. *Ninety percent* of tuna, swordfish, marlin, cod, halibut, and flounder have been fished out since large-scale industrial fishing began! These changes endanger the structure and foundation of marine ecosystems and thus threaten us now and in the future.

Over exploitation and mismanagement of fisheries has already led to some major fisheries collapsing. The cod fishery off Newfoundland, Canada, collapsed in 1992, leading to 40,000 job losses. The cod stocks in the North Sea and the Baltic Sea are now headed in the same direction and are close to complete collapse.

Instead of finding long-term solutions to these problems, the fishing industry's eyes are now turning to the Pacific! Politicians continue to ignore the advice of scientists about how these fisheries should be managed.

Scientific evidence on the status of western and central Pacific Ocean tuna stocks suggests that Big Eye and Yellow Fin tuna are now over-fished. Unless WCPO nations take urgent measures to control fishing in their waters, we could lose these cherished resources.

It's estimated that by the year 2050 the world's population will increase to 9 billion, of which 60% will live within 60 kilometers of the sea. The agriculture and industrial activities required to support this population will increase the already significant pressures on fertile coastal regions.

Another significant impact of human activity upon the oceans is marine pollution. It's not just oil pollution from accidental oil spills and illegally discharged tank cleaning wastes. Despite the visibility of oil spills upon marine environments, these are dwarfed by those of pollutants introduced from other sources such as domestic sewage, industrial waste discharges, urban and industrial runoffs, explosions, sea dumping operations, oil production, mining, agricultural nutrients and pesticides, and radioactive discharges.

Land based sources are estimated to account for about 44% of the pollutants entering the sea, and atmospheric inputs account for an estimated 33%. Maritime transport accounts for only about 12%.[1]

Impacts of these pollutants vary. Nutrient pollution from sewage discharges and agriculture can result in dangerous and unsightly "blooms" of algae in coastal waters. As these blooms die and decay they use up the oxygen in the water. This has led to many areas turning into "creeping dead zones" (CDZ) where oxygen dissolved in the water falls to levels unable to sustain marine life. Industrial pollution also contributes to these dead zones by discharging substances, which as they degrade, also use up the dissolved oxygen.

Radioactive contamination in the sea has many causes. Historically, the testing of nuclear weapons has been a contributing factor. The normal operation of nuclear power plants also pollutes the sea, but by far the biggest sources of man-made radioactive elements in the sea are the nuclear fuel processing plants at La Hague in France and at Sellafield in the UK, whose discharges have resulted in the widespread contamination of living marine resources over a wide area. Radioactive elements traceable to processing can be found in seaweeds as far away as the west coast of Greenland and along the coast of Norway.

The introduction of man-made chemicals into our oceans involves a huge number of substances. Sixty-three thousand different chemicals are thought to be in use worldwide, with 3,000 accounting for 90% of the total production tonnage. *Each year, up to 1,000 new synthetic chemicals are brought onto the market!* Of all these chemicals, 4,500 fall into the most serious category. These chemicals, known as persistent organic pollutants (POP's) are resistant to break down and have the potential to accumulate in the tissues of living organisms (all marine life and eventually humans), causing hormone disruption, which in turn causes reproductive problems, induces cancer, suppresses the immune system, and interferes with normal development of children.

POP's can also be transported long distances through the atmosphere and are usually deposited in cold regions. As a result, Inuit populations in the Arctic are among the most heavily contaminated people on the planet, since they rely on fat rich marine food sources such as fish and seals. POP's include the highly toxic dioxins and PCBs (polychlorinated biphenyls) together with various pesticides such as DDT and dieldrin. These chemicals are also thought to be responsible for some polar bear populations failing to reproduce normally. Seafood consumed by people is also affected by POP's. Oily fish tend to accumulate POP's in their bodies, which are then passed on to human consumers.

Trace mineral pollution from metal mining, production, and processing industries also damages the health of marine plants and animals, rendering some seafood unfit for human consumption. This contribution from human activities is very significant. The amount of mercury introduced into the environment by industrial enterprises is about four times the amount released through natural processes such as weathering and erosion.

The most visible and familiar form of ocean pollution is oil pollution caused by tanker accidents and tank washing at sea. In addition to visible gross short-term impacts, severe long-term problems are also caused. Biological impacts from the Exxon Valdez spill in 1989 can still be identified 20 years after the event. The Prestige, which sank off the coast of Spain in late 2002, resulted in huge economic losses as it polluted more than 100 beaches in France and Spain, effectively destroying the local fishing industry. Ramifications from BP's Gulf of Mexico oil well disaster could be globally catastrophic.

Individual species of sea life are now being threatened by the fishing industry and the polluting of our oceans. The population of the Blue Whales of the Antarctic is at less than 1% of their original abundance, despite 40 years of complete protection. The West Pacific Gray Whale hovers on the edge of extinction, with just over 100 remaining.

In 2003, Stephen Palumbi and his colleagues used DNA samples to estimate that humpback whales could have numbered 1.5 million prior to the onset of commercial whaling.[1] Humpback whales presently number only 20,000. Whaling is no longer the only threat to whales. Human impact on the oceans has dramatically changed in the last half-century since whales have been protected. Known environmental threats to whales include global warming, pollution, over-fishing, ozone depletion, and noise such as sonar weaponry and ship strikes. Industrial fishing threatens their food supply and also puts whales at risk of entanglement in fishing gear. Humans can't even think of eating whale meat. Their blubber is so highly contaminated with organochlorines, such as PCBs and pesticides that it is classified as toxic waste. Organochlorines are known to damage the development of children and affect reproduction.

Despite these threats an increasing number of nations in the International Whale Commission (IWC) are voting for an immediate resumption of commercial whaling!

Expectations for the recovery of whale populations have been based on the assumption that except for commercial whaling, their place in the sea is as secure as it was 100 years ago. Sadly, this assumption is no longer valid. This is why all forms of whaling must be stopped, immediately.

There's a growing body of scientific evidence that demonstrates that the establishment of large-scale networks of marine reserves is urgently needed to protect marine species and their habitats and could be the key to reversing global fisheries' decline. Marine reserves can benefit adjacent factories from both the "spillover" of adult and juvenile fish beyond resort boundaries and through the export of eggs and larvae. Inside these reserves, populations increase in size and individuals live longer, grow larger and develop increased reproductive potential. Marine reserves can also benefit highly migratory species such as sharks, tuna, and billfish, if they are created in places where these species are highly vulnerable, such as nursery grounds, spotting sites, and seamounts.

Large-scale marine reserves are areas that are closed to all extractive users, such as fishing and mining, as well as disposal activities. Marine reserves (MR's) are not just about overfishing, even if one of the primary reasons for creating marine reserves is to preserve fish stocks. They're increasingly seen as an essential global tool to protect the marine environment from pollution, caused particularly by the disposal of wastes, radioactive wastes, munitions, and carbon dioxide.

Plastics are also a major threat to our oceans. The very thing that makes plastics useful to consumers, their durability and stability, also makes them a major problem to marine environments. Around 100,000,000 *tons* of plastics are produced each year, of which about 10% ends up in the sea! Take a walk along any beach, anywhere in the world, and you'll see washed ashore plastic bags, bottles and containers, plastic drums, expanded polystyrene packing, polypropylene foam pieces, and other discarded plastics. Together with traffic cones, disposable lighters, and vehicle tires, all carried ashore by wind and tide. These items don't degrade like natural materials. At sea and onshore, under sunlight, wave action, and mechanical abrasion, they simply break down slowly into even smaller particles. A single one liter drink bottle could break down into enough small fragments to put one fragment on every mile of beach in the entire world!

The North Pacific subtropical gyre, in which water circulates clockwise in a slow spiral, covers a large area of the Pacific. Winds are light and the ocean's current tends to force any floating debris into the low energy central area of the gyre. This debris, in astounding quantities, is equivalent to an area the size of Texas and is swirling slowly around in a circle. This gyre has been dubbed "the Asian Trash Trail, the Trash Vortex, or the Eastern Garbage Patch."

Perhaps this wouldn't be such a problem if the plastics had no ill effects. Unfortunately, these plastics are consumed by seabirds and other animals that mistake them for food. Many seabirds and their chicks have been found dead, their stomachs filled with plastic bottle caps, lighters, and balloons. A turtle found dead in Hawaii had over 1,000 pieces of plastic in its stomach and intestines. It's estimated that over one million seabirds and 100,000 marine mammals and sea turtles are killed each year by ingestion or entanglement of plastics. Imagine chewing and swallowing a piece of plastic. The thought of chewing plastic, tasting the chemicals from which it was made, and sensing the texture of the plastic being chewed makes me ill, let alone the thought of swallowing it!

Plastics also act as "chemical sponges," and concentrate many of the most damaging pollutants found in the world's oceans, the POP's. Any animal eating these pieces of plastic debris will also be taking in highly toxic pollutants.

Floating plastics can carry organisms far from their normal habitat, where they can become a nuisance species. Seventy percent of plastics sink to the ocean floor. In the North Sea alone, Dutch scientists have counted around 110 pieces of litter for every square kilometer, a staggering 600,000 tons! Plastics can also smother the sea bottom and kill marine life that lives there.

The issue of plastic debris is one of the urgent needs we must address. On a personal level, we must avoid buying non-recyclable plastics and dispose of our waste responsibly. The most important thing we must do is demand that all manufacturers have a plan to recycle all their containers, *and everyone must recycle their plastics!* Obviously we need to change our disposal habits and immediately stop ocean dumping of trash and garbage!

On a global level, we must stop all countries from dumping any type of pollution into Earth's oceans. We must stop overfishing and start rebuilding our fish stocks. We must retrace our steps and eliminate all the problems we've caused in the past.

Life on the planet started in the oceans. It would be a monumental mistake for mankind to cause the end of life there. We only have one Earth; there's not another like it in the entire universe. Its inhabitants need to quit trashing its land, atmosphere, and oceans! If we don't stop these travesties, most of us will be exterminated by God, a higher power, or Mother Nature herself. Earth is an absolute miracle of creation. Please help save our planet, if not for us, then for our children and future generations and for every other living creation on Earth!

20

TOXIC CHEMICALS

Toxic chemicals in our environment threaten our rivers, lakes, atmosphere, land, and oceans, and ultimately us and the future. The production, trade, use, and release of many synthetic chemicals are all now widely recognized as global threats to human health and the environment, yet the world's chemical industries continue to produce and release thousands of chemical compounds every year, in most cases with very little or no testing and understanding of their impact on people and the environment.[1]

We now have a chance to win a global precedence, unfortunately not here in the USA, but in Europe, where they are requiring companies to phase out and substitute the most toxic chemicals with safer alternatives. The United States must follow their example and do this now, with all toxic chemicals. Fighting toxic chemical pollution must be a world effort.

The world is manufacturing more and more electronic products every year. This has caused a dangerous explosion in the electronic scrap (e-waste) containing toxic chemicals and heavy metals which can't be disposed of or recycled safely.[2] We must press leading electronics companies to change their methods of production and disposal in order to turn back the toxic tide of e-waste. Poor people in Chinese villages sit over small fires next to their huts and hillsides of electronic scrap from which they melt down metals to be sold to recyclers. Leftover toxic residue is simply poured onto the ground of the dumpsites where they live. We must fight to ensure an end to toxic trade to regions of the world that are least equipped to deal with these inevitable pollutions.

Our lakes, rivers, and underground aquifers continue to be vulnerable to water pollution from direct discharges and diffuse "nonpoint" sources of pollution.[2] Pollution coming from pipes or other readily identifiable discharge sources is a direct or "point source" discharge. Pollution that escapes from agricultural fields, construction sites, city streets, contaminated sediment areas, seeping landfills, or other "diffuse" (thinly scattered) sources is called "non-point source" pollution.

Since Congress passed the Clean Water Act in 1972, great strides have been made in controlling direct discharges. Better controls and enforcement to eliminate these direct discharges are vital, since the sources add large amounts of toxic pollution to our waters. Diffuse sources of pollution are becoming a bigger problem since they aren't as easy to identify and control.

Citizens must get involved in local and state water quality standards and processes by pressing for stronger limits, laws, and enforcements. Citizens must identify and report potential permit violations in our communities. We must not allow any human activity that could harm the quality of our rivers, aquifers, lakes, and waterways. Our children's futures will depend on what we do now.

One large contributor to our water supply pollution is lawn care pesticides. We're exposing our children, pets, and water supplies to toxic pesticides that threaten public health and the environment. Millions of households with the desire to have a perfect lawn are exacerbating the problem. Children, pets, and the environment need to be protected from dangerous pesticides. Lawn care and landscaping services can give us healthy lawns with non-toxic organic programs. Groups like the Northeastern Organic Farming Association (NOFA) train and certify professionals who offer pesticide-free services.

Residential and commercial customers must refuse to use lawn products from manufacturers who choose to make and sell toxic chemicals. We need to force legislation to eliminate all toxic chemical uses. These manufacturers must also be forced to disclose all ingredients of their products, including so-called inert ingredients.

Our communities need to demand reform on manufacturing and use of all toxic chemicals. We must demand:
-Cleanup of all hazardous waste sites
-Stop construction of new landfills which handle any toxic material

-Stop the spraying of toxic chemicals and pesticides
-Halting the land application of toxic sludge, including incineration
-Closing down leaking and unsafe landfills
-Stopping polluting mining and quarrying activities
-Eliminating commercial toxic chemical use, discharge and emissions
-Cleaning up polluting power plants
-Stopping pollution from asphalt and concrete plants
-Stop air pollution from fossil burning power plants
-Stop building public and residential structures on polluted land
-Stiffen laws against illegal toxic chemical dumping
-Stop production and use of gas guzzling vehicles
-Stop disposal of plastics and toxic chemicals in our oceans
-Stop incineration of plastics and toxic substances

These are only some solutions to help the problems we face with pollution. We *must* implement major changes in the United States and other countries' lifestyles!

First, we must identify all sources of toxic chemical production and use and eliminate it all, completely. If we don't manufacture and use toxic chemicals, we won't pollute with them. Until we can phase out all of these substances, we must take it upon ourselves, each and every one of us, to dispose of these toxic chemicals in the best manner technology provides.

Toxic chemicals now in our ground could take up to 120 years to show up since our groundwater moves so slowly. We could be cleaning up existing contamination and fighting its consequences for decades. We don't need to be adding more, forcing our children and grandchildren to deal with problems caused by our stupidity and neglect.

Second, we need to develop a system for recycling every possible piece of litter we dump into our landfills. We must force all manufacturers to make all product containers recyclable or biodegradable. We must recycle all the paper, glass, metal, plastics, and other products that we can. Landfills must truly become "sanitary landfills." If we can't recycle or biodegrade an item, it shouldn't be manufactured or produced!

If a manufacturer or producer supplies a product, it must have a planned way of disposing of or recycling the product and its container once its use has expired. If any item can't be safely recycled or disposed of and be environmentally friendly, we simply don't produce or use it anymore.

Recycling needs to include items that are now disposed of, such as fats, oils, and greases (FOG's). The Water Protection Association refers to these as "residential pollution factor" (or RPF) because American households discard approximately 105 million gallons of FOG into our landfills and sewer systems each month! This equates to 1.26 billion gallons of FOG per year! Most American residents consider current waste disposal methods of these fats, oils, and greases to be "normal and inconsequential." We couldn't be more wrong, considering over 100 million households in the United States are doing the same thing! Municipalities, government agencies, and environmental groups need to acknowledge RPF as a major cause of water contamination and should correct the cause, rather than just cleaning up the results and symptoms.

Most American residents dispose of these FOG's by using solvents and degreasers to dilute the oil, then either pour it down the drain or sewer, put it in a container and then dispose of it in the trash, or sop it up with paper towels and throw it directly into an outdoor trash can or bin. Regardless of how we dispose of these FOG's, a major portion of it continually gets into the environment, either unchecked or uncontained. Most citizens don't realize they're polluting their own water resources and are the cause of a very large portion of pollution.

We must realize that water, oils, and soil do not mix! Households discarding these massive amounts of FOG annually create pollution "domino effects." Fat clogged sewer pipes overflow and result in contamination of our water resources. Landfills are filled with containers of FOG that are smashed or eventually leak into the ground. Landfills can't adequately process liquids due to "natural hydro-geological settings," liquid pressures, and polyethylene dissolving chemicals from household waste collection. Too often, landfills flood and overflow. Purge systems fail, plastic bottoms split under enormous pressures, and toxins leak into our groundwater.

To successfully protect our water resources and environment, new FOG disposal policies need to be put into effect and enforced. Solidification and encapsulation are the answers! Solidification of the FOG's prevents them from entering our water resources and the environment. Once these FOG's are solidified or encapsulated, our cities and counties must get them to our recycling centers, whether we do this by trash collection or delivery by individuals. These FOG's, once solidified into solid waste, can be reused by asphalt manufacturing plants, rubber industries, and coal or oil burning energy plants, thus reducing "ash hazards."

Stopping FOG contamination will require acceptance of personal responsibility and individual awareness of its cause. Changing disposal methods of these FOG's may be one of the hardest items to add to anyone's to do list, but correct disposal of these FOG's will save the creation of billions of gallons of toxic liquid waste and minimize soil and water contamination. All homes should have grease traps built into their plumbing systems that could be cleaned periodically. People wouldn't pour grease and oil down their drains if they had to clean it out of their grease traps later.

Today, the world is searching for new ways to stop landfill seepage and toxic waste runoff and building new types of landfills to better contain toxic chemicals. We must quit putting toxic substances and chemicals into landfills so that we don't have to worry about their consequences in the future!

The majority of these changes should be implemented by local and state leaders, government officials, and corporate leaders, but there are many things we can do as individuals, most of which are common sense. Electing the correct officials would be a good start.

We must stop polluting our lands, oceans, rivers, atmosphere, and waterways with toxic chemicals and all types of pollution. Scientists say we've almost reached a tipping point, where the damages we're inflicting to Earth will soon be irreversible. What kind of world will our children and grandchildren inherit if we pass this point? The people of the world need to stop trashing Earth, before Mother Nature stops us from finishing the job!

21

POPULATION GROWTH

This may not be a popular chapter of this book, since many people won't like reading and facing the facts concerning the reality of an overpopulated Earth. Everyone must realize that if our population continues to grow at the same rate as it has in previous years, eventually we *will* use all of the planet's resources and run out of habitable land! Scientists calculate that as other countries become industrialized, and these countries start using our planet's resources as America does now, we'll need the resources of *five more Earths* to accommodate their needs![1]

The general public views population growth as an inevitable part of life, and we must plan around it. When will people finally realize that overpopulation of the planet will result in many unsolvable problems, and believe it or not, already has? How much longer can this continue before we do something about it? Will we wait until our planet finally runs out of resources?

This scenario reminds me of an early episode of Star Trek. My dad got me hooked on the TV series back in the 1970s; we both loved the show's futuristic values. In this episode, Captain Kirk beamed down to a planet where the population had grown so much that each person had only ten square feet in which to exist. Many people of that world had never been alone in their entire lives! If we don't change our views now, someday this could be us! The sooner we wake up to these facts, the less damage we'll cause to the planet.

The population of the United States alone has grown to just over 309 million, for a total of 6 billion people on the planet. Continuing at this rate, the population of the United States will be 450 million ten years from now, and Earth's population will have reached 9 billion!

Earth's resources can't sustain this population growth forever. Our planet can safely support in a sustainable way and at a reasonable standard of living, *about one half of the present population!*

We've lost half of the world's forests, wetlands, and grasslands. We're systematically eliminating the world's ecosystems. If we continue to lose many more species, we will tear the underlying fabric of nature. Severing the planet's chains of life will have huge repercussions for the people of Earth.

Until we have the technology and capability to colonize other worlds, we must conserve our natural resources by using them less and having less people using them! We owe it to our children and future generations to address and fix the problem now. Waiting will only compound the problem.

China's population boom resulted in the "one child per couple law," which has definitely reduced their population explosion. In the free world, enacting laws on how many children parents could have wouldn't be tolerated, but China unquestionably has the correct idea. As it is now, there aren't enough resources to support the population of the planet. Not only do we need to control our population growth, we must also *decrease* Earth's population to a sustainable point!

I designed a diagram to depict population growth where each couple had only one child. After having one child, one of each couple would "get fixed," resulting in only one child per couple. Twenty years later, their children would also have only one child. If this plan continued for 140 years, there wouldn't be many people remaining! My diagram shows that in order to keep existing population numbers the same, each couple would need to have at least two children, not accounting for untimely deaths. Also, there are people who wouldn't have children, so if all couples who desired kids conceived only two children, our population would still slowly decrease.

As I stated previously, it wouldn't be probable that governments of the free world would implement a one child only law, but it's time for us to see that adapting a similar concept is the only way we can keep Earth salvageable for our future generations. I'm not stating that it should be made a law, but it must be a goal that everyone strives for. The time has come for *voluntary* implementation of this concept! If the American people can realize it's the right option, then the world will follow. We can't continue overpopulating Earth; we can't even take care of all the mouths that need to be fed today! Telling people how many children they can bring into the world would not be allowed, but showing them why they should have only one or two children would be an intelligent way to create better lives for our children and future generations.

Education is most of the answer. One hundred percent of births must be planned births! Parental planning for teenagers is a must. First, teenagers need to be taught higher morals and standards. Second, birth control must be practiced, and contraceptives should be supplied to the world, free.

My mother gave birth to nine children. Her nine children brought twenty-four children into the world, and her grandchildren now have forty-three children. That's sixty-seven people descending from my parents! Had this plan been in effect when my parents married, the number of their descendants could have been as little as *three*, far from today's total of *sixty-seven!* My family means everything to me. I wouldn't desire to change the events of the past. Had this plan been envisioned years ago, many of my siblings and relatives would not exist, including me, but we must now think of our future generations, not ourselves!

Overpopulating Earth and destroying its resources will only lead to a required cleansing of the planet. Unless we desire to be eradicated like an infestation, we must change our views on population growth. *Expansion of our cities must also be curbed.* If our cities grow unchecked, eventually we will run out of habitable land. Our country's infrastructure (highways, bridges, roads, and sewage, electrical, and water systems) and inner city residential areas are deteriorating beyond the point of repair, and must be replaced *rather than excavating new land and expanding cities' borders.*

If we start solving these problems today, ten years from now we'll have a housing and resource surplus, and the planet will be well on its way to recovery. As members of the now overpopulated Earth, we have a moral obligation to *our children and future generations*, to voluntarily have only one or two children per couple!

22
NUCLEAR POWER AND NUCLEAR WEAPONS

The first thing that most of us envision when we hear the word "nuclear" is a picture of nuclear destruction. After researching 2012 prophecies for many years and discovering many predictions that concern nuclear war, I believe that mankind shouldn't be tampering with atomic energy. Nuclear destruction of the world would be an absolutely horrible nightmare!

HBO's documentary called *White Light / Black Rain: the Destruction of Hiroshima and Nagasaki* reveals the horrific power we have created.[1] Japanese families tell stories of the unimaginable events of the bombing of Hiroshima and Nagasaki. Family members, chatting as they ate a meal, were suddenly and violently thrown hundreds of feet as their house disintegrated around them. Arms and legs were torn off of their loved ones' bodies. People's skin and muscles were melted and burned to their bones.

Unbelievable images were shown and heart-wrenching stories told by Japanese people who were only small children when we dropped the atomic bombs on their cities. Thousands of people, half or completely burnt, lay screaming for help, many of them trapped under debris. Thousands were smashed by collapsed buildings. After the explosions, people were running everywhere in the streets, their skin and muscles melted, mutilated, and burnt. They were all dazed and in a state of shock, not knowing what had happened. As far as the eye could see there was complete devastation. Fires burned everywhere. The only escape from the fire was the rivers. People burned beyond recognition plunged into the waters. A confused mother walked down the street carrying her baby in her arms. Its head was missing. People's skin sagged and melted, many with their eyes falling out of their sockets.

These were all civilian people. They weren't the Japanese army, they were just common people. Why did we drop these bombs on populated cities? The Japanese could have easily seen the destruction caused by these bombs had they been dropped in other areas that weren't as densely populated. The American government didn't realized the everlasting horror that they were about to unleash on the Japanese people.

To hear and see the stories of what these people experienced was absolutely incredible! We must all take our hats off to them and pray to God that our families, countrymen, and the people of the world never have to experience the results of nuclear war for themselves. And this was only the beginning of the nightmare.

People who survived the blasts became ill from radioactive fallout. Japanese doctors had never seen these diseases, for which there wasn't a cure. People's gums became swollen and bled profusely. They lost their hair and many of their internal organs shut down.

These bombings were the saddest and most completely unbelievable tragedies that mankind has ever witnessed. Watching this documentary is highly recommended. We must all realize the destructive capability of the weapons we've created and that these bearers of doom could instantly destroy civilization as we know it.

The constant threat of nuclear war has diminished since the breakup of the Soviet Union, but we're still threatened by nuclear attacks from communist countries, dictatorships, terrorists, accidental triggering of a nuclear war, and mishaps that could occur at the sites of our nuclear power plants.

Besides the problem of possible accidents, nuclear power plants also have major problems with nuclear waste storage and disposal.[2] Viable long-term solutions for storage and disposal of nuclear waste have not yet been found. This is because the time period for storage is incredibly long, on the order of thousands of years. Waste must be stored this long due to the extreme amount of time necessary for the material to become non-lethal. There are several ways that nuclear waste is stored, of which all methods are temporary. We're currently leaving all storage and disposal problems of the nuclear waste we've created up to future generations. They aren't going to appreciate this.

Spent fuel rods from nuclear reactors are the most radioactive of all nuclear wastes, giving off 99% of the total radiation of the nuclei inside, despite their small sizes. There isn't any permanent storage as of now for the spent rods. When spent fuel rods are removed from the reactor core, they're extremely hot and must be cooled down. Most nuclear power plants have a temporary storage pool next to the reactor. The spent rods are placed in this pool, which is filled with boric acid that helps to absorb some of the radiation given off by the radioactive nuclei inside the spent rods. The rods must be cooled in these pools for six months, but because there aren't any permanent storage sites, *they often stay there for years!* Many plants have been forced to enlarge their pools to make room for newly spent rods. As pools fill, major problems develop. If the rods are too close to each other, the remaining nuclear fuel could go critical, starting a nuclear chain reaction. Rods must be well monitored, and pools mustn't become too crowded. Permanent disposal of the spent rods becomes more important as the pools become more packed.

Another method used to store the spent fuel rods, which eliminates overcrowding of pools, is called dry storage. The waste is put in reinforced casks or entombed in concrete bunkers. This is after the waste has already spent about five years cooling in the pools! These casks are usually also located near the reactor site.

Many ideas exist on what to do with nuclear waste. Low-level waste, which usually loses most of its radioactivity in a couple hundred years, is often buried underground. High-level waste, compromised mostly of spent fuel rods, is much harder to dispose. Some plans include burying the waste under the ocean floor, storing it underground, or shooting it into outer space. If stored underground, it must be stored in an area with no water flow, since it would erode the containers and carry waste into our environment. Also, a disposal site must be found that doesn't have any geological activity. We can't put a waste disposal site near a fault line, because an earthquake could release buried waste into the environment in the future.

In the United States, a permanent storage site has been selected at Yucca Mountain, Nevada. Yucca Mountain is an extremely dry area, which minimizes the possibility of water seeping through the rock and corroding the casks. If the casks do get corroded, there would be hardly any water flow to carry away the nuclear waste. Though Yucca Mountain is near a fault line, the fault is believed to be inactive. There are also several volcanoes in the vicinity, but it is believed they won't erupt during the next 10,000 years. Naturally, the people in Nevada are highly opposed to the nuclear waste repository, as we would be if we lived there.

The scariest thing about nuclear power plants is the possibility of something going wrong. When reactor systems fail, the nuclear core goes into meltdown, the fuel rods actually turn to liquid, and the steel walls of the reactor melt. In a complete reactor meltdown, temperatures reach about 2700°C and the extremely hot, molten uranium fuel rods melt through the bottom of the reactor and sink about *50 feet into the ground* beneath the power plant. The molten uranium reacts with groundwater, producing large explosions of radioactive steam and debris that affect nearby and downwind cities and populated areas. Two major meltdowns have occurred; one at 3 Mile Island in the United States, and one at Chernobyl in the former Soviet Union. No one is really sure how much of the escaped radioactive waste was released into the Susquehanna River.

The effects of the Chernobyl accident were immense. Radiation released from the accident was 200 times that of the Hiroshima and Nagasaki nuclear bombs combined! The fallout was far-reaching. For a time, radiation levels in Scotland were *10,000 times the norm!* Thirty lives were lost, many of which were from radiation poisoning. Over 2,500 deaths were caused by the fallout. Cancer cases were significant in surrounding areas.

Another method of dealing with spent nuclear fuel, which is highly debated, is reprocessing the spent nuclear fuel. Mary Olsen, from the Nuclear Policy Research Institute and the Nuclear Information and Research Service, has written several articles on reprocessing spent nuclear fuel. They were very enlightening and revealed many facts on the reprocessing issue. Here are a few facts from

Mary's articles on reprocessing.[3]

According to Mary, every reprocessing site (France, UK, Russia, and soon Japan will have the largest sites) is an environmental catastrophe waiting to happen, with massive releases of radioactivity into the air, land, and water. High worker radiation exposures and residues are also possible. Reprocessing also creates stockpiles of nuclear weapons-usable Plutonium. President Carter banned reprocessing, as a nuclear nonproliferation measure. President Reagan lifted the ban, but no commercial interest has pursued it since it isn't a profitable enterprise.

In this reprocessing procedure, fuel rods are chopped up and then dissolved in nitric acid. The resulting highly radioactive and caustic stew is then processed to remove the plutonium and uranium, leaving the highly radioactive fission products in the liquid.

Reprocessing is *not* recycling. The formation of fission products in these fuel rods makes high-level waste fundamentally different from the uranium it came from. It's not possible to remake the original fuel from high-level waste, and thus it is not a cycle!

Reprocessing doesn't reduce radioactivity, it just dilutes the waste without any actual reduction of radioactivity. Contrarily, reprocessing doesn't reduce waste volume. Fuel pellet volume is magnified by a factor of 100 to 100,000! The resulting "dilution" allows the reclassification from "high-level" to the so-called "low level" waste category, which is still deadly!

High-level nuclear waste contains so much lethal radioactivity that the plutonium inside the waste fuel rods is effectively safeguarded. Separating out the plutonium makes it available for nuclear weapons use. For the United States to reverse more than 30 years of policy against recovering plutonium also reverses the moral authority with which the United States calls on other nations to refrain from this activity. North Korea and Iran are the most recent examples of countries ready to join the "nuclear weapons club." Reprocessing is a direct contradiction to United States' reprimands of these countries for nuclear proliferation. The obvious intent of the Bush/Cheney team to return to full-scale production of nuclear weapons has added to this atomic hypocrisy.

Reprocessing creates *millions* of gallons of highly radioactive, caustic, destabilized high-level waste that history shows will leak and evaporate, and may not even be contained for a generation. This is not a solution.

Other negative aspects of reprocessing that worry the members of the Nuclear Policy Research Institute make me very wary of having any reprocessing plant in my backyard. The Institute says wherever reprocessing has taken place, it has resulted in huge amounts of radioactive waste and environmental degradation in and around the facilities involved. The Sellafield plant in Britain is responsible for converting large parts of the Irish Sea into a biologically dead body of water. The Hanford Nuclear Reservation in Washington is a toxic contaminated wasteland. Of the 177 underground tanks stored there, about 70 have ruptured, leaking waste into the surrounding soil and groundwater. The adjoining Columbia River is considered to be the most nuclear polluted river in the Western Hemisphere.

The Bush administration and DOE representatives claimed that the Uranium Extraction Plus (or UREX+) method of reprocessing will reduce the radioactive waste produced by nuclear power plants. This is strongly contested by scientists. According to UCS, reprocessing does not reduce the need for storage and disposal of radioactive waste.

Philip Finck, the Deputy Associate Laboratory Director for Argonne National Laboratory, told a congressional hearing that he expected the increase in the number of nuclear power plants would mean the United States will need up to nine more Yucca Mountain type repositories by the end of the century!

After comprehending all this information, we should all agree that there must be a better way to get our electricity than nuclear power. Hoping that we don't have any accidents at our nuclear power plant sites and earthquake activity around Yucca Mountain isn't enough. Fault lines exist there, and if a pole shift of the planet occurs in 2012, there will be massive radioactive leakage from the site, and just because the area is dry now doesn't mean it will be dry two years from now. By then it could be under the ocean! Also, failsafe and shutdown systems won't work well under water. Many of our nation's reactors could go into meltdown after being hit by floods.

Some say that contamination of smaller areas of our environment is better than all of Earth dying from the effects of global warming. We have enough resources of uranium to last at least another century. By then, maybe we'll have better technology to create our energy so that we won't need to use fossil fuels or nuclear power. We must eliminate all emissions of greenhouse gases *and* all nuclear capabilities!

Another nuclear controversy now exists, concerning the building of Generation IV reactors. Also called fast-breeder reactors, Generation IV reactors use high energy neutrons to transmute more of the U238 into elements, such as plutonium, for further fission.[4] Generation IV reactors can use reprocessed fuel from Generation I to III reactors and extract 90% more energy from the spent waste, leaving it dangerous for only 200 years instead of 10,000. The volume of the waste created by Generation IV reactors is much less than previous generation reactors. Research and development for these systems was stopped by Jimmy Carter when reprocessing was banned in the United States, but other countries continue designing and working with Generation IV reactors. There are several commercial Generation IV plants around the world with different basic designs. Maybe the United States should look closely at these newer type reactors. It would surely be more feasible to store nuclear waste for 200 years than for the thousands of years our previous nuclear waste would require.

It's hard for me to believe that nuclear power plants were built knowing that their waste would be deadly for thousands of years. Nuclear waste that's deadly for 200 years doesn't cut it either. Until we have the technology to safely eliminate nuclear waste, nuclear power plants producing deadly waste that must be stored for thousands of years must be shut down immediately.

The nuclear weapons race is no longer needed and has become more of a possible nightmare than a protection. It should top of our list of things to eliminate. Many of this book's 2012 chapters contain information on future prophecies that deal with nuclear war in the end of days. A pole shift of the planet would be frightening, but world-wide nuclear war is a horror beyond imagination. We could rebuild the world after super earthquakes tear apart all continents on the planet, but rebuilding our civilization after a nuclear holocaust would be an immeasurably harder task.

There are over 30,000 nuclear warheads in the world that belong to nine countries: the United States, the Russian Federation, the United Kingdom, China, Israel, France, India, Pakistan, and North Korea. Just over 20,000 of these warheads could be used against the United States. This equates to a possible 400 nuclear warheads detonating *per state* if a nuclear war was accidentally triggered! Visualize a nuclear missile detonating in the center of your city. Imagine the devastation and instantaneous loss of thousands of lives, possibly *ten times* the lives lost on 9/11/2001, *per bomb.*

Over 2,000 nuclear weapons tests have been conducted in the past and have contaminated our oceans and lands. People living near these test sites have suffered from cancers, stillbirths, miscarriages, and many other health problems. Polled by Lake, Sosin, and Snell, 87% of Americans believe the United States should negotiate an agreement to eliminate nuclear weapons and 87% of Japanese, polled by Asahi Shimbun, said they agreed that all nuclear weapons states should eliminate such weapons. Ninety-two percent of Australians and Norwegians polled, and 93% of Canadians polled, all agreed with abolishing nuclear weapons.

We must eliminate all nuclear weapons from all countries, *now*, before the prophecies concerning nuclear war come true. The Hopi Indians prophesied the coming of the True White Brother, who will come with his two great helpers. The Hopi say that if the True White Brother and his helpers fail, *nuclear war will be our fate!*

Albert Einstein also had something to say about nuclear weapons. He said, "I do not know how the Third World War will be fought, but I can tell you what they will use in the fourth… *rocks!*"

23

VOTING AND THE

ELECTORAL COLLEGE

In the 2004 presidential election, Al Gore received more individual votes from American citizens than did President George Bush. Many people in the United States didn't even bother to vote, because they knew for a fact that their vote wouldn't count. Knowing that one vote won't make a difference is a frightening reason why too many Americans don't vote at all. If our country is to make the changes necessary in order to prevent the world's destruction, *everyone's voice must be heard!* This means changing our voting system so that everyone's vote counts!

There's a much better system available for voting in a new president than our existing system. This system is called, "Direct Election with Instant Runoff Voting".[1] Our country should change to this system. When people don't vote for a new president, they also don't vote for their state representatives. If every person's vote counted, many more people would vote, not only ensuring the election of the presidential candidate with the popular vote, but also the election of state representatives whose objectives coincide with the goals of the President and the country.

After comparing our present system with the new system proposed, you'll agree that the new system is *much* simpler and results in a more "fair" outcome to the election.

In today's system, when a United States citizen votes for President or Vice President, ballots show the names of the Presidential and Vice Presidential candidates, although actually electing a slate of "electors" that represent them in each state. These electors combine to form the Electoral College. Our Electoral College was established in Article II, section 1 of the U.S. Constitution and was later modified by the 12th and 23rd amendments.

The number of electors in each state is determined by adding the number of representatives the state has in both the House and the Senate. The number of representatives allocated to each state corresponds to that state's population as a percentage of total United States population and is amended every decade when a U.S. Census is taken. The number of Senators for each state is always two.

Usually at state conventions, each political party with a candidate on the ballot appoints a set of electors. The number of electors in a state, itself determined by the number of representatives that each state sends to Congress (based on state population), also decides the number of electoral votes allotted to each state.

After the election, the electors in each state from the party with the most votes in turn cast votes for their Presidential and Vice-Presidential picks. Even worse than this tedious and roundabout process is the fact that technically the electors don't even have to vote for the winner of the popular vote in their state! And even though the public votes for the party as a whole, the electors cast individual votes on separate ballots for the President and Vice President. This has become important in several elections where electors voted for candidates other than those to which they had pledged.

Most often, state electors cast every Electoral College vote allocated to his or her state to the candidate who won the popular vote in that state. This is known as the "winner takes all" or "unit rule allocation of electors."

Today, Maine and Nebraska are the only exceptions to the rule that a state can vote for one candidate. These two states use an alternative method called the Congressional District Method, where a state divides itself into a number of districts, allocating one of its statewide electoral votes to each district. The winner of each district is awarded that district's electoral vote, and the winner of the state-wide vote is then awarded the state's remaining two electoral votes. However, statewide winners have consistently swept all of the state's districts as well, so neither state has ever split its electoral votes.

The electors for each state cast their votes in mid-December, after which the votes are sealed and sent to the Senate. On January 6, the president of the U.S. Senate opens all sealed envelopes containing the electoral votes and reads them aloud. In order to be elected President or Vice President, a candidate must have an absolute majority, 51% of the electoral votes for that position.

A majority is never guaranteed within the Electoral College. An election with no majority can occur in one of two ways; if two candidates tie with 269 electoral votes each, or if three or more candidates receive electoral votes (in this case we might say that a candidate won a "plurality" of the votes, but this is not sufficient). If no candidate receives a majority of electoral votes, the decision is deferred to the U.S. Congress. The House of Representatives selects the President, choosing between the top three candidates, and Senate selects the Vice President, choosing between the top two contenders. In the House selection, each state receives only one vote, and an absolute majority of the states (26), is required to elect the President.

However, a majority vote is not guaranteed in Congress either! States could feasibly cast 25 votes to each candidate, or states could split between three in such a way that no one candidate receives a majority vote. If the House can't reach a consensus to fill the Presidential vacancy by January 20, the newly-elected Vice President serves as President until the House is able to make a decision. If the Vice President has not been decided either, the sitting Speaker of the House is appointed President until Congress is able to make a decision. If the President has been elected, but no Vice President has been selected, then the President appoints the Vice President and must wait for approval by Congress. *Wow! What a process!*

If we converted to a Direct Election system with Instant Runoff Voting, the process would be much simpler, and would result in a true reflection of the majority's desires. In this direct election system, IRV can be used for Presidential elections with or without the Electoral College. Many people say eliminate the Electoral College!

In a simple and quick Direct Election, voters would *rank their preferences* for president rather than marking only one candidate! For example, if three presidential candidates were listed on a ballot, some voters might choose candidate B for their first choice, candidate C for their second preference, and candidate A for their third selection. Other voters may rank the three candidates differently. Then, when the votes are counted, if no single candidate had the majority, *the candidate with the lowest amount of votes is eliminated!* The ballots are then counted again, this time counting the second choice votes for those ballots. This process is repeated until a candidate receives a majority vote, reducing the time and money wasted in a normal runoff election! Wouldn't you agree that this is a much simpler voting system? The various parties submit their candidates, we vote, and we're done! And everyone's vote counts!

This IRV system would solve many complications inherent in the Electoral College, as well as the problems introduced by some of the other alternatives. It would end the "spoiler dynamic" of third party and independent candidates and consistently produce a majority vote, a nationwide winner. The spoiler dynamic is the effect that comes into play when there are more than two candidates receiving votes and the "winner" of the election is not the majority's favorite candidate. For example, in an election where only two candidates compete, and candidate A receives 51% of the votes cast, candidate A would be declared the winner, since candidate B had only 49% of the vote. If a third "spoiler" candidate would have entered the race, he or she may have taken away votes from candidate A, resulting in candidate B being declared the winner, even though the people that voted for candidate C don't care for candidate B! Direct Elections with IRV would allow voters to select their favorite candidate without ensuring a vote for their least favorite, as often happens when the spoiler dynamic is a factor and a voter prefers a third candidate the most.

I strongly support abolishing the Electoral College and replacing it with Direct Elections and IRV, and recommend getting involved with the Center for Voting and Democracy, Fair Vote. This organization is working to simplify our voting systems for a fairer outcome in elections.

The only other popular option would be Direct Vote with Plurality Rule. This method would abolish the Electoral College and instead allow each person to cast one vote for the candidate of their choice. The candidate with the most nationwide votes would win the election, with or without a majority of the votes. This option would require a Constitutional amendment and would therefore need the support of two thirds of Congress and three fourths of the states.

This method would more accurately reflect the popular will of the nation, but it would need substantial bipartisan support. More people would vote, knowing their vote had a better chance of making a difference. This would be especially encouraging to people who hold a minority political orientation compared to most of their state; these individuals would be more likely to cast a vote knowing that it would help their candidate even if the rest of their state didn't.

A direct vote, however, would not eliminate the entrenchment of the two party system or the "spoiler" considerations of minor parties and independent candidates. In a close race, voting for a candidate from a minor party could reinforce the same spoiler dynamic as exists today within the present system. Using only direct voting, it's very probable that a winner could be declared with only a small plurality of votes rather than the strong majority guaranteed with my proposal. Direct Election with Instant Runoff Voting means that voters can express degrees of preference for a variety of candidates. In effect, citizens can support more than one candidate. No more choosing the lesser of two evils!

Once a voting system like this is implemented, it could be adopted by the people to retake control of the government. Today, our Senate and Congress decide the outcome of many crucial issues that would be better directed to the people! Nationwide votes could be taken on many issues as well as presidential elections. It's time that the people of this nation say what they really think about the economy, housing, drugs, and health care. We can only see an accurate reflection of the true desires of our citizens when people vote on these issues themselves, rather than for sparkling personalities who are supposed to have their constituency's best interests in mind.

If America is to change, the voices of the common people must be heard. Unless we elect the correct officials, ones which represent the president's and our own goals, change won't occur. The time has come for everyone's vote to count, and every American must vote! In our present system, one individual's vote doesn't mean much. In a "direct election," one individual's vote could determine the outcome of the race! If we're to change America's current path to destruction, everyone's voice must be heard, and everyone's vote must count!

24

SEX OFFENDERS

Sex offenders are everywhere! Laws that force sex offenders to register their addresses allow us to see where they live and operate. Upon viewing a registry map of my hometown, which has a population of about 50,000, I was astounded to see all the nearby homes where sex offenders live! The number of offenders listed is staggering! How bad has the problem become?

There are many crimes where people say that punishments should be more severe. This is definitely one crime that requires harsher penalties. Punishment needs to fit the crime. Most of these sex offenders are scarring people emotionally and physically for life, and need punishment that not only fits the crime, but will deter these barbaric atrocities. In instances where we know someone is a habitual sex offender (which is almost always a man) and his guilt has been proven well beyond a shadow of doubt, there is only one thing left to do. Castrate them! Surgically remove or disable their testicles!

I'm referring to instances where we have videos of the crime, physical evidence, several witnesses, and DNA evidence, with guilt being established well beyond any doubt whatsoever. These guys would be the repeat offenders, the ones that have been caught frequently and have built solid cases against themselves. Give them the choice of castration or the death penalty! If they wish to live and can't be trusted to control their deviant sexual desires, then all of their sexual cravings should be removed, by removing or disabling their testicles! The thought of having their testicles disabled for sexual offenses could deter them from committing the crime in the first place. Why do I believe that castration would eliminate our country's problem with habitual sex offenders? We must again learn from other countries successes.

The Czech Republic practices surgical castration of convicted sex offenders.[1] According to the human-rights forum, Council of Europe, the central European country physically castrated almost 100 prisoners from 1998 to 2008. The Czech Republic defends this course of action, saying that it is both *voluntary and effective*. Dr. Martin Holly, director of the Psychiatric Hospital Bohnice in Prague, says *NONE* of the nearly 100 sex offenders who had voluntarily been physically castrated had committed further offenses! One serial offender said that being castrated was the "best decision" he had ever made. He stated, "On the one hand you have to protect the potential victims and on the other hand I wanted to be protected from myself, I wanted to live like a normal person."[1]

German researcher A. Langelüddeke preformed a large study in 1963 involving 1,036 sex offenders.[2] Physical castration resulted in a 20-year re-offense rate of less than 3%, versus 80% in the group that was not castrated. Obviously, castration of sexual offenders *dramatically* reduces reoccurring offenses! This practice should be implemented in the United States!

Minor sex offenses, where a slip of judgment occurred and the perpetrator is truly remorseful for their social misbehavior, admitted their problem, and is willing to get psychological help would obviously be dealt with in a less severe manner, but the offender would know that his next offense wouldn't go so easy. Some minor sex offenses deserve leniency, such as an 18-year-old male who had consensual sex with his 17-year-old girlfriend after being in a five-year relationship. Poor decisions may have been made, but the act was certainly not an offense against humanity. The people we despise are the sexual predators who force their victims to have nonconsensual sex. These people's delusional behavior must be terminated!

The nation must adopt a zero tolerance policy for sex offenders. The death penalty should be imposed for major sex offenses and castration for committing violent sex offenses. Repeat sexual offenders would be bumped up to the next category, closer to the death penalty. No one would want to discover that they were a part of sentencing an innocent man to castration or death, so guilt would need to be established well beyond any possible doubt. Most people will agree that if a person perpetrates any crime monstrous enough to warrant castration, they deserve the death penalty, and requesting castration (or being required to be castrated) should be the only way that they might be saved from execution.

Sex offenders usually have warped senses of reality. Specials aired on the news shows 20/20 and Prime Time, where they revealed Internet predators that were seeking out underage teenagers for sex. What were these sexual predators thinking! When caught, a few of them said, "I have daughters of my own, I would never have gone through with it!" *Totally disgusting!* Guys with daughters the age of their sexual victims! What kind of monsters has society created? Hopefully their daughters aren't being abused! Thinking about the problem makes me believe that some type of legal prostitution would prevent *some* of these atrocities. If these men had a legal place to go, where they could find a sexual (and possibly emotional) outlet for their desires, then they wouldn't be preying on innocent victims.

Basic flaws exist in most sexual predators' minds and thoughts. First, they believe that no one knows what they're thinking and that their thoughts are theirs alone. This is a misconception that they carry around with themselves. Everyone's minds and thoughts are connected to the Cosmos. God, your guardian angels, and your relatives that have passed on, all have the capability of sharing your thoughts. Chapter 2: Prophecies of Edgar Cayce, tells of how Cayce would go into trances, where he tapped into the eternal consciousness of the Universe and gave answers to questions using knowledge given to him from the Cosmos. He also stated that he was able to go into any person's mind, anywhere, anytime, by tapping into that person's subconscious mind through the consciousness of the Universe.

Have you had the chance to see a psychic artist draw a picture of a person's deceased relative, the person desiring proof of the afterlife? In order to perform this psychic's job, you would need to read the person's mind for which you were drawing the picture, be able to tap into the eternal consciousness of the Universe, or be able to see dead people's spirits. This should show sexual offenders that other people, here and on the other side, can share their thoughts!

There must also be a common fault in the thought patterns of these offenders. It seems that they don't care about the feelings of the person they're abusing. They aren't able to see their victim's state of mind. It's almost like they don't realize their victims are real people! They're at the center of their own universe and everything revolves around them. Somewhere during their lives, these people missed critical information and weren't taught proper feelings, morals, and ideals.

Not believing in God or an afterlife can also be a major cause of sexual predators' disillusions. These ailing minds need to realize that they are not alone in their thoughts. They should be ashamed and put these deviant sexual thoughts completely out of their heads! These people take life for granted and haven't been taught that life is precious. They may believe that in the end, nothing really matters, and all we do is just dust in the wind.

These people don't have a basic purpose in life. They don't know why they're here on Earth and stumble through life without an understanding of the big picture of our existence. They feel other people's lives are as insignificant as their own and don't think of the ramifications of their acts. They don't expect any consequences for their actions, unless they're caught and prosecuted. These people need to realize life does have a purpose and there is an afterlife, where mankind will be accountable for his or her actions.

Some people believe that there wasn't a pre-existence before we were born, but I believe we all knew each other in what was our "eternal" pre-existence (it must have seemed like it was forever!). The Bible's Jeremiah 1:5 states "Before I formed thee in the womb I knew thee." Also being scientific minded, I believe Einstein when he said, "Energy can be created and its form changed, but once energy is created it can never be destroyed." Maybe we were created in the womb, but once our energy lives as an entity, it can change form, but it can never be destroyed. An afterlife definitely exists!

It's obvious to me that the key to stopping sexual abuse is education. Isn't that crazy? Education is the answer to so many things! Sexual desire has been around since the beginning of time, almost describable as a primitive animal instinct, brought on by certain circumstances that must be controlled by modern-day thought. As our society progresses, animal instinct and nature's primitive desires must be dominated by superior wisdom and knowledge. We aren't animals running around with propagation and feeding being the only thoughts on our minds. There is no place in a modern society for sexual misconduct and abuse, and these sexual offenders must be educated and reformed, or removed from society permanently! If the offender's acts are a result of chemical imbalance rather than an educational problem, castration will most likely be the cure.

A zero-tolerance policy for sexual misconduct is needed immediately! We must swiftly pass new, tougher laws, with hard hitting national campaigns that let the public know we won't tolerate the abuse of our citizens anymore, and any such acts against humanity will result in removal of the problem, permanently. Whether this means the death penalty, removal of their testicles, or permanent removal from our society, these should be the new zero tolerance laws.

We must also rethink our policies on prostitution. Prostitution should be legally available (but not advertised nor advised!). Most big cities have prostitution, legal or not. If sexual predators had a way to release their sexual tensions through legal accessible means, they wouldn't be attacking our daughters and spouses. After researching many different sources, I learned that cities with legal prostitution have 25% fewer sexual crimes than cities where prostitution is limited or unavailable.[3] Wouldn't you much rather have these offenders release their tensions with a willing participant rather than an unwilling victim? Sure, it sounds like the lesser of two evils, but we would be in better condition with legal prostitution rather than what we have now.

Laws against prostitution violate Americans' fundamental rights of individual liberty and personal privacy. Our forefathers envisioned a society where people can live without intrusion from government, provided they don't harm others. We live in a "free" society; the government shouldn't be telling people that they can't charge a fee for a service they otherwise give away free. This issue is comparable to issues like birth control and abortion and involves people's fundamental rights to control their own bodies and decide the best manner to carry out their lives.

Some religious people would say that people shouldn't have sex until they're married. Some people never get married. Does this mean that these people should go their entire lives without having experienced sex?

As mankind progresses, hopefully sooner rather than later, we'll have enough knowledge and morals where this type of behavior will no longer exist. Until then, we must shut this problem down by being more lenient about some controversies, such as monitored and controlled prostitution, and by being stricter about other issues, such as making major sexual crimes punishable by death or castration! If God does cleanse the planet in 2012, these people will surely be among the ones who are eradicated!

Conclusion

The upcoming year of 2012 will usher in many changes. Whether these "apocalyptic" changes are physical, spiritual, or both remain to be seen. We may never discover whether or not the actions we take today save the planet from physical cataclysmic destruction. As evidence to support this statement, I submit that most of the world's population is completely oblivious to the fact that Sister Lucia of Fatima, with help and guidance from the Blessed Virgin Mary, convinced Mikhail Gorbachev of the former Soviet Union to end communism there. She prevented global nuclear war and the destruction of many nations, including the United States (see Chapter 5: Our Lady and the Children of Fatima). If actions we take in the near future *do* save the planet from destruction, after the threat passes, many people will state that there was never anything to worry about to begin with; surely hoards will be completely oblivious to the fact that others saved them from doom and destruction.

Regardless of the outcome of 2012, immediate changes are absolutely necessary, and each and every one of us must ensure we build the best possible future for the world! If the year 2012 (2013 according to Maya elders) passes without any physical earth changes, we will have at least saved ourselves, our future generations, and the planet, and the year will be remembered as a great year of change.

One of the main conclusions that should be reached from reading this book is that we must stop trashing the planet! Most of us will be exterminated as an infestation unless we change our unsustainable, irresponsible ways. Everyone has an obligation to do his or her part. People of the world must stop disposing of garbage and pollutants into our oceans, lakes, rivers, and soil, and quit over-fishing our deteriorating oceans!

If everyone isn't presently recycling everything they can, they must start now! People must take the time to separate their plastics, aluminum cans, glass, metal cans, and paper, and get them to recyclers. If communities don't provide separate pickups for these items, citizens should petition for a change. Our communities must get involved in recycling everything possible! Once people start recycling items rather than disposing of them, they will feel more committed in taking care of the planet and tackling other responsibilities will come easier.

We must contact our state representatives and press for changes. Representatives should enact legislation forcing all manufacturers to create recyclable containers for all their products. Manufacturers must also be forced to quit producing toxic chemicals! If we don't produce these chemicals, we won't ingest them. We must stop all contributions to global warming, no matter what the cost to our economics. What good are economics with a trashed Earth?

Our government is completely out of control and its spending habits have become absolutely unsustainable! We must retake control of our government and let our leaders know that they are not our shepherds. We *can* actually think for ourselves! The government needs to look out for the common people, not the rich who now pay for their lifestyles. *We must replace all politicians who are impeding the world's progress and are presently "doing business as usual!"* Will the representatives that we have elected support the "People's bailout"? If not, they must be replaced! Questioning our state representatives and governors would be a good start!

The time has truly come for "the People's bailout"! Chapter 12: Housing shows that for about the same cost, rather than following through with stimulus packages now proposed, the Commonwealth could paid off the average American's home mortgage and purchase homes for all our country's renters (at a cost of $100,000 per American adult). The chapter also shows that if the plan is implemented, it would *barely* phase the dollar amount of our country's total unfunded obligations and debts, and from a retrospective position five years from now, we would have accomplished this vision for free!

Over 67% of the country's citizens don't live in a home with a clear title. In a nationwide vote, this could be the majority vote needed to change this situation. Many of the 33% of our country's citizens who own clear home titles wouldn't be selfish and greedy and would be more than happy to help other people who haven't been as lucky as they have. It's very possible that more than 85% of Americans would favor an initiative such as this. Eliminating housing expenses for all Americans is the *only* way we will ever escape from the deep economic canyon our government has dug for us! We could also include any American who desires to be a part of this bailout, regardless of whether they have their homes paid off or not, with little change in our country's total unfunded debt.

President Obama's Bipartisan Deficit Reduction Commission, which was formed to study the national deficit and draft a proposal to reduce it, has cowardly recommended cuts in many benefits, hikes in taxes, and raising the minimum age requirement for Social Security eligibility. These politically divisive recommendations aren't the fixes people wanted to hear. Representative Jan Schakowsky, one of the eighteen commission members, told New York Times, "I think every member of the commission would agree that this is not the plan."[3] Financial analysts across the country have stated that the only way the nation will eliminate its debts is by *doubling both taxes and the nation's productivity.* Neither is feasible in this economy. Doubling everyone's taxes, cutting benefits, and extending age eligibility requirements for Social Security aren't the answers. The solution is the People's bailout! After enacting the plan, the nation's productivity *would* double, and we could *then* afford to double the country's tax revenue! We could more than double our tax revenue by both implementing the People's bailout *and* eliminating income tax, changing to a sales tax only (the latter of which other industrialized nations have successfully done)! If people had the choice of doubling their taxes now, *or paying off their homes*, and they knew that paying off their homes would put the country in much better shape now and further ahead in the long run, what would their decision be? You know my opinion!

Many people will believe that the ideas in the second half of this book that pertain to the People's bailout and solving our country's and the world's problems are very virtuous, but are unrealistic. They may think that the radical ideas seem too hard to enact, because many of the wealthy that control the country would be firmly opposed to such changes. Commonly held economic theory holds that most people are selfish, greedy, and uncaring about other people's problems. Others may say that changing the country's ways of exploiting the planet and its resources would hurt our economy.

Sticking with our *unsustainable* ways is unrealistic! The country's finances have plummeted off a cliff into a nearly inescapable chasm, and the trashing of our planet has almost reached a point of no return! Also, the wealthy would benefit from these changes as much as the poor. Unless a person is *extremely* wealthy, he or she needs a good economy to sustain his or her lifestyle. Though some might be afraid of losing their status, wealth, and accomplishments, this could not be further from the truth! With a little compassion and a few unselfish acts (such as paying off the average American's home), we could free everyone from their daily grind, creating massive amounts of extra money and spending that would benefit the rich as well as the poor. Our country's economy is built on spending! If everyone's home were paid off, people would have loads of extra money to spend! *Our economy would blossom!* Wealthy people may actually become wealthier! Which would further the country more: continuing present stimulus plans that we will pay on forever, resulting in little change for the average American, or eliminating housing costs for the average American, *FOREVER?*

The main conclusion that should be reached from the prophecies of 2012, which we have been *privileged* to receive is that these predictions were intended to create awareness and change. Warnings must be heeded and alterations made in order to prevent the gloomy foreseen timeline from occurring. It has been clearly shown that there are two paths mankind can travel. Many prophecies in this book have been painstakingly passed down *for thousands of years*, so that we might see these two possible futures and make the changes necessary to obtain the correct result. The Maya have foretold the outcome of December 21, 2012, for more than 5,000 years!

These predictions were given to us in order to convince us to change our current path of greed, selfishness, and destruction. We are meant to pave a new path that leads the world to paradise and peace for a thousand years. I pray to God that we will have the courage to make these changes, which will start with everyone realizing the magnitude of the scientific and historical evidence presented in many of this book's chapters, along with common sense in others, which show astonishing track records of psychics and ancient civilizations throughout the centuries who have given us warnings of events to occur in 2012 (or 2013). These prophecies were meant to awaken us to the realization that we must change our thoughtless ways, *now!* We must also understand that overpopulation of Earth is overburdening our planet's resources and overstressing our societies. These dire problems must be dealt with *immediately*!

We have trashed the planet! We are exterminating ecosystems around the world, resulting in the depletion and extinction of many of Earth's species. Scientists say more than two thirds of the species of plants and animals around the world will be extinct by the year 2100, and that we will soon pass a tipping point—a point of no return—where the destruction that we have caused to the planet will be *irreversible!* Humans are becoming more of a destructive force to the planet than any comet or asteroid collision of the past (Earth has recovered from them, but it may not survive the damage we are inflicting upon it)! The planet has evolved for *millions* of years, and we have almost destroyed it in less than a century! We must immediately stop all irresponsible actions against our planet, or a higher power will force us to do so!

After researching the different aspects of the upcoming date of December 21, 2012, my belief is that *civilization as we know it will not end on this day.* The date may only be a reference point that has been given to us in order to draw our attention to this time period. Everyone must realize that the Sun started its transit through the Galactic equator in 1980 and will travel through the Galactic equator for a total of 36 years. In my opinion, the world won't be clear of destruction until after the year 2016. At this time, our transitional "cleansing" period will have passed and a new age will have begun for the world. If I had to pick the exact date for an "apocalyptic" event to occur, the end of days *or a new beginning* (the latter of which I envision), I would listen to the words of Maya elders, who say that "judgment day" will occur on March 31, 2013.

Maya elder Don Alejandro Cirilo Perez Oxlaj, head of the National Council of Elders of Guatemala, has been sent as a messenger from the council of elders to warn the world that we must change the way we live and take care of Earth if we're to avert our self-destruction. He stated:

Now let's speak about the future. We, the traditional Maya elders, and all indigenous peoples in the world, meditate on the future. We don't think only for today, the present, we think for tomorrow for our children, grand children, and future generations. We see a dark shadow approaching, a shadow that will cause a lot of harm. It is the great contamination. All this is due to manâs creation. We are digging our own graves. On March 31, 2013, the Sun will be hidden for a period of 60-70 hours and this is when we shall enter the period of the Fifth Sun. Then you will realize that what the Maya speak are facts and not false preaching.[1]

This is an extremely bold declaration. Knowing its origination should make us very leery of this date. Sixty to seventy hours is a long time for the Sun's rays to be "hidden." Could this be caused by an approaching asteroid or a galactic super wave? Complex changes inside the Sun as it experiences its upcoming solar flare cycle could also cause a darkening of the Sun.

Our planet is now in an "out-of-balance state" and will remain so until it nears the Great Galactic Alignment's end. If we had the capability to test the strength of the gravitational fields of the other planets in our solar system, we would find that their fields have weakened also. Exactly how long Earth's out-of-balance state will last is unknown. At any time during the out-of-balance state, Earth could be hit by solar flares, a comet, an asteroid, a galactic super wave, or any combination of the four, which could easily burn one third of Earth's surface and possibly cause a reversal of its poles.

On August 1, 2010, almost the entire Earth-facing side of the Sun erupted in a tumult of activity. NASA scientists observed a 28-hour period of shock waves, gigantic solar flare explosions (including a C-3 class solar flare), multiple filaments of magnetism lifting off the stellar surface, a large-scale shaking of the solar corona, a coronal mass ejection, and a solar "tsunami" that shook the Sun. They have named the event "The Great Eruption."[4] Scientists say the activity is an omen that the Sun is "waking up" and heading for another "solar maximum" cycle in 2013. And so the fun begins!

Now that the Sun is waking up, we must do the same. Another sign has recently been presented to us, a precursor of what we are to witness in 2012, if not sooner. On March 11, 2011, Japan's earthquake and tsunami gave us live pictures from a *real* 2012 movie. The horror and reality of their situation has taken time to sink into our minds. As I viewed more and more video footage of the catastrophe, all I could say is "Oh my Lord..... Lord, please help us!

Edgar Cayce predicted that the beginning of our planet's earth changes (in the end of days) would start with major changes in the South Sea (China, Japan). He stated that "the greater part of Japan must go into the sea." After seeing this prophecy come to pass, I'm starting to envision the destruction that Cayce foresaw for America and Europe. It will be very hard for many people to admit the fact that destruction far beyond what we have seen in Japan could soon happen to us, but the sooner we accept the possibility, the better off we will be. The question then arises, "How far do we go?" *Storage of food, water, medicine, and supplies would be a good start!*

The world can learn many lessons from Japan's disaster. First, we must admit that many predictions concerning the events of the year 2012 are coming to life. We must also learn from the Japanese people. If such a tragedy happened in our country, would our citizens show the resolve that the Japanese have, or would our country fall into chaos? We haven't seen any videos from Japan of looting or pillaging, only frightened and caring people. Grocery store shelves were empty, but there weren't any riots. Let's hope the rest of the world would act similar in the same circumstances.

One of the most valuable lessons that the world should gain from this nightmare is that nuclear reactors around the globe aren't as safe as we believed them to be. As I stated in this book's chapter on nuclear power, just because nuclear power sites reside on dry land now, doesn't mean that they will stay dry in 2012. Two nuclear meltdowns occurred in Japan after several of their nuclear power plants were submerged by tsunami flood waters. We must eliminate all nuclear threats before December 2012, including shutting down all nuclear plants and eliminating all nuclear warheads and missiles!

The Hopi say that global nuclear war could also occur in the end of days. As I envisioned variations of this book's cover image, I debated between painting an asteroid, comet, solar flare, or super wave approaching Earth, or painting the site of a nuclear explosion. I decided to paint my worst fear, global nuclear war. The world could more easily recover from the other disasters. Imagining the horrors of Hiroshima and Nagasaki (described in Chapter 22: Nuclear Power and Nuclear Weapons) on a global scale is enough to make anyone ill. We may not have the capability to avert global destruction caused by natural forces, but we can prevent global nuclear devastation.

Sometime during the next few years, nuclear war could break out between Iran and Israel. If so, Iran will be destroyed, as foretold in the Dead Sea Scrolls and many Bible codes. North Korea may receive the same fate unless they correct their human rights issues. I'm not sure if the United States will be involved with these wars, or whether nuclear war will encompass the globe, but the Hopi say it's a possibility that can be averted. On September 17, 2010, headlines read, "Russia: We will provide Syria with advanced missiles despite Israel, U.S. protests." Other recent headlines from ABC News on October 20, 2010, say our government believes that Venezuela has the right to Russian nuclear aid. Venezuela's leader, Hugo Chavez, was recently photographed making an alliance with the Iranian president, President Ahmadinejad. The two are joining so that they might "change the world order." Many people believe that the Bible's book of Ezekiel (Chapter 38-39) speaks of battles in the end of days when the righteous people of the world will defeat an alliance between Russia and various Arab nations. Nuclear war *and* a pole shift in 2012 would absolutely devastate the planet!

If a pole reversal of Earth occurs, regardless of its cause, Earth's crust will rotate around the core of the planet. Earthquakes with magnitudes beyond comprehension will rock every continent. Cities and mountains will be leveled as our planet physically turns upside down. Earth's plates will shift, large areas of land will fall into the seas, and other landmasses will appear from beneath the oceans. Volcanoes and super volcanoes will erupt, tidal waves will slam the shores of all countries, and no land will be unscathed. We must also realize that the Yellowstone super volcano could blow at any time, independent of any asteroid, comet, or solar flare impact. To *preview* the disaster scenarios that could happen in the next few years, watch Roland Emmerich's block buster movie *2012*. The special effects are amazing!

Survival of the initial physical pole reversal would depend upon a person's location. Living in higher elevations away from the coasts, the Mississippi River, and the Great Lakes would result in a better chance of survival. Areas of high volcanic activity, such as Hawaii and Yellowstone Park should be avoided. If you haven't yet looked on the Internet for an image of Stan Deyo's future map of the United States, *Hopi Sea Level*, and you're concerned about your location, take a quick look. The map is *very* impressive! The map's web-site is listed in this book's notes.[2]

After Earth's poles reverse and the planet stabilizes, Earth would then rotate in the opposite direction (it would spin in the same direction, but its orientation to the solar system would be reversed and upside-down; the Sun would rise in the West rather than the East). The atmosphere would be filled with debris, which would block the Sun's rays and plunge us into several months of winter. A two-year reserve of food, medicine, supplies, and other essentials such as a heat source for cooking and heating would be required to survive until civilization restructured itself. Many areas of the United States would become central areas of rebuilding, including lands of the Hopi Indians.

It may be that Earth's pole shift (and the eruption of the Yellowstone super volcano) is inevitable and that a higher power will prevent any further destruction, but mankind's actions in the next two years will be the primary determinant of our future living conditions. The only "entity" that can stop the devastation meant to cleanse the planet will be a higher power, which will prevent ruin, *if* we do indeed change our "evil" ways.

Our technologies are now progressing at very high rates. We will have advanced further in the next ten years than we have in the previous 200 years. As these technologies develop, we must take care of our planet. New technologies must function in harmony with the ecosystems of Earth. Fifty years from now, human intelligence levels and our New Age morals, ethics, and standards will make today's times seem like the dark ages. Greed and selfishness will no longer exist. Wars, crime, and violence will be a thing of the past. There will be no homeless or hungry. *Everyone will rise in the morning with a positive attitude, eager to do their part to better the world!* Families will be secure in the knowledge that housing and health care are provided. New technologies will make all jobs and careers enjoyable with plenty of assistance available for every undertaking. Having more material possessions than everyone else will no longer be glamorized and everyone will have the minimal essentials necessary for comfortable lifestyles.

All governments will be controlled by their people, rather than the people being controlled by their government. Human rights will be equally realized for everyone around the world. Segregation and country borders will cease to exist after population growth is well under control. The population of Earth will be less than half of today's numbers; mankind will have finally realized that population growth can't continue forever. The rebuilding of our Earth's atmosphere and ecosystems will be complete, the consciousness of the planet having been awakened and put to good use. These visions may be 50 years away, but Americans can make them realities much sooner. In order to do so, we must band together and make our voices heard.

People who are very religious constitute over 70% of the country's population, and most others at least believe in God or some type of higher power. All these people must join hands and eradicate the "evils" of the world. Christians know deep inside their hearts that greed, selfishness, and materialism are condemnable morals and are the "evils" we must all work on eliminating in our daily lives. Jesus taught that everyone should help the less fortunate as themselves so that someday greed and selfishness will no longer exist.

The Bible says that in the end of days, God will vanquish the devil and evil once and for all, eliminating all the evil ways of the world, and an army of 200 million led by Jesus will fight the last battle against evil. This eradication of evil and the devil *symbolizes* the changes Americans will make in the world in the next few years, evolving from our selfish, primitive, "evil" ways to a path that leads to spiritual enlightenment, happiness, contentment, and paradise. The army of 200 million is our country's work force of 200 million, and led by Jesus' teachings we shall eradicate all "evils" from the world, such as poverty, greed, and homelessness!

Americans must now lead the way to eliminate selfishness from our societies. We must immediately solve our country's problems so that we can then tackle the problems of the world. With everyone working together for the benefit of mankind, our new policies of no poverty, homelessness, or hunger shall rock and change the world (rather than a pole shift of Earth)!

One principal factor in making these necessary changes is our support for our president, President Barack Obama. Throughout history, the president of the United States has held considerable power to influence the world's politics. President Obama has his work cut out for him with many self-promoting politicians backed by greedy corporations fighting his every move. Americans across the nation must stand up with the President and show our politicians (Republicans and Democrats alike) that we want massive change now! Most citizens' opinions are more in line with President Obama's views than many people believe. We must stand by him as he introduces any ideas to better the lives of the common person.

The word "apocalypse" means a disclosure *to certain privileged persons* of something hidden from the majority of mankind. If the cleansing of Earth and the destruction of civilization is to be averted, we must pass on the information we have been privileged to receive to everyone possible. Please help me do so in the hopes of reawakening humanity and changing our current path to self-destruction!

I can't stress enough that the first step in saving the world is fixing the country's economy by implementing the People's housing bailout. If every American who believes that enacting this system would repair the economy (and everyone's outlook on life) united and spread the word to their family and friends, we could quickly make home ownership a reality for every American adult, rather than just an American dream! Other countries in the same financial trouble as the United States could also implement the People's bailout to fix their economies. How long it takes for each adult across the nation (and around the world?) to receive their check for the People's bailout is up to us. Please help pass this book's information to friends and family as soon as possible! Many people deserve tears of joy from paying off their homes, purchasing homes, or receiving "extreme home makeovers," and they all deserve them, *now!*

Changing our destructive, greedy, and selfish ways will determine the outcome of the future. Which of the two paths we travel is our choice. We can continue on our current path of self-annihilation or change direction to the path that leads to world peace and living in harmony with the planet. Two paths, one future, which shall we choose? With big changes in our moral standards and our ways of thinking, we *can* save the world!

One of Nostradamus' quatrains gives us hope that mankind can change. According to the prophet, in order to transform the world, we must expel "the cunning ones." The cunning ones are many of our politicians who are currently "doing business as usual," and they will impede the country's economic recovery unless they are replaced. 2012 will be a great year of change, including major changes in our government. The quatrain reads:

The transformation will be very difficult.
Cities and provinces will gain by the changes,
Their hearts held high, prudence reestablished,
The cunning ones expelled.
The sea, the land restored, as human harmony awakens.

Lyrics from Led Zeppelin's legendary song *Stairway to Heaven* say it all:

And a new day will dawn,
For those who stand long,
And the forests will echo with laughter!
Yes, there are two paths you can go by,
But in the long run,
There's still time to change the road you're on!
Dear lady can you hear the wind blow,
And did you know,
Your stairway lies on the whispering wind!

About the Author

They call me Bruce. I live near the Grand Tetons and Yellowstone National Park with my lovely wife, three children, a cat, a dog, and a demanding guinea pig that answers to the name Pepe. We spend a lot of time in Hawaii; I love painting Hawaiian scenery. My dream has forever been to move there permanently, but the kids have always had other plans. With all its volcanic activity, Hawaii may not be the best place to live in 2012 (or 2013?).

In the last 25 years, I've created five successful businesses, most of which operated simultaneously. I owner contracted all of their properties, remodeled the buildings to suit the business' needs, designed and painted their signs, and now manage all daily business, advertising, book keeping, and deal with all of the problems and obstacles that arise. Two of my businesses were luxury businesses, which collapsed with the Twin Towers. Since 9/11, my other businesses' profits have slowly declined with the economy.

I am *absolutely* fed up with the failing economy, the state of the world today, and the government's inability to solve the country's problems. I constantly hear people gripe about the injustices that most of us endure, but I don't hear any solutions. That's where this book enters the picture!

I wrote *Two Paths* in order to lead Americans down a new path and to supply logical solutions to resolve the country's problems, so that everyone might live the American dream, rather than the nightmares that many of us face daily.

BIBLIOGRAPHY

-Arguelles, José. The Mayan Factor: Path beyond Technology. Santa Fe, New Mexico: Bear & Co., 1987.

-Bauval, Robert. and Gilbert, Adrian. The Orion Mystery: Unlocking the Secrets of the Pyramids. London: Mandarin, 1995.

-Browne, Sylvia. End Of Days: Predictions and Prophecies about the End of the World. New York: Penguin Books, 2008.

-Cheetham, Erica. The Prophecies of Nostradamus. New York: Perigee / Wideview Books, 1973.

-Cheetham, Erica. The Final Prophecies of Nostradamus. New York; Perigee Books, 1989.

-Coe, Michael D. The Maya. London: Thames and Hudson, 1996.

-Drosnin, Michael. The Bible Code. London: Weidenfeld and Nicholson, 2002.

-Geryl, Patrick, and Gino Ratinckx. The Orion Prophecy: Will the World Be Destroyed in 2012? Kempton, Illinois: Adventures Unlimited Press, 2001.

-Geryl, Patrick. How to Survive 2012: Tactics and Survival Places for the Coming Pole Shift. Kempton, Illinois: Adventures Unlimited Press, 2007.

-Hogue, John. Nostradamus and the Millennium: Predictions of the Future. Garden City, New York: Dolphin / Doubleday, 1987.

-Hogue, John. Nostradamus: The Complete Prophecies. Shaftesbury, England: Element Books LTD, 1997.

-Jenkins, John Major. Galactic Alignment: The Transformation of Consciousness According to Mayan, Egyptian, and Vedic Traditions. Rochester, Vermont: Bear & Co., 2002.

-Jenkins, John Major. Maya Cosmogenesis 2012: The True Meaning of the Maya Calendar End Date. Santa Fe, New Mexico: Bear & Co., 1998.

-LaViolette, Paul. The Earth under Fire: Humanity's Survival of the Apocalypse. New York: Starlane Publications, 1997.

-Mardyks, Raymond, and Alana-Leah, Stacia. Maya Calendar: Voice of the Galaxy. Sedona, Arizona: Star Heart Publications, 1999.

-Missler, Chuck. Cosmic Codes: Hidden Messages from the Edge of Eternity. Coeur de Alene: Koinonia House, 2004.

-Parker, Julia and Derek. Parker's Astrology: The Essential Guide to Using Astrology in Your Daily Life. New York: Dorling Kindersley, 1991.

-Shak, Moshe. Bible Code's Breakthrough: Amazing Matrices. 2004.

-Stray, Geoff. Beyond 2012: Catastrophe or Awakening? Rochester, Vermont: Bear & Co., 2009.

-Waters, Frank. The Book of the Hopi. New York: Ballantine Books, Inc. 1963.

NOTES

PART 1

THE 2012 PHENOMENON

(1) - Phillips, Tony. <u>NASA Solar Storm Warning 2012 - Solar Maximum</u>.
http://www.2012supplies.com/what_is_2012/solar_maxim.html
- NASA 2012 Sun solar flare predictions
(2) - <u>Solar Flares May Pack a Bigger Punch</u>.
http//agonist.org/20060307/solar_flares_may_pack_a_bigger_punch
- Solar flare predictions
(3) - Shiga, David. Major Solar Storm Could Cause Lasting Damage.
<u>New Scientist</u>. 12 Jan 2009.
- Solar flare activity - magazine article
(4) - <u>Earthquake Hazards Program</u>. U.S. Geological Survey.
http://earthquake.usgs.gov/earthquakes/recenteqsww/
- Recent earthquake information
(5) - <u>2012: Countdown to Armageddon</u>. National Geographic.
http://channel.nationalgeographic.com/episode/2012-countdown-to-armageddon-4438/meet-the-expert-maloof
- Princeton University pole shift studies
(6) - Unsolved Mysteries. I researched this episode to no avail, television episodes over 20 years old are apparently hard to find. If anyone has any information on this episode or its characters, please contact me. I would love to find copies of these original maps.

(7) - Deyo, Stan. "Hopi" Sea Level. http://www.millennium-ark.net/news/07_prophecy/070207.hopi_sea_level.html
- Future map of the United States
(8) - Phillips, Tony Dr. Solar Storm Warning. NASA.
http//science.nasa.gov/science-news/science-at-nasa/2006/10mar_stormwarning/
- Solar Flares to be a doozey

Chapter 1- Earth's Decreasing Magnetic Field

(1) - The South Atlantic Anomaly. NASA, Atmospheric Science Data Center.
http://eosweb.larc.nasa.gov/hpdocs/misr/misr_html/darkmap.html
- The South Atlantic Anomaly
(2) - Magnetic Storm. NOVA.
http://www.pbs.org/wgbh/nova/magnetic/reversals.html
- Professor Gary Glatzmaier
(3) - Sington, David. Magnetic storm.
http://www.pbs.org/wgbh/nova/transcripts/3016_magnetic.html
- Clay pot magnetite studies
(4) - Researcher Jeremy Bloxham. Harvard Science.
http://www.harvardscience.harvard.edu/director/researchers/jeremy-bloxham
- Professor Jeremy Bloxham
(5) - Snelling, Andrew A. Fossil Magnetism Reveals Rapid Reversals of the Earth's Magnetic Field.
http://www.answersingenesis.org/creation/v13/13/fossil.asp
- Lava flow magnetite studies
(6) - KSPT Contract with European Space Agency on Swarm. Kongsberg, World Class.
http://www.spacetech.no/news_store/kspt-contract-with-european-space-agency-on-swarm
 - European Space Agency
(7) - Johnson, Kimberly. Earth's Core, Magnetic Field Changing Fast, Study Says.

http://news.nationalgeographic.com/news/PF/76158139.html
- Professor Nils Olson - Danish National Space Center

Chapter 2- Prophecies of Edgar Cayce

(1) - Edgar Cayce's A.R.E. Association for Research and
Enlightenment. http://www.edgarcayce.org/
(2) - "The Other Nostradamus". Decoding the Past. Mathilde Bittner.
Harlan Saperstein.
- John Hogue, Dale Beyerstein, Mark Thurston. The History Channel.
28 Nov 2005.
(3) - Exodus 2006, Bible Codes and the End Times.
http://exodus2006.com/
(4) - Morgana's Observatory. Edgar Cayce Earth Changes
http://www.dreamscape.com/morgana/index.htm
-Predictions

Chapter 3- Prophecies of the Hopi Indians

(1) - Browne, Sylvia and Waters, Frank. (see books)
- Reverend David Young and White Feather prophecies
(2) - Allen, Nick. Al Gore 'Profiting' From Climate Change Agenda.
http://www.telegraph.co.uk/earth/environment/climatechange/64
96196/Al-Gore-profiting-from-climate-change-agenda.html
(3) – Native American Names. Spotted Wolf's Corner.
http://www.snowwowl.com/swolfNAnamesandmeanings2.html
-Meaning of Pahana
(4) – Jordan, Robert. Seven Spokes: A Wheel of Time Chronology.
http://www.sevenspokes.com/chronology/creation.html
- Seven spoke Wheel of Time

Chapter 4- The Bible Codes

(1) - Witztum, Doron; Rips, Eliyahu; and Rosenberg, Yoav.
Equidistant Letter Sequences In the Book of Genesis. Statistical

Science. May 1999:
http://www.math.washington.edu/~greenber/biblecode.html/
- Article in Statistical Science Magazine
(2) - Torah Code Info. Endtime Ministries, Christian Resource Center.
http://www.despatch.cth.com.au/ articles_v/torah_extracts.htm
#official
- Public statements - Witztum, Rips, and Gans
(3) - Exodus 2006, Bible Codes and the End Times.
http://exodus2006.com/
- Bible code authors
- LOrd KyrON -Juan of Spain - Bible Code Researcher
- Fabrice Bect -France- Bible Code Researcher
(4) - "The Bible Code: Predicting Armageddon". History's Mysteries.
Danny Gold and Matthew Asner. Harlan Saperstein. Brendan McKay,
Eliyahu Rips, Mordechai Gafini, Art Levitt, Professor M. Maralick, Roy
A. Reinhold. History Channel. 13 Sept 2003.
(5) - "The Bible Codes II: Apocalypse and Beyond". History's
Mysteries. Danny Gold and Matthew Asner. Harlan Saperstein. (cast
listed below) History Channel. April 2004.
- Chaim Ber Michoel Dov Weismandel
- Eliyahu Rips -Professor at Hebrew University, Jerusalem
- Doron Witztum -Physicist - Jerusalem College of Technology
- Yoav Rosenberg -Jerusalem College of Technology
- Harold Gans -Former Senior Math. Cryptologist for the U.S. Gov.
Dept. of Defense
- Professor Brendan McKay -Department of Computer Science at the
Australian National University
- Moshe Shak - Author of "The Bible Code Breakthrough"
(6) - Missler, Chuck. Meaning of Names in Genesis 5.
http://www.khouse.org/articles/2000/284/
 - Names in Genesis
 (7) - Greene, Susan and Briggs, Bill. Carnage Puts Spotlight on
Trench Coat Mafia. http://www.pulitzer.org/archieves/6296
- Columbine massacre

Chapter 5- Our Lady and the Children of Fatima

(1) - De Marchi, John. "The True Story of Fatima". Catechetical Guild. 1952. Page 147.
- Article concerning statement from Avelino de Almeida
(2) - De Marchi, John. "The True Story of Fatima". Catechetical Guild. 1952. Page 144.
- Article concerning statement from Dr. Domingos Pinto Coelho
(3) - The Fatima Prophecies - Three Secrets of Fatima. Unexplained Mysteries. http://theunexplainedmysteries.com/fatima-prophecies.html
- Story and quotes of Sister Lucia and Fatima
(4) - The Abdication of Nicholas II.
http://wwi.lib.byu.edu/index.php/The_Abdication_of_Nicholas_II
- Facts on Czar Nicholas II
(5) - "Fatima Secrets Unveiled". History's Mysteries. Matthew Asner and Danny Gold. Harlan Sapperstein. Suaann Finnka, David Ackroyd, Father Nicholas Gruner, Mary Kriz, Dr. Joe Nickell, Father Michael Hearst. The History Channel. 13 June 01.

Chapter 6- Prophecies of the Maya and the Egyptians

(1) - Jenkins, John Major. Mayan mysteries.
http://www.newdawnmagazine.com/article/mayan_mysteries_galactic_alignments.html
- Joseph Goodman - Maya researcher 1891
(2) - Sanction News. The Truth about 2012.
http://www.allvoices.com/contributed-news/5870005-the-truth-behind-2012
- Maud Worcestor Makemson
(3) - Rohl, David. "The Mountain of the Arc". The Daily Express. 13 Mar 1999.
- newspaper article concerning evidence of the great flood of Noah's day
(4) - Lost King of the Maya. Nova. Feb 2001.

http://www.pbs.org/wgbh/nova/maya/copan.html
- David Stewart -Mayan scholar
(5) - <u>2012 Information</u>. Project Camelot. 7 Aug 2008.
http://2012info.ca/articles/?p=34
- Don Alejandro, Wondering Wolf prophecies
(6) - <u>Solar System Dynamics</u>. The Jet Propulsion Laboratory, NASA,
California Institute of Technology. http://ssd.jpl.nasa.gov/sedb.cgi?=
99942
- Discoverers of Apophis
(7) - <u>Predicting Apophis' Encounters in 2029 and 2036</u>. Near Earth
Object Program, NASA. http://neo.jpl.nasa.gov/apophis/
(8) - <u>The Kolbrin Bible.</u>
http://graceheart.stormloader.com/kolbrinExcerpt.pdf.
- Descriptions of the Destroyer

Chapter 7- The Roman Oracle: Sibyl

(1) - <u>Sibylline Oracles</u>. New Advent.
http://www.newadvent.org/cathen/13770a/htm
- History of the Sibyls
(2) - "Doomsday 2012: The End of Days." <u>Decoding the Past</u>. Jeff
Schiro. Phil Crowley. Daniel Pinchbeck, Lauren Mora, R.J. Stewart,
Jason Boyett. The History Channel. 2007.
- Sibyl Predictions and history

Chapter 8- The Lost Book of Nostradamus

(1) - "Lost Book of Nostradamus". Kreg Lauterbach. James Lurie.
Vincent Bridges. History Channel. 28 Oct 2007.
- Enza Massa
(2) - Crystal, Ellie. <u>The Lost Book of Nostradamus</u>.
http://www.crystalinks.com/lostbookofnostradamus.html
- Burning tower image
(3) – Smelyakov, Sergey and Karpenko, Yuri. <u>The Auric Time Scale &
the Mayan Factor.</u>

http://cura.free.fr/xx/20smely2.html
-Spiral bifurcation points

<u>Chapter 9- Prophecies of the Book of Revelation</u>

(1) - "Seven Signs of the Apocalypse". Tim Prokop. Joe Falasca. Jon Barton, Alina Dorian, Armand Dorian. History Channel. 5 Jan 2009.
(2) - Deventer, Jack Van. <u>The Dispensational Origins of Modern Premillennialism and John Nelson Darby</u>. http://www.sullivan-county.com/news/cathouse/darby.htm
- John Nelson Darby, the Rapture
(3) - Brehm, William D. <u>When Will Jesus Come Again?</u>. Bread upon the Waters Ministry.
http://www.be-ready.org/when.html
- Book of Daniel Prophecies, date of end of days
(4) - The Dome of the Rock was built on the Temple Mount in 691A.D. There was another mosque built on the Temple Mount before the Dome. It's been calculated that its year of construction was 677A.D. If we use the later date of 691A.D. for our reference date for "the time that the daily sacrifice shall be taken away," this would put the end of days to occur in 2026, and not in 2012, but using this later date as a reference doesn't correlate. Using this date, the Six-Day War of June 1967, in which Israel recaptured Jerusalem from the Jordanians, wouldn't have occurred until 14 years later in 1981. Since we know that Israel indeed took control of Jerusalem in 1967, and not in 1981, the 677A.D. construction date and 2012 end date seem to be more accurate.
(5) - "Armageddon Battle Plan". <u>Nostradamus Effect.</u> Luke Ellis. Phil Crowley. Michael Baigent, Azzen Yadin, Ken Spiro, Robert Eisenman. History Channel. 9 Dec 2009.
(6) – Holden, Michael. <u>God Did Not Create the Universe, Says Hawking.</u>
http://news.yahoo.com/s/nm/20100902/lf_nm_life/us_britain_hawking
-God creating the Universe

<u>PART 2</u>

<u>Introduction</u>

(1) - Morgana's Observatory. Edgar Cayce Earth Changes
http://www.dreamscape.com/morgana/index.htm
-Predictions

<u>Chapter 10- President Barack Obama</u>

(1) - Cook, Philip J. And Ludwig, Jens. <u>Guns in America: National
Survey on Private Ownership and Use of Firearms</u>.
http://www.smallarmssurvey.org/files/portal/issueareas/victims/
victims_pdf_/1997_cook_ludwig.pdf
- Gun survey statistics
(2) - Walther, Harry Pastor. <u>Satan's Rapture</u>. The Church of
Philadelphia. http://www.satansrapture.com/obama.htm
- Bible code predictions of assassination attempts on Obama
(3) - <u>Obama Assassination Attempt</u>. Mahalo.
http://www.mahalo.com/obama-assassination-threat

<u>Chapter 11- The Economy</u>

(1) - "America the Story of Us". The History Channel. 2008.
- 2008 Stock market crash with comparisons to 1929 crash
(2) - Villarreal, Pamela. <u>Social Security and Medicare Projections:
2009</u>. http://www.ncpa.org/pub/ba662
- Total unfunded debt figures for United States
(3) - Goldman, David. <u>CNNMoney.com's Bailout Tracker</u>.
http://moneycnn.com/news/storysupplement/economy/bailouttra
cker/
- Final bailout costs plus stimulus money
(4) - <u>U.S. Debt Clock</u>. http://www.usdebtclock.org/index.html

(5) - Haberman, Maggie. "Oh, No! Debt Ceiling Soars As Dow Sinks". New York Post. 5 Feb 2010.
- New debt ceiling information

(6) - DeNavas-Walt, Carmen; Proctor, Bernadette D.; Smith, Jessica C., Income, Poverty, and Health Insurance Coverage in the United States': 2008. U.S. Census Bureau.
http://www.census.gov/prod/2009pubs/P60-236.pdf
- Government statistics on income levels

(7) - "Seven Deadly Sins". Tim Evans. History Channel. 2008.
- Yerkes Institute of Atlanta - Capuchin monkey studies
- Jessica Tracy - authentic and hubristic pride
- Laurie Santos - Yale University Capuchin monkey studies

(8) - Sins, Seven Deadly Sins. Bible Information.
http://www.bibleinfo.com/en/content/what-are-seven-deadly-sins
- Pope Gregory's seven deadly sins

(9) - Miqz, Pete. US Consumer Spending – The Growth Rate on Consumer Spending. http://ecinearticles.com/?us-consumer-spending-the-growth-rate-report- on-consumer-spending&id=4512320
- Spending percentage of the economy

(10) - Thera, Nyanaponika. The Roots of Good and Evil.
http://www.buddhanet.net/pdf_file/roots_goodevil.pdf
- Lao Tzu saying

(11) - Aristotle.
http://philosophy.ucdavis.edu/mattey/phii001/arietlec.htm
- Aristotle saying

(12) - Luby, Bill. VIX Drops 30% in Five Days for Eighth Time in 19 Years. http://www.dailymarkets.com/stocks/2008/12/01/vix-drops-30-in-five-days-for-eight-times-in-19-years/
- Declining stock markets

(13) - Foreclosures Jump 55% in July. CBS News.
http://cbs3.com/national/foreclosure.rate.doubles.2.794775.html
- Home foreclosures

(14) -Pendell, Aaron D. Herbert Hoover's Legacy.
http://american.historysuite101.com/article.cfm/hoover_and_the_d

epression
- Andrew Mellon
(15) - Bierman, Harold Jr. <u>The 1929 Stock Market Crash</u>.
http://eh.net/encyclopedia/article/bierman.crash
- Stock market bubble
(16) - <u>Report: Home Values Drop 30%</u>. Sacramento Business Journal.
http://www.dotbiz
journals.com/Sacramento/stories/2008/05/daily46.html
- Housing values
(17) - <u>Wal-Mart Reports Fourth Quarter and Fiscal Year 2010
Results.</u> Trading Markets.
http://www.tradingmarkets.com/news/press-
release/wmt_walmart-reports-fourth-quarter-and-fiscal-year-2010-
results-785718.html
- Wal-Mart profit figures
(18) - Ruffing, Kathy; Cox, Chris; Horny, James. <u>The Right Target:
Stabilize the Federal Debt.</u> http://www.cbpp.org/files/01-12-
10bud.pdf
- Medicare costs expand
(19) - <u>Fact Sheet, Medicare, Social Security Financial Status.</u>
Republican Caucus – The Committee on the Budget.
http://house.gov/budget_republicans/press/2007/pr20080325med
ss.pdf
- Revenue projections
(20) - Chantrill, Christopher. <u>Budgeted US Federal Deficit Current –
Historical – As Percentage GDP</u>.
http://www.usgovernmentspending.com/us_deficit
- GPD comparisons
(21) - Bell, Shannon. <u>Rasmussen Poll: Capitalism Versus Socialism,
50% Prefer Capitalism.</u> http://www.rightpundits.com/?p= 3699
- Polls for socialism and capitalism
 (22) - <u>Income, Poverty, and Health Insurance Coverage in the United
States.</u> U.S. Census Bureau.
http://www.census.gov/prod/2009pubs/p60-236.pdf
- Average American incomes

(23) - <u>Labor Force Statistics from the Current Population Survey.</u> Bureau of Labor Statistics – US Department of Labor. http://www.bls.gov/cps/
- Jobless rates in the United States

(24) - Kyl, Jon. <u>More Government Spending, More Debt Means Less For Tomorrow.</u> http://www.nationalledger.com/cgi-bin/artman/exec/view.cgi?archive=43&num=28945
- National debt will double then triple

(25) - <u>US Forecast 2010.</u> Institute for Economic Competitiveness – University of Central Florida. http://issuu.com/ucfbusiness/docs/usforecast_feb10
- GPD comparisons from 1940 to today

(26) – Ritchie, Joshua. <u>The Financial Burden of the Penny.</u> http://www.mint.com/blog/trends/penny-cost-to-make-06212010/
-Cost of making coins

Chapter 12- Housing

(1) - Goldman, David. <u>CNNMoney.com's Bailout Tracker</u>. http://moneycnn.com/news/storysupplement/economy/bailouttracker/
- Final bailout costs plus stimulus money

(2) - <u>Housing Vacancies and Homeownership (CPS/HVS)</u>. U.S. Census Bureau. http://www.census.gov/hhes/www/housing/hvs/annual08/ann08ind.html
- Government statistics on housing

(3) - "United States: Age and Sex". *2007 American Community Survey One Year Estimate*. United States Census Bureau. Retrieved January 10, 2009.

(4) - <u>Home Mortgage Rates.</u> Mortgage Calculator. http://www.mortgagecalculator.org/mortgage-rates/maryland.php
- Average Home Value in U.S.

(5) - <u>34 Banks Fail in 2009: Bank United Collapses.</u> Rediff Business.

http://business.rediff.com/report/2009/may/22/bcrisis-34-us-banks-fail-in-2009.htm
- Number of collapsed banks since 2008
(6) - Boorstein, Michelle. *Americans May Be More Religious Than They Realize.* http://www.washingtonpost.com/wp-dyn/content/article/2006/09/11/AR2006091100459.html
- Number of religious people in the U.S.
(7) - <u>Mankind Using Earth's Resources At Alarming Rate.</u> France 24. http://www.france24.com/en/node/4932275http://www.france24.com/en/node/4932275
- Mankind using Earth's resources at alarming rates
(8) - <u>U.S. Debt Clock.</u> http://www.usdebtclock.org/index.html
- Total Unfunded Obligations per U.S. citizen
(9) - <u>How to Own Your Home Years Sooner.</u> The Mortgage Revolt. http://www.thegreatmortgagerevolt.com/01/13/how-to-own-your-home-years-sooner/
(10) - <u>Stoeppelwerth, Walt.</u> Markup Redux. http://www.remodeling.hw.net/markup/markup-redux.aspx
- Contractor's markup rates
(11) - DeNavas-Walt, Carmen; Proctor, Bernadette D.; Smith, Jessica C., <u>Income, Poverty, and Health Insurance Coverage in the United States': 2008.</u> U.S. Census Bureau. http://www.census.gov/prod/2009pubs/P60-236.pdf
- Government statistics on income levels

<u>Chapter 13- Health Care</u>

(1) - Palmer, Karen S. <u>O, Canada, Healthcare Myths from the Great White North.</u> California Physicians Alliance. http://www.thirdworldtraveler.com/health/o_canada_kp.html
- Karen S. Palmer MPH, MS -California Physicians Alliance
(2) – <u>Annual Average Revenue Per Employee in Insurance Agencies in the US is Close to $200,000.</u> All Business. A D&B Co. http://www.allbusiness.com/company-activities-management/financial-performance/5376235-1.html

-Insurance company profits

<u>Chapter 14- Our Country's Drug Problem</u>

(1) - <u>Working to Reform Marijuana Laws; Faq's</u>. Norml, The National Organization for the Reform of Marijuana Laws.
http://www.norml.org/index.cfm?group_id= 3418
(2) - <u>Exodus 2006, Bible Codes and the End Times</u>.
http://exodus2006.com/
- Iciple -USA -Bible Code Researcher
(3) - <u>Marlowe, Eric.</u> 85 to 95% of Crime is Driven by Illegal Narcotics.
http://wcs.wayuga.com/en/08162006/wide/2589/
- Drug related crime
(4) - <u>Cannon, Lou.</u> Daryl Gates: The LAPD Chief Who Stayed Too Long. http://www.politicsdaily.com/2010/04/27/daryl-gates-the-lapd-chief-who-stayed-too-long/print
- Daryl Gates statement

<u>Chapter 15- Foreign-Made Products</u>

(1)- PETA. www.peta.org (click on the pictures on the main page, be prepared to be shocked and horrified!)

<u>Chapter 18- Global Warming</u>

(1) - "Global Warming". Guy Pepper, Tom Brokaw. Discovery Channel, NBC News. 2006.
- Stephan Harrison -Glaciologist
- Mark Serreze -National Snow and Ice Data Center-Boulder, Co.
- Stephen Pacala -Director-Princeton Environmental Institute
- Dr. Nick Lunn -Canadian Wildlife Service
- Professor Peter Cox -Hadley Center for Climate Research-Exeter, England
- Dr. Jim Hansen -Climate Scientist
- Jeremy Bloxham -Harvard Geophysicist

- Svante Arrhenius -Swedish Scientist
- Charlie Keeling –Climatologist

Chapter 19- Our Oceans

(1) - <u>Defending Our Oceans</u>. Greenpeace International.
http://www.greenpeace.org/international/campaigns/oceans/
- Dr. Daniel Pauly
- Stephen Palumbi -Humpback Whale Studies

Chapter 20- Toxic Chemicals

(1) - <u>Eliminate Toxic Chemicals</u>. Greenpeace International.
http://www.greenpeace.org/international/campaigns/toxics/
(2) - <u>The Great Lakes Water Quality Agreement: Promises to Keep, Challenges to Meet</u>. Great Lakes Basin's Environmental Community.
http://www.greatlakes.org/document.doc?=1
- Toxic chemicals

Chapter 21 – Population Growth

(1) - <u>Mankind Using Earth's Resources At Alarming Rate.</u> France 24.
http://www.france24.com/en/node/4932275
- Mankind using Earth's resources at alarming rates

Chapter 22- Nuclear Power and Nuclear Weapons

(1) - "White Light / Black Rain; the Destruction of Hiroshima and Nagasaki". HBO Documentary Films. Okazaki, Steven. Home Box Office, HBO. 6 Aug 2007.
(2) - Oser, Wendy; and Brown, Molly Young. <u>A Background Briefing on Radioactive Pollution</u>. Nuclear Guardianship Library.
http://www.nonukes.org/metatoc.htm
- Radioactive pollution information
(3) - <u>Reprocessing Is Not a Cycle</u>. NPRI, Nuclear Policy Research

Institute. Mary Olsen. Info@nuclearpolicy.org/mox (This website is currently for sale and not accessible, information was accessed in 2007, the next website listed contains similar information from Mary Olsen.)
- Macy, Francis and Joanna. <u>The Politics of Nuclear Waste - an Interview with Mary Olsen</u>. http://www.nonukes.org/r06polnu.htm
(4) - Picha, Roppon. <u>Fission Focus; Generation 4 Reactors</u>.http://www.tint.or.th/adv/fission/g4.html
- Generation 4 reactor information

<u>Chapter 23- Voting and the Electoral College</u>

(1) - <u>Instant Runoff Voting</u>. Fairvote, The Center for Voting and Democracy. http://www.fairvote.org/instant-runoff-voting/

<u>Chapter 24- Sex Offenders</u>

(1) - Council of Europe Anti-torture Committee Publishes Report on the Czech Republic. Council of Europe.
http://www.cpt.coe.int/documents/cze/2009-02-05-eng.htm
-Czech Republic castration studies
(2) - Bradford, J.M.W. <u>The Paraphilias, Obsessive Compulsive Spectrum Disorder, and the Treatment of Sexually Deviant Behaviors.</u>
http://www.brainphysics.com/research/ocpara_bradford99.html
-German castration studies
(3) - Cundiff, Kirby R. <u>Prostitution and Sex Crimes</u>.
http://www.independent.org/publications/working_papers/article.asp?id=1300
-Legalized prostitution leads to less sexual crimes

<u>Conclusion</u>

(1) - Deyo, Stan. <u>"Hopi" Sea Level</u>. http://www.millennium-ark.net/news/07_prophecy/070207.hopi_sea_level.html

- Future map of the United States
(2) - <u>2012 Information</u>. Project Camelot. 7 Aug 2008.
http://2012info.ca/articles/?p=34
- Don Alejandro, Wondering Wolf prophecies
 (3) – Cohn, Michael. <u>Deficit Commission is at a Loss.</u>
http://www.webcpa.com/Debits_Credits/Deficit-Commission-Loss-
56309-1.html
(4) – <u>Amazing Fast Eruption on the Sun Photographed.</u> Space.com.,
msnbc.com.,
http://www.msnbc.msn.com/id/38575669/ns/technology_and_scie
nce-space/

<u>Other Suggested Authors</u>
<u>*(Also See Authors in Bibliography List!)*</u>

- Jay Weidner
- John Peterson
- Lawrence Joseph
- Vincent Bridges
- Gregg Braden